PUBLISHER
MADE EASY

Making Your Ideas Come to Life

James Bernstein

Bernstein, James
Publisher Made Easy
Book 13 in the Computers Made Easy series

For more information on reproducing sections of this book or sales of this book,
go to www.onlinecomputertips.com

Contents

Introduction

Microsoft Publisher has been around for many years and is commonly used for making things such as flyers, brochures and business cards. Microsoft has kept it fairly easy to use and if you are used to Microsoft Word then you shouldn't have much of a problem getting the hang of Publisher.

Creating professional looking publications is fairly simple and that's one of the things that makes Publisher such a great tool to use to help promote your business or even make things like calendars or holiday cards. Of course it takes a little know how to add some flair to your publications to really make your work stand out and even that is not too difficult once you get the hang of how things work.

The goal of this book is to teach you how to get up and running with Publisher and show you how all the tools and menu options work, so you know where you need to go to do what you need to do. I will go over how to create various types of publications as well as how to add some advanced features to them so you can make yourself look like a pro even if you might not be!

I will be using Publisher 2019 for my examples but if you are using any version from Publisher 2010 and up (maybe even 2007) then it should be fairly easy to follow along since things have not really changed that much in regards to where you go to find the tools needed to get things done.

What this book is not, is a book on advanced Publisher even though I will be going into some of the more advanced features of the software. Then again there is nothing super advanced when it comes to using the software but that is all relative to the person reading this book.

So on that note, let's get started making some eye catching publications that will be sure to wow your friends and family... and maybe even yourself!

Chapter 1 – What is Microsoft Publisher?

If you are reading this book then you most likely have a general idea of what Microsoft Publisher is used for. Or maybe it just happened to come preinstalled on your new computer or you bought the version of Microsoft Office that includes Publisher with it, and you want to learn about what it does. Whatever your reason for wanting to learn about Publisher might be, it's not a bad program to know how to use!

Since the name of the program itself is Publisher, that should give you an idea of what it is used for, creating publications. Publisher is by no means the most professional program you can use to create your publications but for many people, it works quite well and still allows them to create some professional looking content. Plus it's very easy to use and if you are used to the other Microsoft Office software such as Word or PowerPoint then you shouldn't have any trouble getting used to using Publisher.

How Publisher Differs from Word
Speaking of using Microsoft Word, you might be wondering what the difference is between the two. If you open each program side by side you will notice that they look very similar. Figure 1.1 shows each program opened side by side and you can see that they look very similar. Figure 1.2 shows a closer view of the toolbars (called the Ribbon) so you can see the similarities there as well.

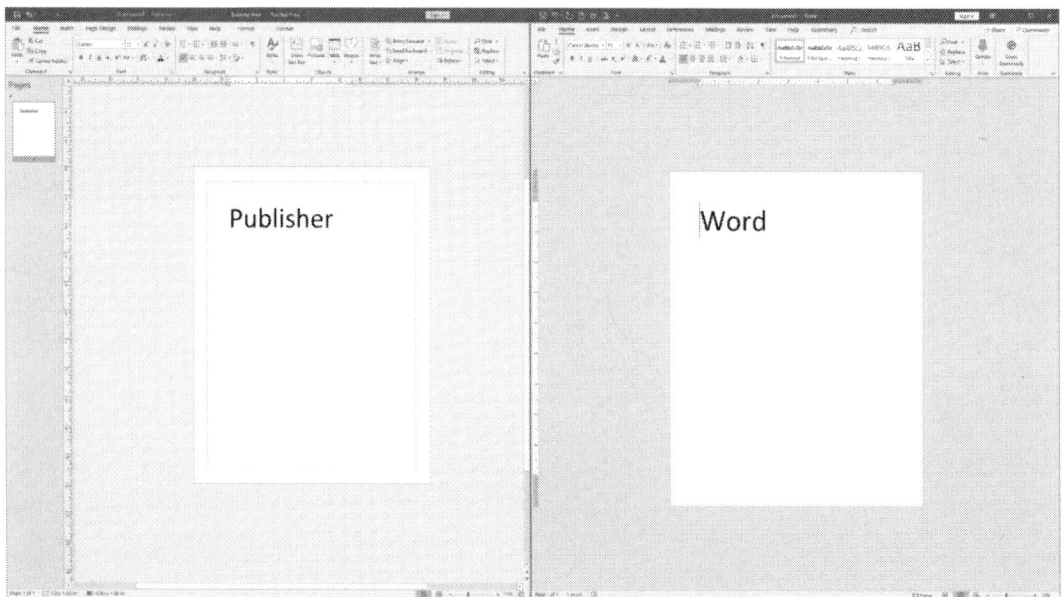

Figure 1.2

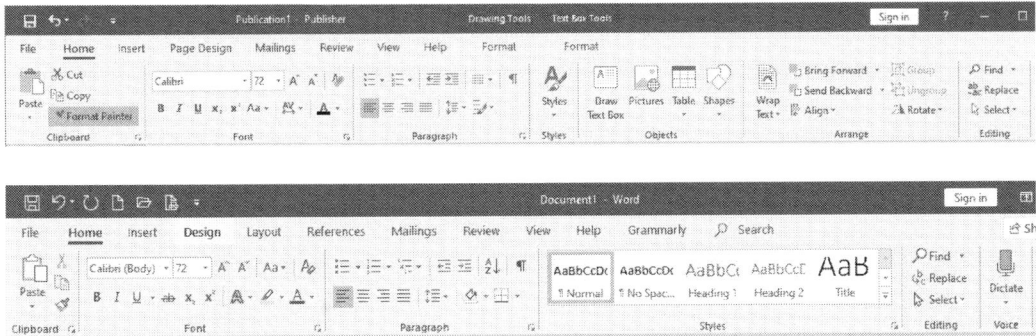

Figure 1.2

You can create many of the same types of documents in both programs, but Publisher makes it easier to design documents that include photos and graphics by allowing you to easily manipulate them on the page since it's not just a text composing type program like Word. I like to think of Publisher as a combination of Word and PowerPoint with Publisher being more designed for printing rather than how PowerPoint is designed for slideshows you would project on a screen.

If you want to learn more about PowerPoint then check out my book titled **PowerPoint Made Easy**. It is an easy to follow step by step guide that will help to get you started creating professional looking presentations.
https://www.amazon.com/dp/1698139276

While both Word and Publisher will let you place text and pictures anywhere you like on the screen and create various types of documents such as flyers and brochures, Publisher has more features that allow you to create various types of documents\publications with less hassle since that's what it is designed to do. To me, being able to freely move your text and images around is what really sets the two apart.

Publisher features a *Pages* pane, similar to the PowerPoint slide deck that lets you easily view and organize the pages in your publications (figure 1.3). It also has features like Page Parts, Advertisements and Business Information that allow you to add some style to your publications with just a few quicks. These features will be discussed in more detail later on, but I included a few examples in figure 1.4.

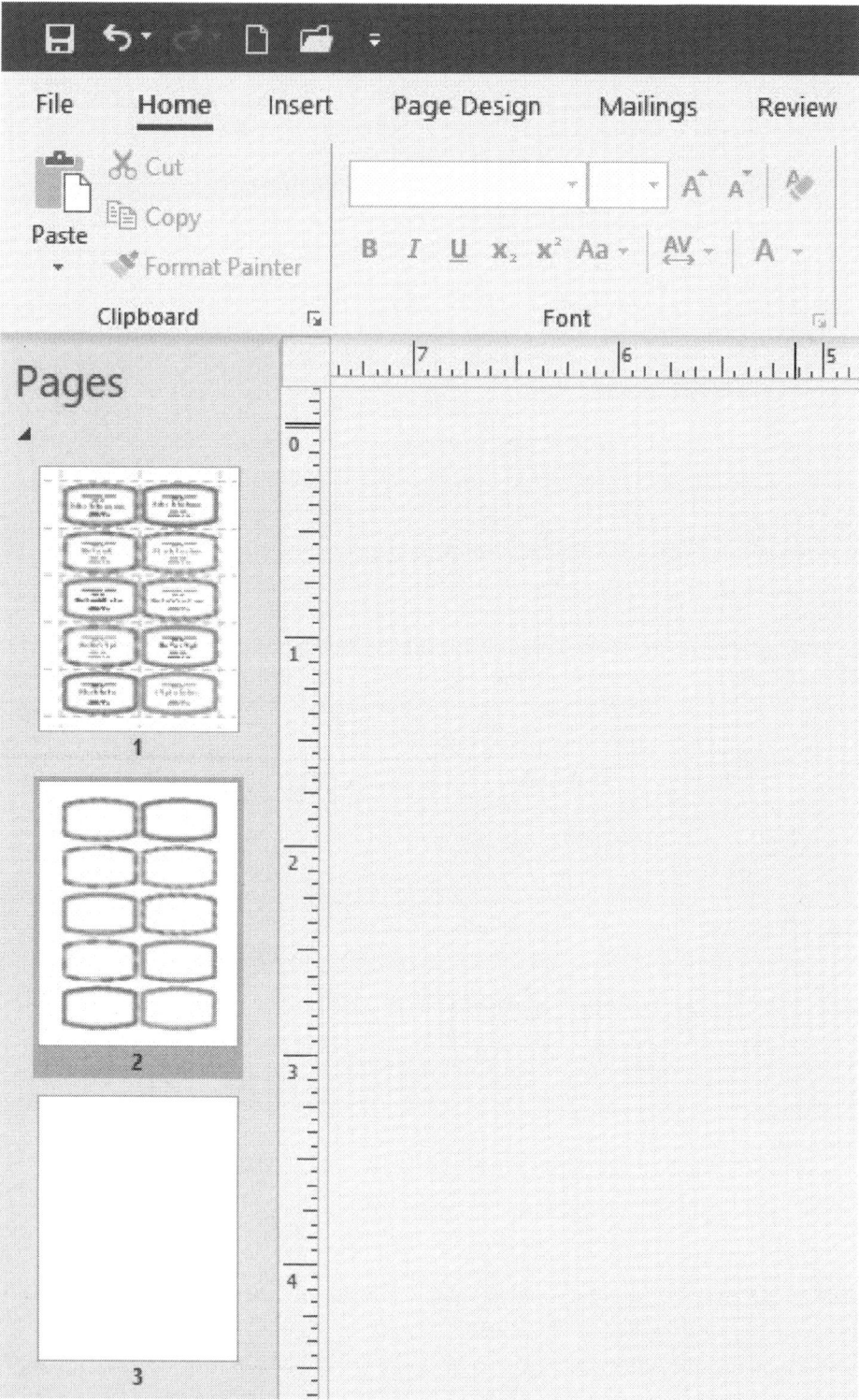

Figure 1.3

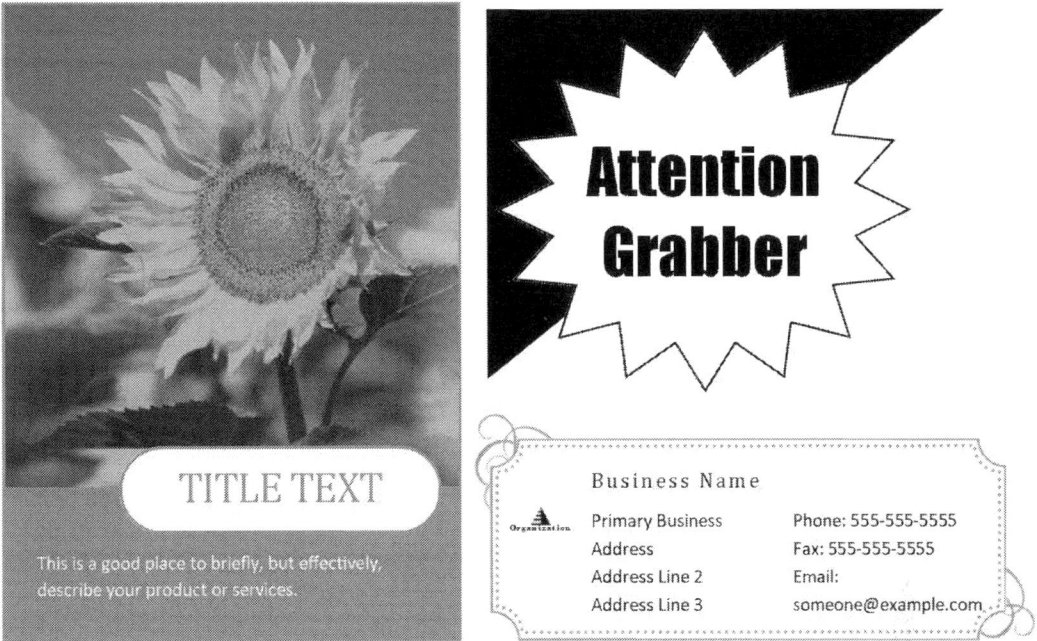

Figure 1.4

Types of Publications You Can Create with Publisher

There are countless publication types you can create using Publisher, so if you can think of it, you can most likely create it. Since you can create publications from scratch then all you need to do is use your imagination to make your ideas come to life.

If you don't feel like thinking about it too much then you can simply use one of the built in templates to get you going on your design. Then you can edit and customize the template to make it your own. When you go to the *File* tab and then to *New*, you will be presented with many templates based on a variety of publication types such as posters, cards, flyers, labels, banners and so on as seen in figure 1.5.

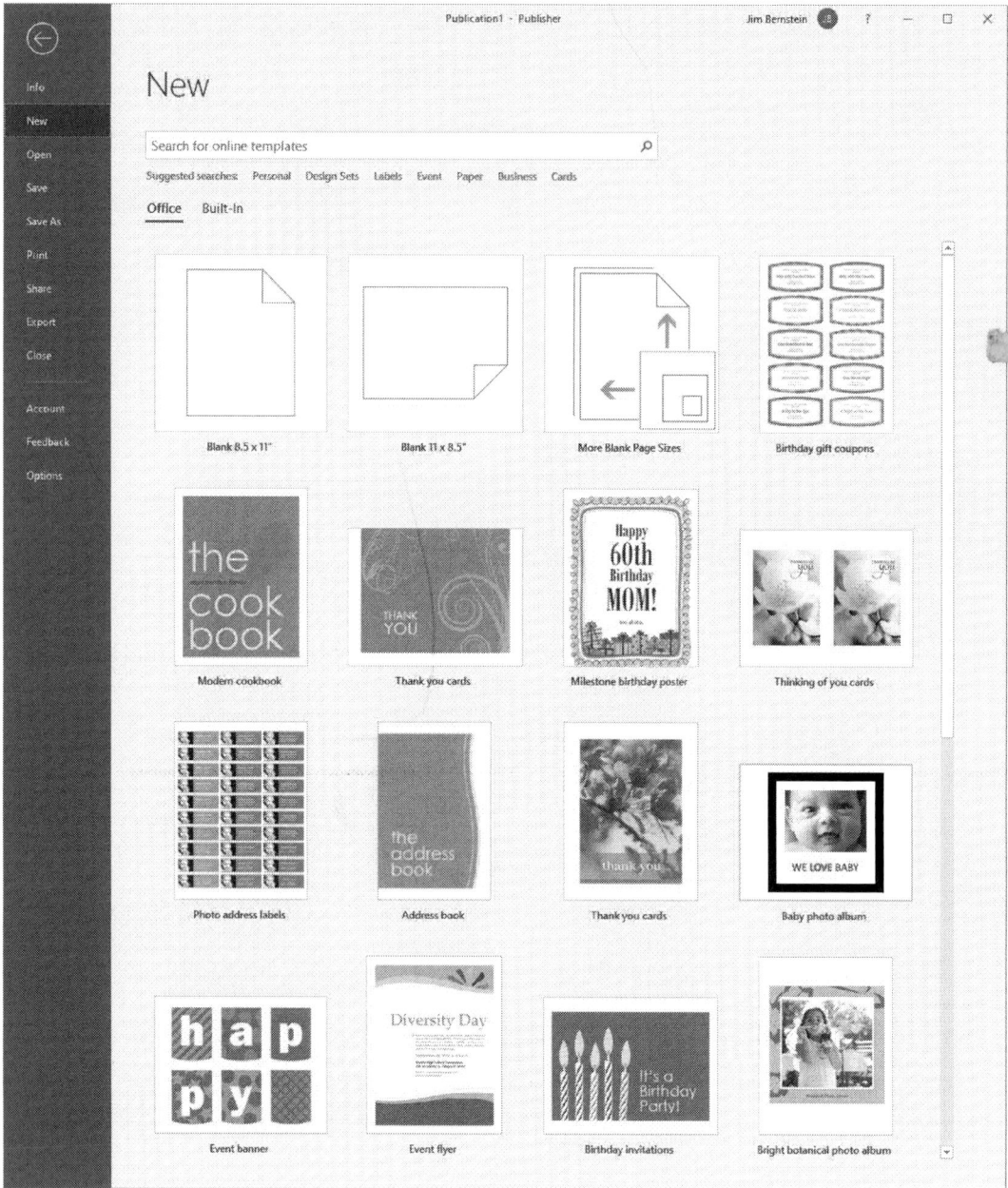

Figure 1.5

If you click on *Built-in* then you will be presented with some more standardized templates and when you click on one of them you will be shown all of the options you have to choose from for that particular template type.

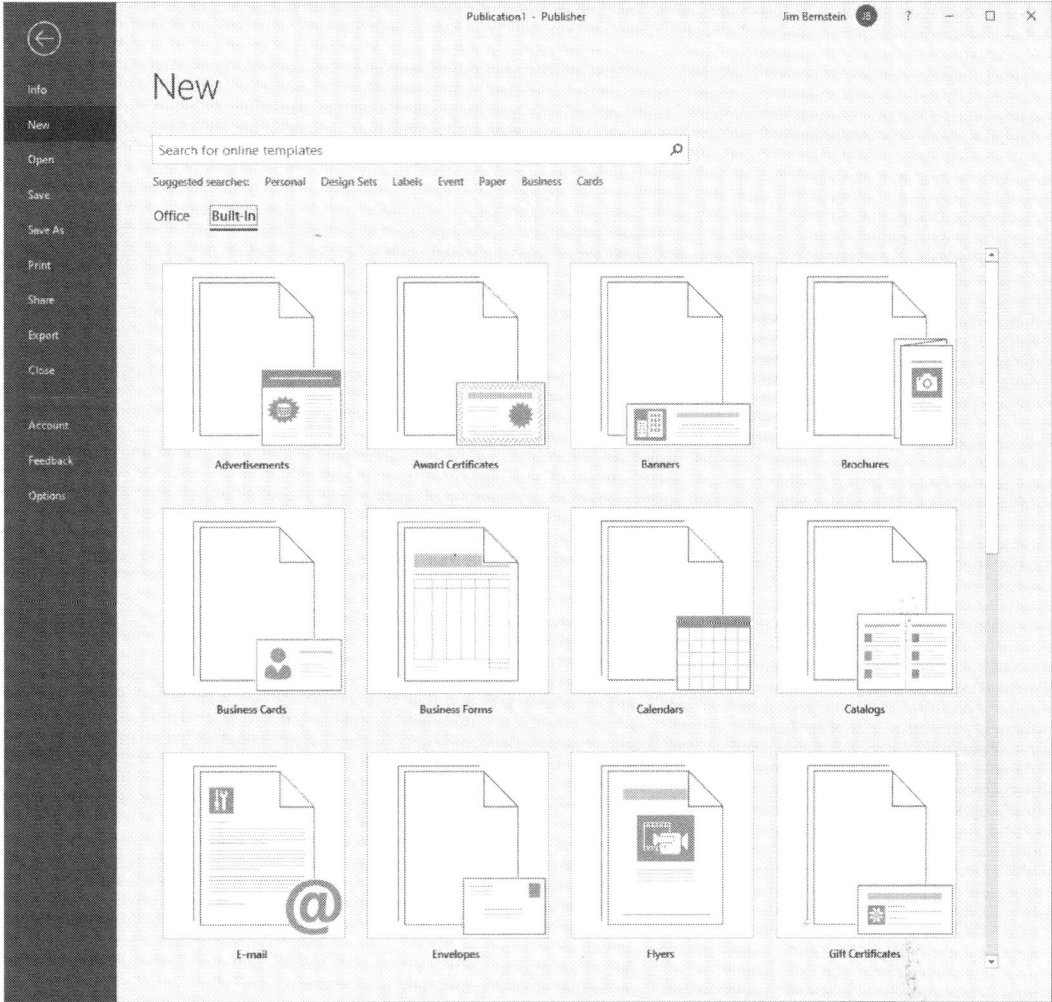

Figure 1.6

If you don't see what you are looking for then all you need to do is type in the kind of publication you are looking for in the search box and see what Publisher can find for you to use. For example, I want to create a calendar so I will type that into the search box and see what Publisher finds for me.

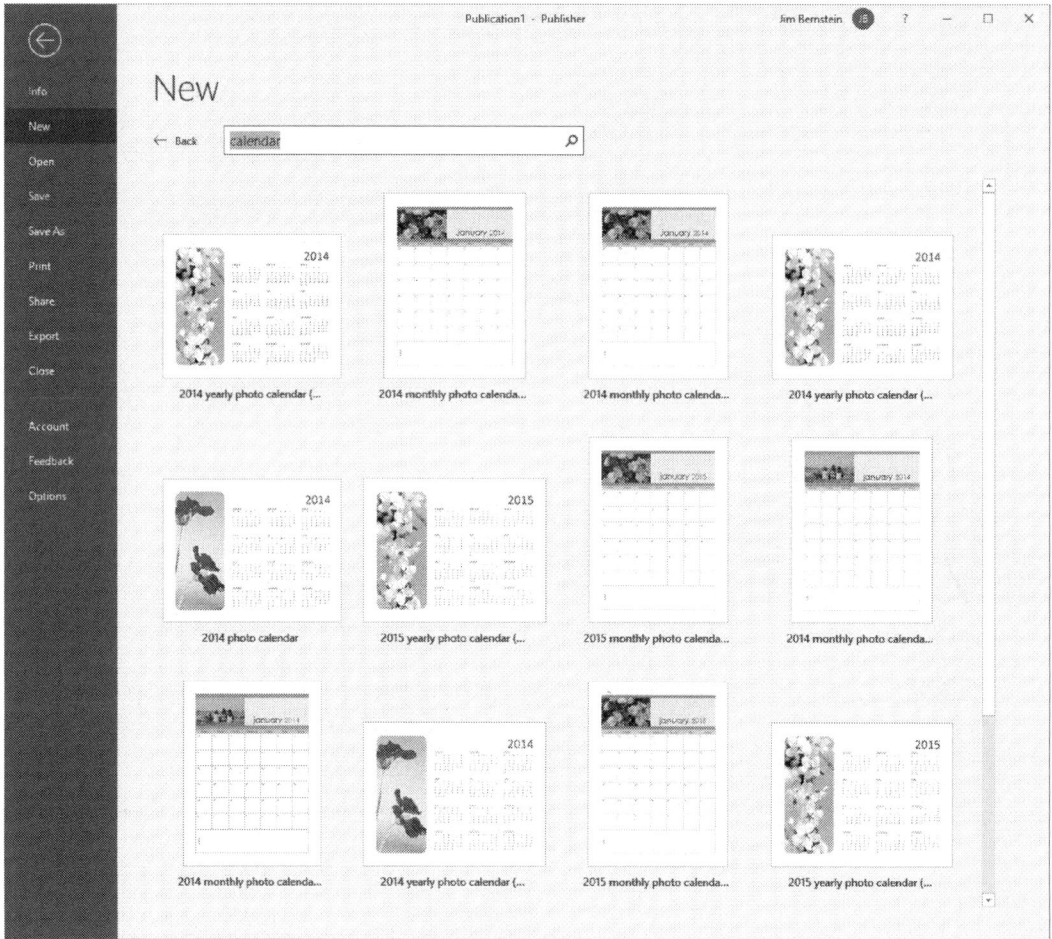

Figure 1.7

As you can see, you have the ability to create just about any type of publication you can think of and it's very easy to find a preconfigured template you like and then just edit it to make it your own.

Chapter 2 – The Publisher Ribbon

Starting with Office 2007, Microsoft completely changed the user interface for its Office software, making many people very upset because they had to learn how to do everything all over again because they added what they called the *Ribbon* to all of their Office programs. If you have only worked with newer versions of Office, then you most likely don't know the difference and assume that the Ribbon was always there.

Before I get into tabs and groups for Publisher in the next chapter, I want to discuss the Ribbon a bit. The Ribbon is the part of Publisher that has all of your icons, tabs, and groups for all of the different things you can do in the software. The Ribbon is shown in figure 2.1 and may look a little different depending on what version of Publisher you are using but should still function the same. Keep in mind that the ribbon for each program (such as Word vs. Excel) will have different options\groups within their tabs and different tabs as well.

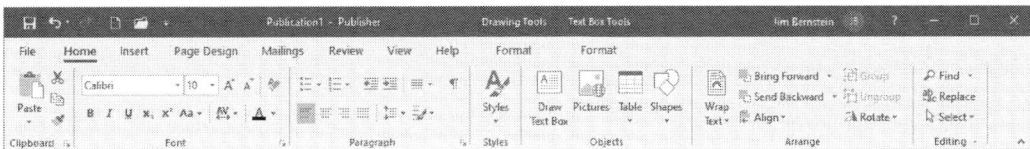

Figure 2.1

As you can see there are various tabs such as File, Home, Insert, Page Design, Mailings and so on. In pre-2019 versions of Publisher, they looked more like actual tabs than they do now. Each tab has its own set of *groups* within it. For example, the Home tab contains the Clipboard, Font, Paragraph, Styles, Objects, Arrange and Editing groups. You can see the names of the groups at the bottom of the Ribbon in figure 2.1.

Within many of the groups, there are other options that can be accessed by clicking on the arrow at the bottom right hand corner of the group. For example, clicking on this arrow in the Font group (figure 2.2) brings up the additional font options as shown in figure 2.3.

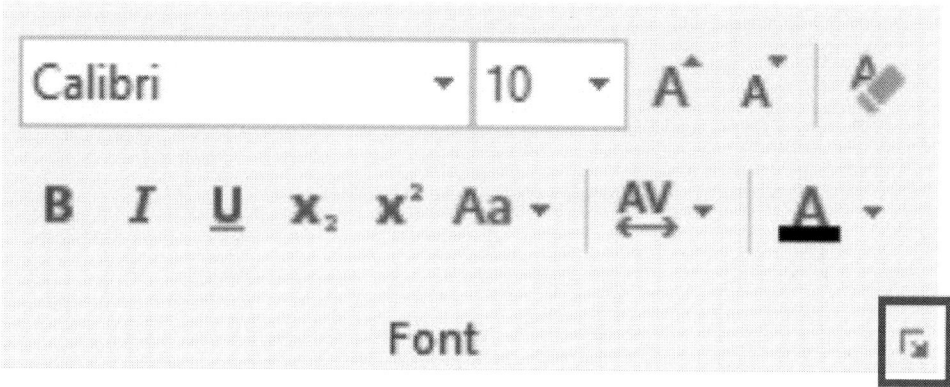

Figure 2.2

Figure 2.3

Customizing the Ribbon

The default ribbon settings will work fine for most people, but if you're the type that likes to customize things whenever possible, then you can add your own tabs and groups to the Ribbon. You can also remove some of the default tabs and groups if you desire.

To customize tabs and groups go to the *File* tab, click on *Options* and then click on the *Customize Ribbon* section. Take a look at figure 2.4 and you will see on the right side it shows your current tabs and then the current groups within those tabs. As you can see, the Home tab has groups named Clipboard, Font, Paragraph, Styles, Objects, Arrange and Editing just like you saw in figure 2.1.

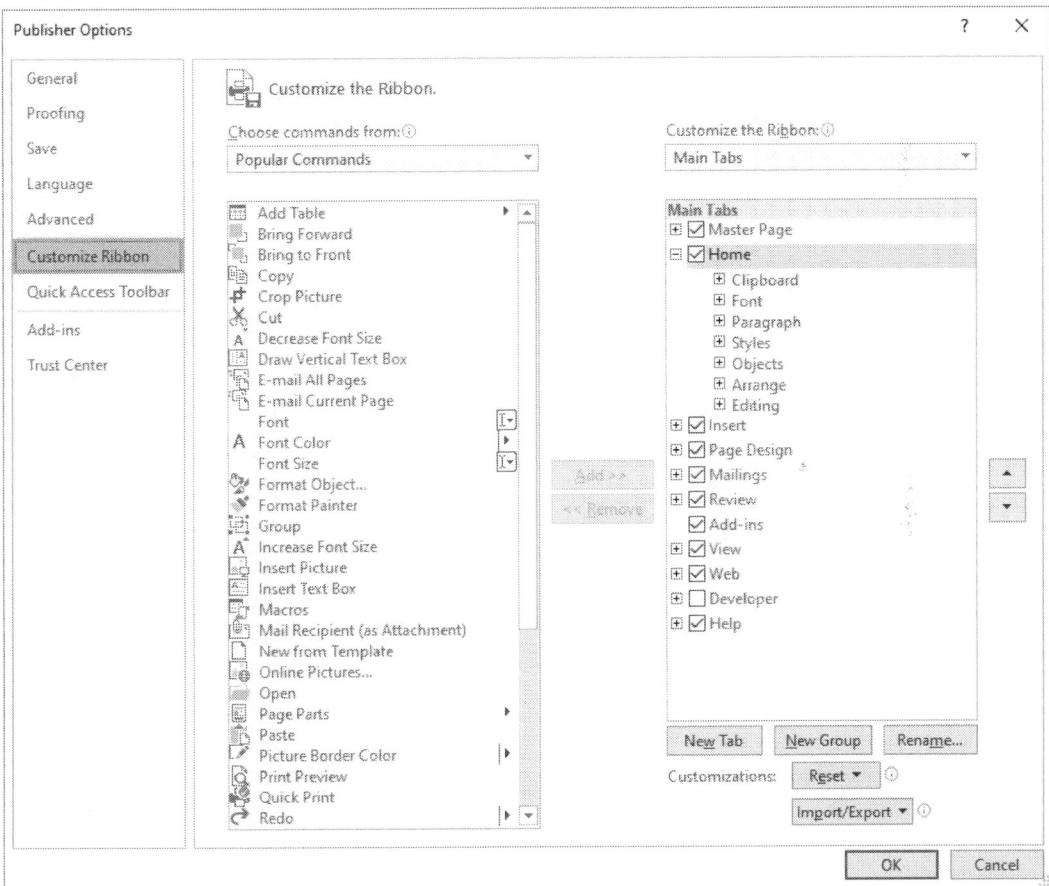

Figure 2.4

To add a new group to an existing tab, click on the tab's name to highlight it and then press the *New Group* button. Then name your group and insert commands from the left side list into your new group by clicking the *Add* button. As you can see in figure 2.5, I made a new group called Custom Group in the Home tab and added the Draw Table and Email commands to that group. Then the results are shown in the ribbon (figure 2.6). By default, Publisher will add this new group to the right of all the other groups.

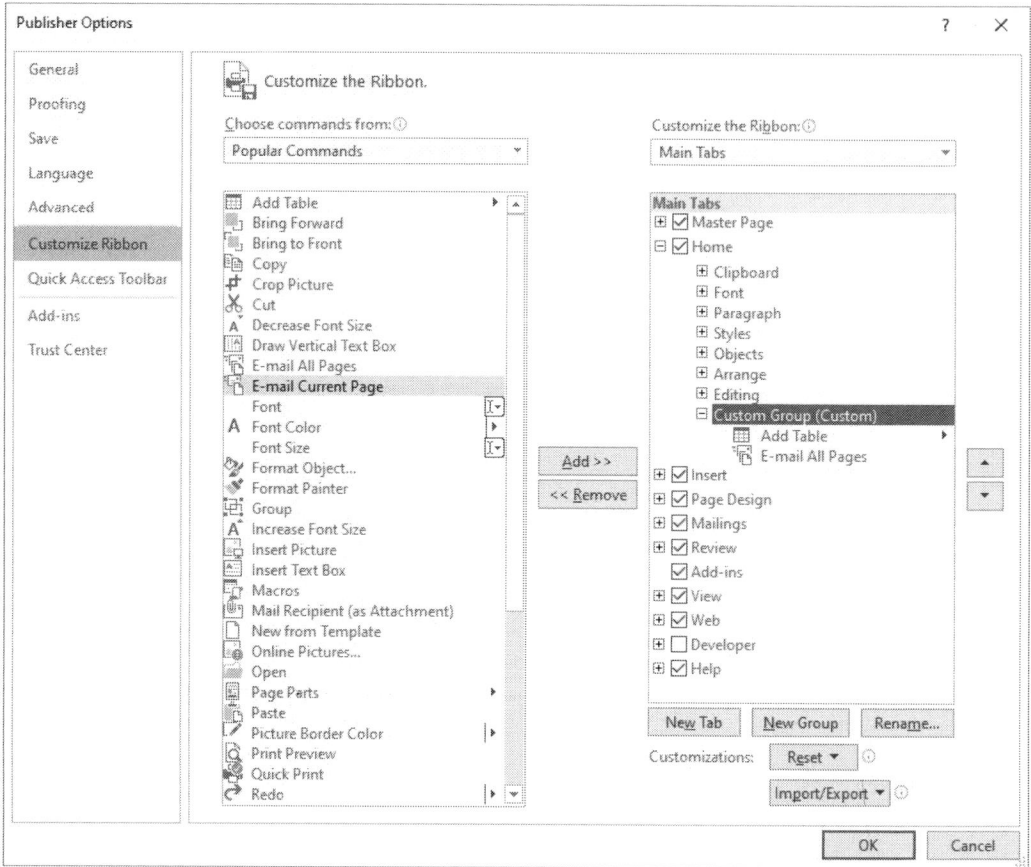

Figure 2.5

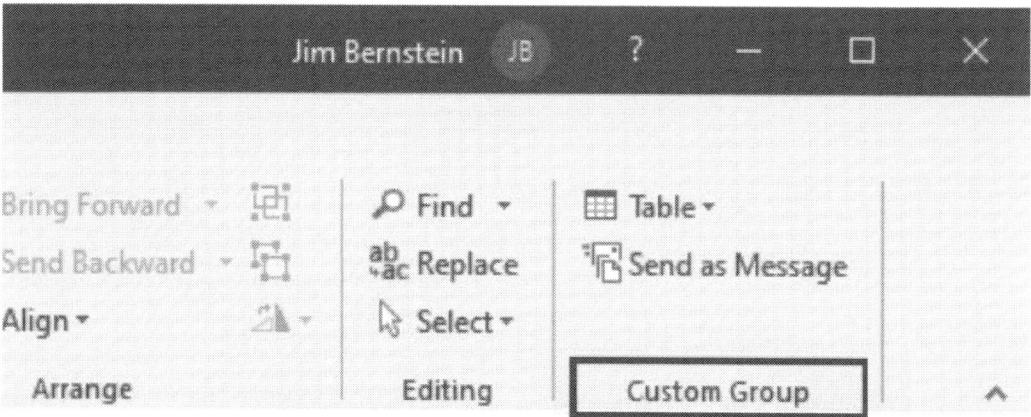

Figure 2.6

You can also remove commands from the right by highlighting them and clicking the *Remove* button. By default, the most popular commands are shown for you to choose from so if you don't see what you are looking for, you can change the setting to show *All Commands*.

Adding a new tab is a similar process, and all you need to do is click on the tab you want to create a new tab next to, then click the *New Tab* button. In figure 2.7 you can see that I created a new tab called *Jim's* next to the Home tab. Then I renamed the group it automatically created within this tab called *Jim's Group* and added the Bring to Front and Group commands to that group. Figure 2.8 shows the results of this new tab creation in the Ribbon.

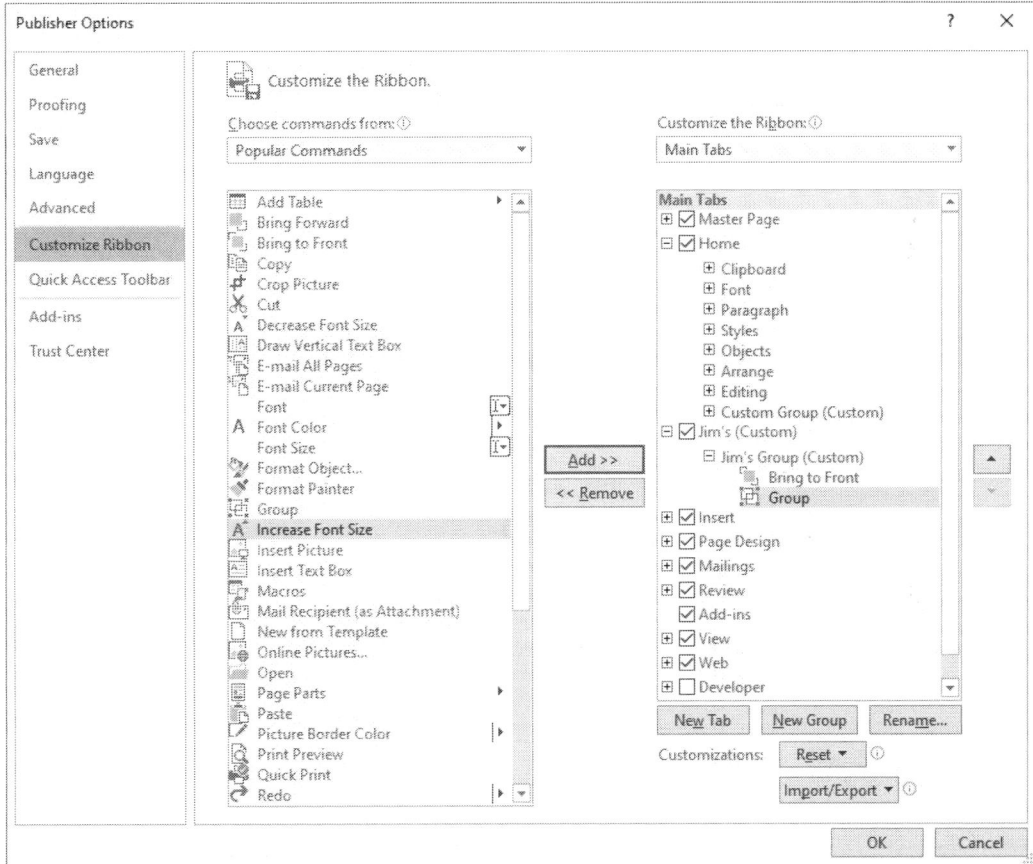

Figure 2.7

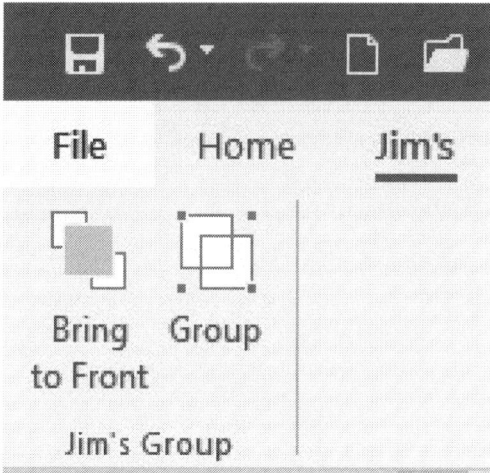

Figure 2.8

Quick Launch Bar

One very useful area of the Ribbon that you will find yourself using all the time is called the Quick Launch Bar. Think of the Quick Launch Bar as the place where you will go to perform the actions that you use the most, such as save, open, and print. If you take a look at figure 2.9, you will see a bunch of icons at the top above the tabs. These are your Quick Launch icons and, as you can see, it makes it easy to group all of the icons you use the most in one place.

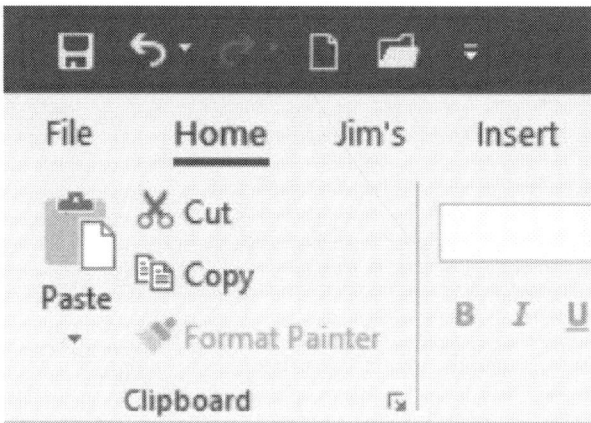

Figure 2.9

The icons do not have names, but since they are the ones you will use all the time, you will get to know exactly what each one does. Plus, if you hover the mouse pointer over the icon, it will tell you what it is used for. If you click the little down arrow to the right of the icons it will bring up a list of all the Quick Launch commands that you have available on your Quick Launch Bar (figure 2.10). Then you can check the ones you want displayed on the Quick Launch Bar or uncheck ones that you don't want to show.

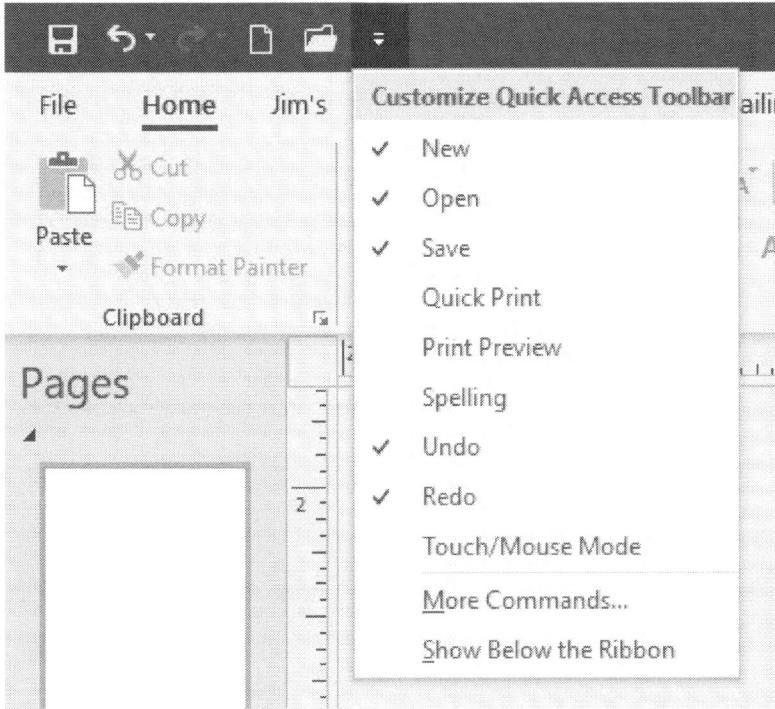

Figure 2.10

If you click on Show Below the Ribbon it will put your Quick Launch icons underneath the ribbon (as shown in figure 2.11).

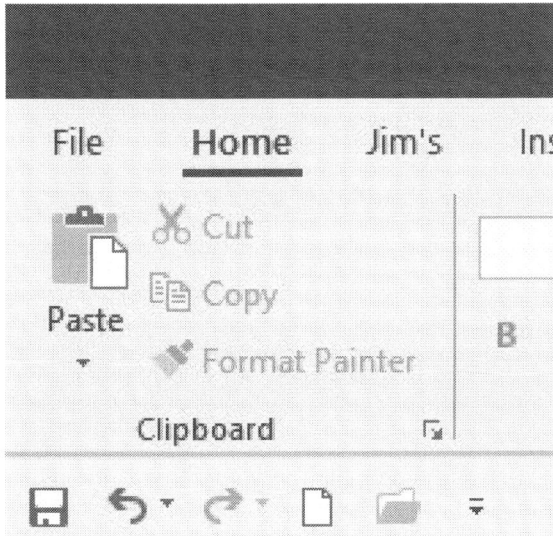

Figure 2.11

Customizing the Quick Launch Bar

Just like with tabs and groups, it's possible to customize the Quick Launch Bar to your liking. When clicking on the down arrow next to the icons (as shown in figure 2.10) there is a choice called *More Commands*. This will take you to the Quick Access Toolbar customization setting, which you can also get to from the File tab and then Options (figure 2.12).

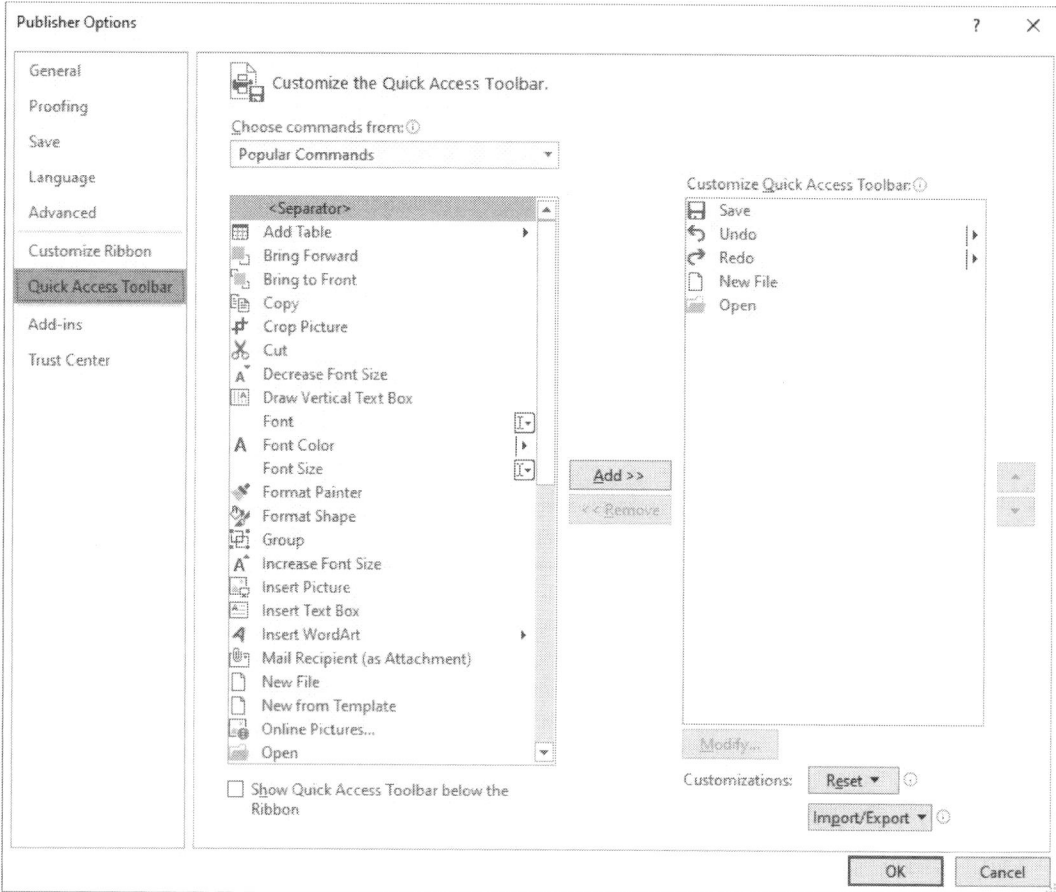

Figure 2.12

From here you can add commands from the right or remove commands from the left by using the *Add* or *Remove* button.

Tip

If you are into shortcuts then one quick way to remove icons from the Quick Launch Bar is to right click them from the bar itself and choose *Remove from Quick Access Toolbar.* This way you don't need to go into the Publisher options to get rid of them.

If you have made changes to the Ribbon or Quick Launch Bar and want to revert things back to the Office default, simply go to the options for either one and then click the button on the bottom of the window that says *Reset* (as you can see in figure 2.12).

One nice feature that Office programs have is that you can import and export your custom settings to be used on another computer that has Office installed. That way you don't need to configure the other computer from scratch if you have made a lot of changes that you like to use.

Hiding the Ribbon
If for some reason, you would like some more real estate on your screen and think the Ribbon is in the way, then it's possible to collapse the Ribbon and only have it show when you need it.

To do so you can press *Ctrl-F1* on your keyboard (Command-F1 for Mac) when you want to hide the Ribbon, or you can click the small up arrow at the very bottom right of the ribbon to collapse it. Then press Ctrl-F1 to bring it back, or right click any tab and clear the checkmark next to *Collapse the Ribbon.* You can also double click any tab to have the ribbon brought back on the screen.

You can also click on the up arrow at the bottom right of the ribbon to have it hidden as shown in figure 2.13.

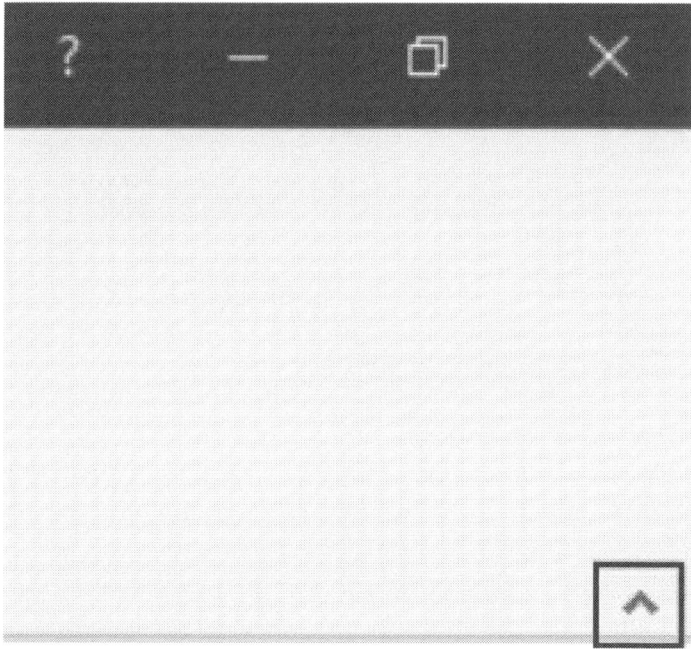

Figure 2.13

The only thing to remember here is that when you click on this arrow to hide the Ribbon that the arrow itself gets hidden so you will need to use one of the previously mentioned methods to get the ribbon back.

Chapter 3 – Tabs and Groups

Like I mentioned earlier, Publisher has its own unique tabs compared to the other Office programs like Word and Excel but there are also some different groups within the tabs that are common to the other Office programs. In this chapter, I will be going over all of the tabs within Publisher as well as the groups contained in these tabs.

File Tab

The File tab is used for things you will do before and after working on your publication. As you can see in figure 3.1, you have various options to choose from such as opening, saving, and printing your publications. Most of these options are obvious, but I want to go over a few that might not be.

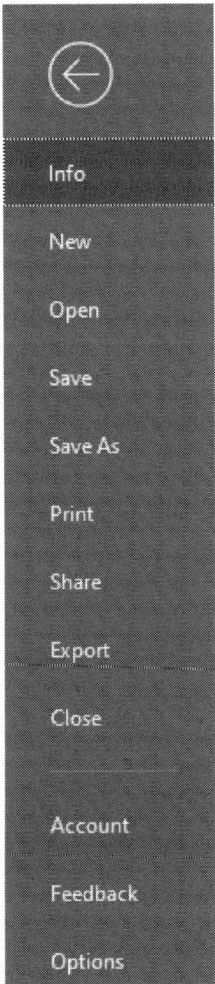

Info

New

Open

Save

Save As

Print

Share

Export

Close

Account

Feedback

Options

Figure 3.1

Info

This section will give you specific information about the publication you are working on such as its size, the number of pages, last modified date, created date, the author, and so on. It also contains other information as listed below.

- **Business Information** – These are personalized sections of information, about yourself or your business, that can be used to quickly fill in various places in your publications, such as business cards and flyers, etc.

- **Design Checker** – Here you can have Publisher review your publication for various design and layout problems. It can be used to identify potential problems and provides options to fix them. You can have it perform general design checks, final publishing checks, website checks and email checks.

- **Embedded Font Information** – If you use non-standard fonts that others might not have on their computer then you can use this tool to embed your fonts within your publication so other people who open your Publisher file will be able to see it the way you intended it to look. You can embed only TrueType fonts, and then only if their licensing allows embedding.

Save As

Publisher allows you to save publications in other formats besides the default Publisher format. You might have noticed that your Publisher publications end in .pub, which is the default file extension for Publisher. If you look at figure 3.2, you can see there are many other formats to choose from, such as a .pub version to be compatible with older versions of Publisher, PDF file, image file, video file and so on. I will be going over these save options in more detail in Chapter 6.

Figure 3.2

Share

If you have a need for others to be able to open, edit or print your publication then you can do so from this section. The Share options will most likely be different depending on what version of Publisher you are using and can be different from other Office programs. I will get into more details on sharing in Chapter 6.

Export

This section is similar to the Save As section where you can save your publication in a different format, except here you are exporting it rather than saving it. Once again, I will be covering this in more detail in Chapter 6.

Account

Here you can get information such as what account you are using with your Publisher and Office software, what version you are running and how updates are applied to your computer. You can also do things like change the default Office background and theme if you want to personalize your software.

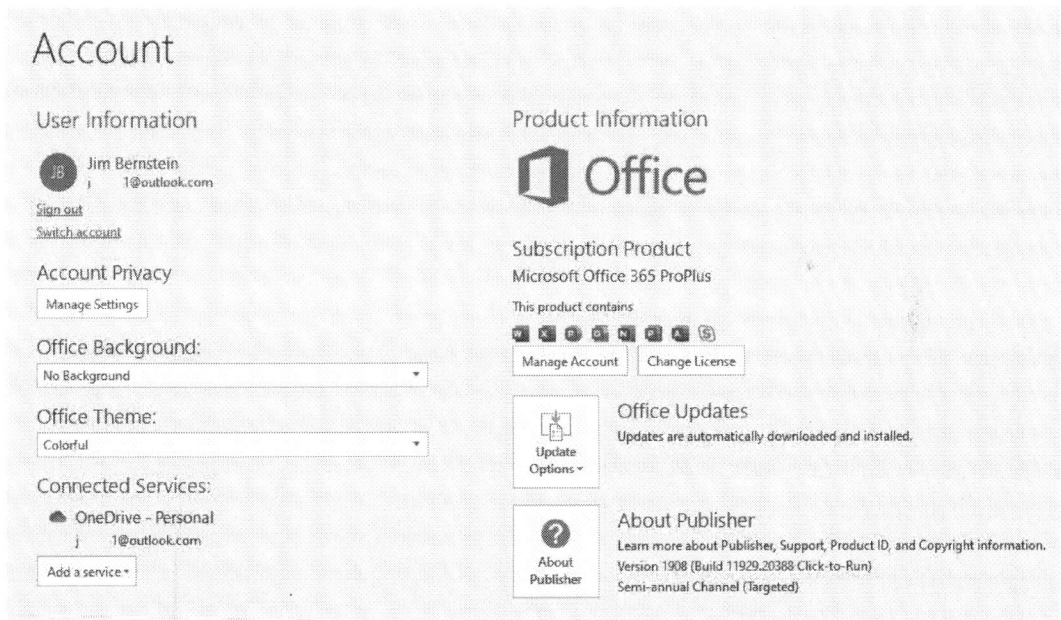

Figure 3.3

Options

I have gone over some of the options when I discussed how to customize the Ribbon and Quick Launch bar, but you can also configure things such as proofing and language options that are beyond the scope of this book. If you are curious you should poke around these options to see what is available for you to configure.

Home Tab

Like all the other Office programs, the Home tab is the default tab that is displayed when you open the program. The Home tab contains many of the more commonly used settings, and that's why Microsoft has made it the default tab when you open any of the Office programs. It has many of the same groups as the other Office programs, but there are some that are specific to Publisher and they should be pretty obvious as we go along. For example, the Page Design group sounds like the type of group that would be specific to Publisher since we are designing our publications.

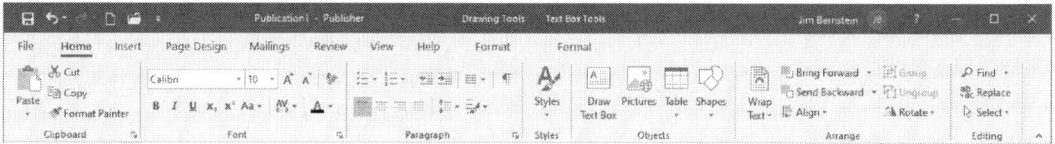
Figure 3.4

Now I will go over each group within the Home tab.

Clipboard

The clipboard is used to hold information such as copied text and images to keep them in memory until you are ready to paste them into your publication or somewhere else. The clipboard will paste the last copied item unless you expand the Clipboard group by clicking on the little arrow to show other items you have copied. From this section, you can paste in different formats, depending on what you are pasting.

Font

Fonts, also known as typestyles, are used to change how the characters look on the screen and when printed. Windows comes with its own default fonts installed and many programs will install additional fonts when you install the actual program, so not every computer will have the same fonts. From the Font section, you can do things such as change the font type, color, and size.

Paragraph

Here you can adjust settings to change the text to align to the left or right, be centered, or be justified on both sides. You can also set text indents, line and paragraph spacing, and create borders from this section.

Styles

Styles apply to your text and are used to format it to look a particular way and to make it stand out from other text. Some examples of styles include Title text, Heading text and bulleted lists. The best way to get an idea of how these styles work is to create a text box, enter in some text and then apply various styles to that text.

Objects

The objects group contains some of the same items you will see on the Insert tab. Here you can insert things such as a text box to enter text or pictures from your computer as well as draw tables and shapes in your publication. I will be showing examples of how to do all of this in Chapter 4.

Arrange

When you add objects such as text boxes, images, shapes, etc. to your publication, you might run into a situation where they start to overlap each other, and you might have one object covered up with or hidden by another object. This happens a lot with image files since they will fill in the extra part of the picture with "white space" to make it a rectangular image. Figure 3.5 shows that I have some text that is being covered up by a dog picture. I need to "rearrange" my objects so the dog is not covering the text.

This is my

important

Figure 3.5

To do this I can either bring the text forward or send the dog backward behind the text. I will now click on my text box and choose the *Bring Forward* option to have it brought forward one level. I can do this as many times as I need until it is brought all the way to the front of all the objects if that is my goal. Or I can just use the *Bring to Front* option to have it brought all the way to the front (top level) in one click. This also works the same when sending objects backward. The results are shown in figure 3.6.

This is my text. It is very important information

Figure 3.6

> **Tip**
>
> One way to get around the problem of the "white space" that many images have around them is to use transparent PNG files. These PNG files don't have the extra white space around the picture. This requires a little photo editing on your part to make your images transparent, but I just wanted to mention it.

Also included in this group is the *Group* option. This can be used to make two or more objects act like one object. Doing this makes it easier to move them around your page all at once so you don't need to move them individually and try and get them all back in the same position. To do this, hold down the Shift key and click on each object until they are all highlighted (figure 3.7). Then click on Group and they will then be grouped together as seen in figure 3.8.

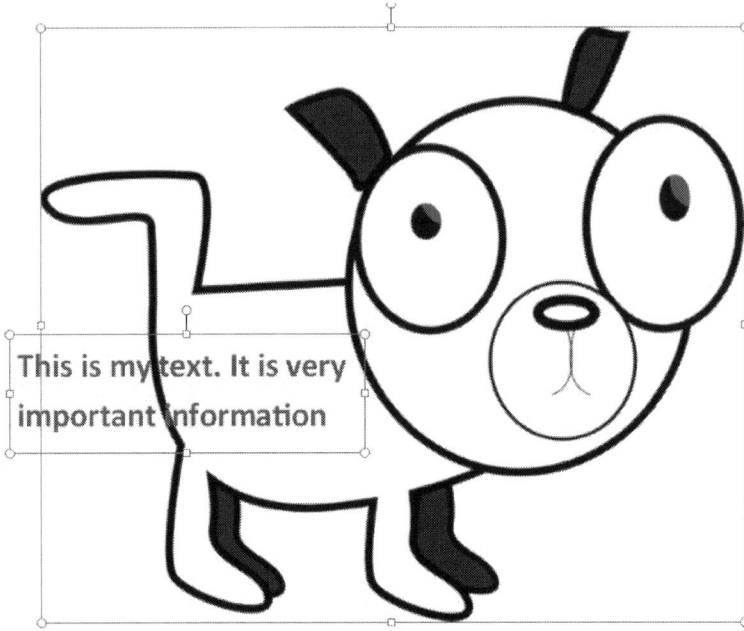

This is my text. It is very important information

Figure 3.7

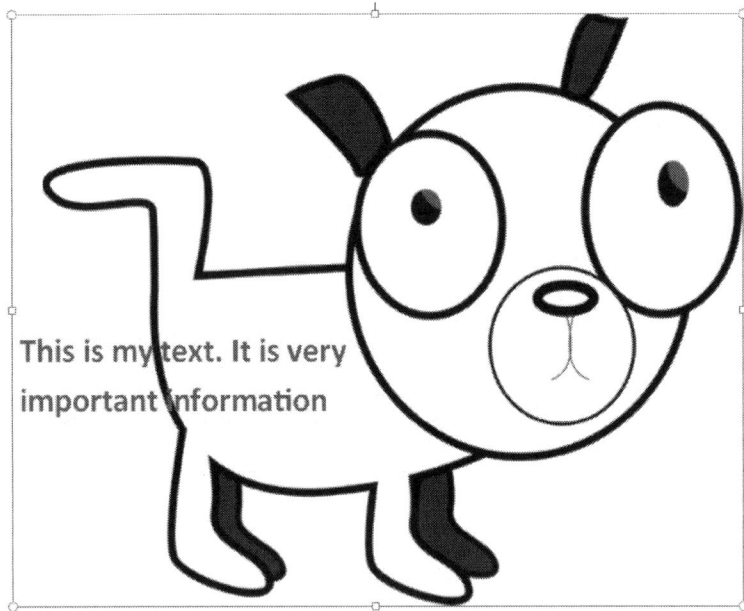

This is my text. It is very important information

Figure 3.8

If you want them all to be individual objects once again then you can select the grouped object and then click on the *Ungroup* button.

The *Rotate* option can be used to do things such as rotate an object left or right 90 degrees or even free rotate the object by hand. You can also do things like flip the object horizontal or vertical as seen in figure 3.9.

Before   After

Figure 3.9

Wrap Text
Here you can adjust how your text wraps around objects and whether or not it wraps around an object, goes behind an object or stays in front of an object.

Dogs (Canis lupus familiaris) are domesticated mammals, not natural wild animals. They were originally bred from wolves. They have been bred by humans for a long time, and were the first animals ever to be domesticated. ... Today, some **dogs** are used as pets, others are used to help humans do their work.

Figure 3.10

Editing
If you have a lot of text and want to find a word or phrase to maybe change it or remind yourself if you even typed it at all, you can use the *Find* feature from the Editing group. Simply click on *Find*, type in the information you are searching for, and it will show you all the results in the document. Then you can click on a particular result and it will take you right to it within the document. The *Replace* feature is great

to use if you want to replace a certain word with another throughout the whole document. For example, let's say you spelled Jon as John and want to replace all the instances of John with Jon. You can do that with the Replace tool. You can also use the *Select* option to quickly select\highlight everything on a page if you want to do a quick move of all your objects or even deleted or copy everything on the page.

Insert Tab

When using Publisher you will be inserting many items such as pictures, text, drawings, etc. into your publication so you will be using the Insert tab quite a bit. Now I will go over each of the groups within the Insert tab.

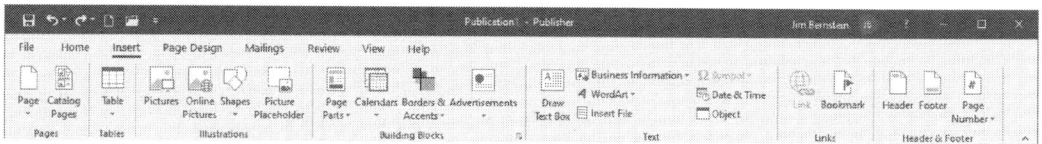

Figure 3.11

Pages

I mentioned earlier in the book how Publisher had Pages that are similar to Slides in PowerPoint and knowing how to use these will help you effectively use Publisher. Pages allow you to easily move between the parts of your publication and give you a way to visually see how things are laid out.

Figure 3.12 shows a newsletter template file that I opened and added some pages to and changed the content around a little. As you can see on the left hand side, there are four pages numbered 1-4 and if I want to go to page 3 for example, all I need to do is click on it in the Pages pane and I will then have that page shown in the main work area.

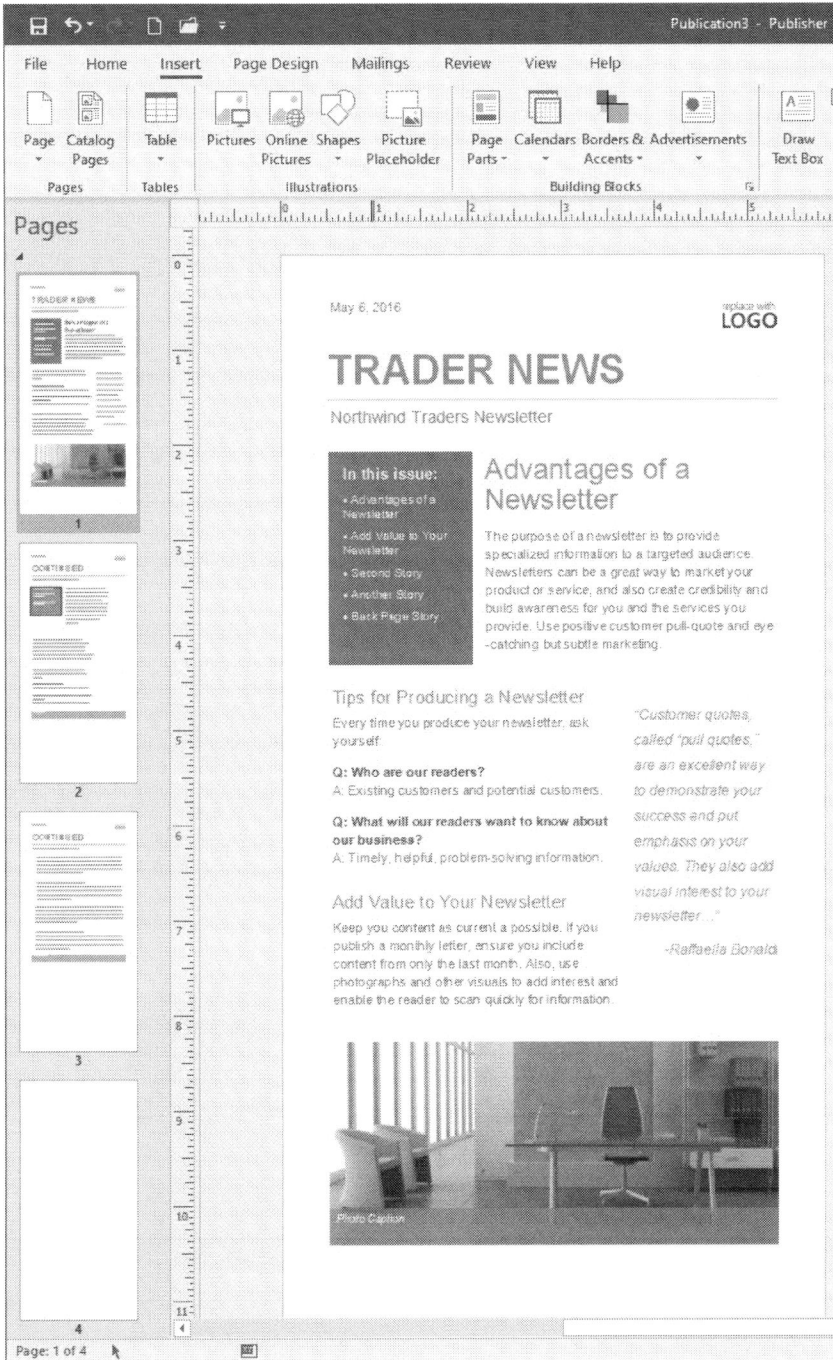

Figure 3.12

Clicking on the Page icon in the Pages group will give me options to insert a blank page, insert a duplicate copy of the page I am on or do a custom insert which is shown in figure 3.13. Here you can fine tune what type of page insert you want to perform.

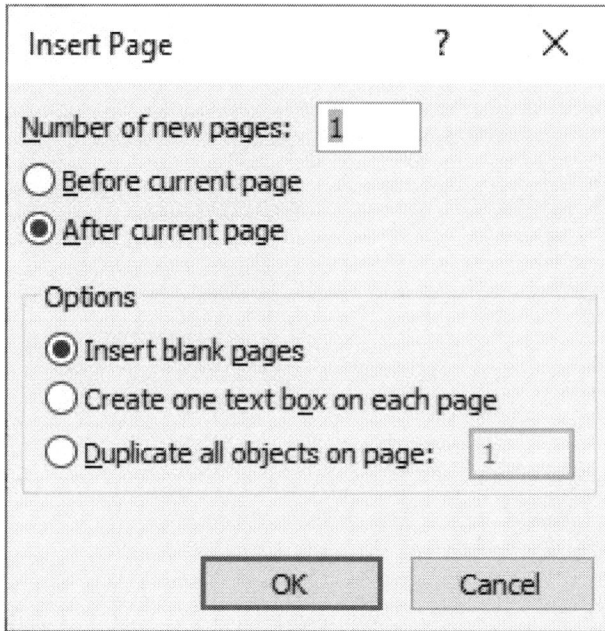

Figure 3.13

Right clicking on a page in the Pages pane will give you additional options as to what you can do with that particular page. Once again you can insert a new page or a duplicate page of the one you right clicked on.

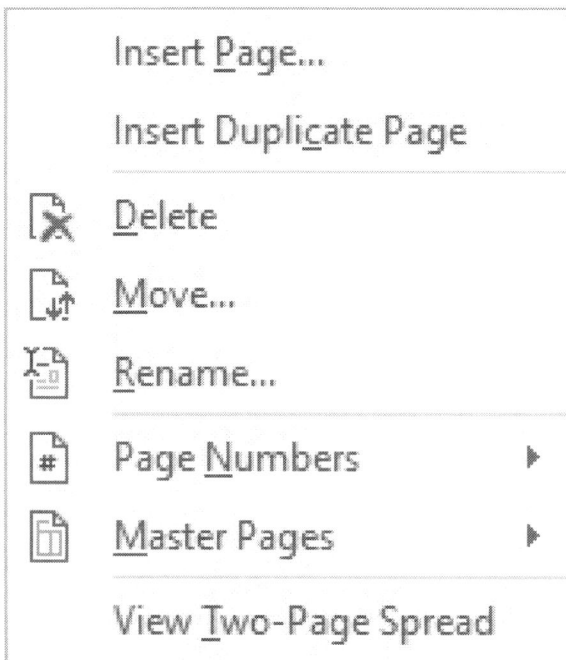

Figure 3.14

Other options you have from here is to delete the page you right clicked on as well as move it to a different position or rename the page. You can also rearrange your pages by clicking on them and dragging them to a different position in the Pages Pane.

You can also add page numbers to your pages if desired and you can also do this from the *Header & Footer* group. *Master Pages* determine how the overall look of the publication is handled and allows you to make publication wide changes from one area. It's similar to the Master slide in PowerPoint and I will be going over Master Pages in Chapter 5.

A *two page spread* is used for viewing two pages that are going to be bound or folded for printing purposes. When two pages are configured this way, the locations of page numbers, running titles, and margins on both pages will be mirrored from each other. Figure 3.15 shows how pages 2 and 3 have been converted to a two page spread.

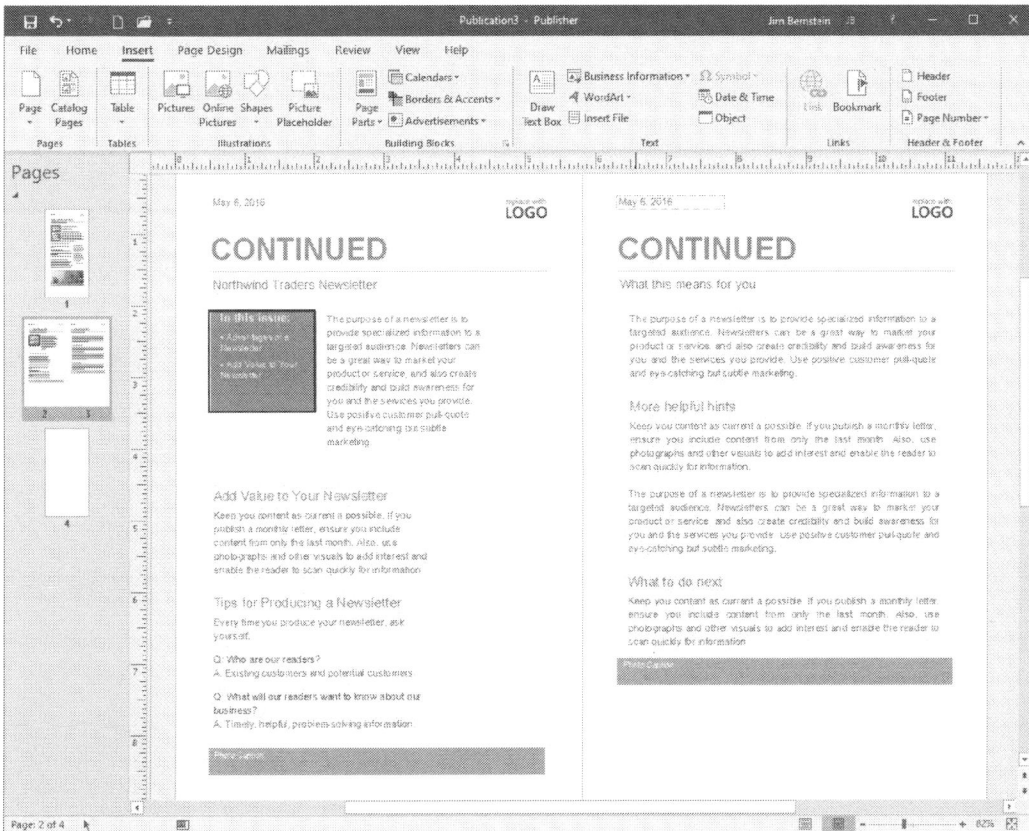
Figure 3.15

When using Publisher or pretty much any software for that matter, right clicking can be used to quickly perform common tasks. Depending on where you right click, the menu options will change to reflect things you can do from that particular area of the program. Give it a try while working on your publication and see how it works!

Catalog Pages

This option can be used to quickly create a catalog for your products by entering in the information about those products or by importing them from a list. I will be going over how to create a catalog in Chapter 4.

Tables

Tables are useful to add to your publication when you need to create a list of items and their related information. Think of using tables the way many people use spreadsheets to store information.

In Publisher, you can either draw a table based on how many rows and columns you need or manually type in the information. I prefer to figure out how many rows and columns I will need and enter the information in manually. You can always add or remove some after you create the table.

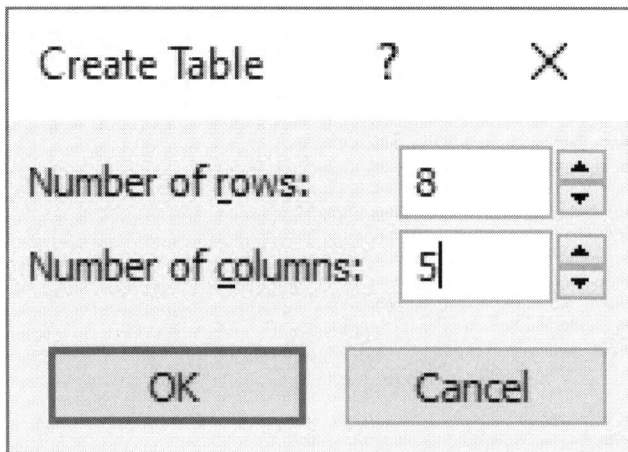

Create Table	?	X
Number of rows:	8	
Number of columns:	5	
OK	Cancel	

Figure 3.16

Figure 3.17 shows how my table looks after I entered in some generic data\text.

Topic 1	Topic 2	Topic 3	Topic 4	Topic 5
Data	Data	Data	Data	Data
Data	Data	Data	Data	Data
Data	Data	Data	Data	Data
Data	Data	Data	Data	Data
Data	Data	Data	Data	Data
Data	Data	Data	Data	Data
Data	Data	Data	Data	Data

Figure 3.17

I'm sure you have noticed that the table looks pretty bland, but it is easy to add some color and other formatting to the table by right clicking on it and choosing *Format Table*. Then you will see the Format Table options as shown in figure 3.18 which allow you to change things like fill and line color, add borders, change cell size and so on.

If you want to change specific cells rather than the entire table, first select those cells before right clicking on them and choosing Format Table. I will now select the first row and add some color, enlarge the text size and make it bold. I will also add a border around all of the cells to make it look more like a table. The results can be seen in figure 3.19.

Format Table

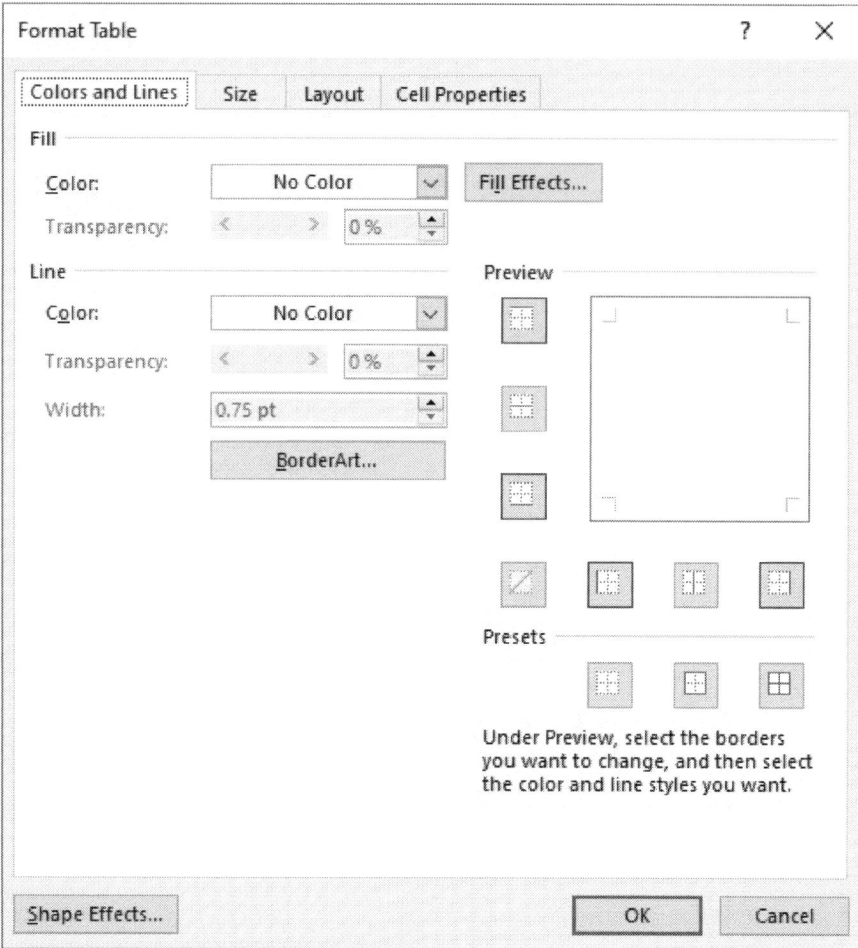

Figure 3.18

Topic 1	Topic 2	Topic 3	Topic 4	Topic 5
Data	Data	Data	Data	Data
Data	Data	Data	Data	Data
Data	Data	Data	Data	Data
Data	Data	Data	Data	Data
Data	Data	Data	Data	Data
Data	Data	Data	Data	Data
Data	Data	Data	Data	Data

Figure 3.19

Illustrations

You will most likely be using the Illustrations section on a regular basis when creating your publications since here is where you can go to insert various pictures and shapes.

When it comes to inserting pictures into your publication, you have a couple of choices. You can use the regular *Pictures* option to insert an image that you have stored on your hard drive, CD\DVD, flash drive, network drive or other local location. As long as you know what the picture file is called and where it is stored, you can easily insert it into your publication.

If you don't have the type of image on your hard drive that you need for your work then you can choose the *Online Pictures* option to go out on the Internet and do a search for the specific type of picture you need. When you select this option it will give you some categories to choose from as shown in figure 3.20. But if you want to look for something more specific then you can type in what you are looking for in the search box and see what kind of results you can find.

If you look at the bottom left of figure 3.20 you will see there is a button that says *OneDrive*. If you have your OneDrive account configured and have any images in there then you can browse your online files and insert images right from your OneDrive account.

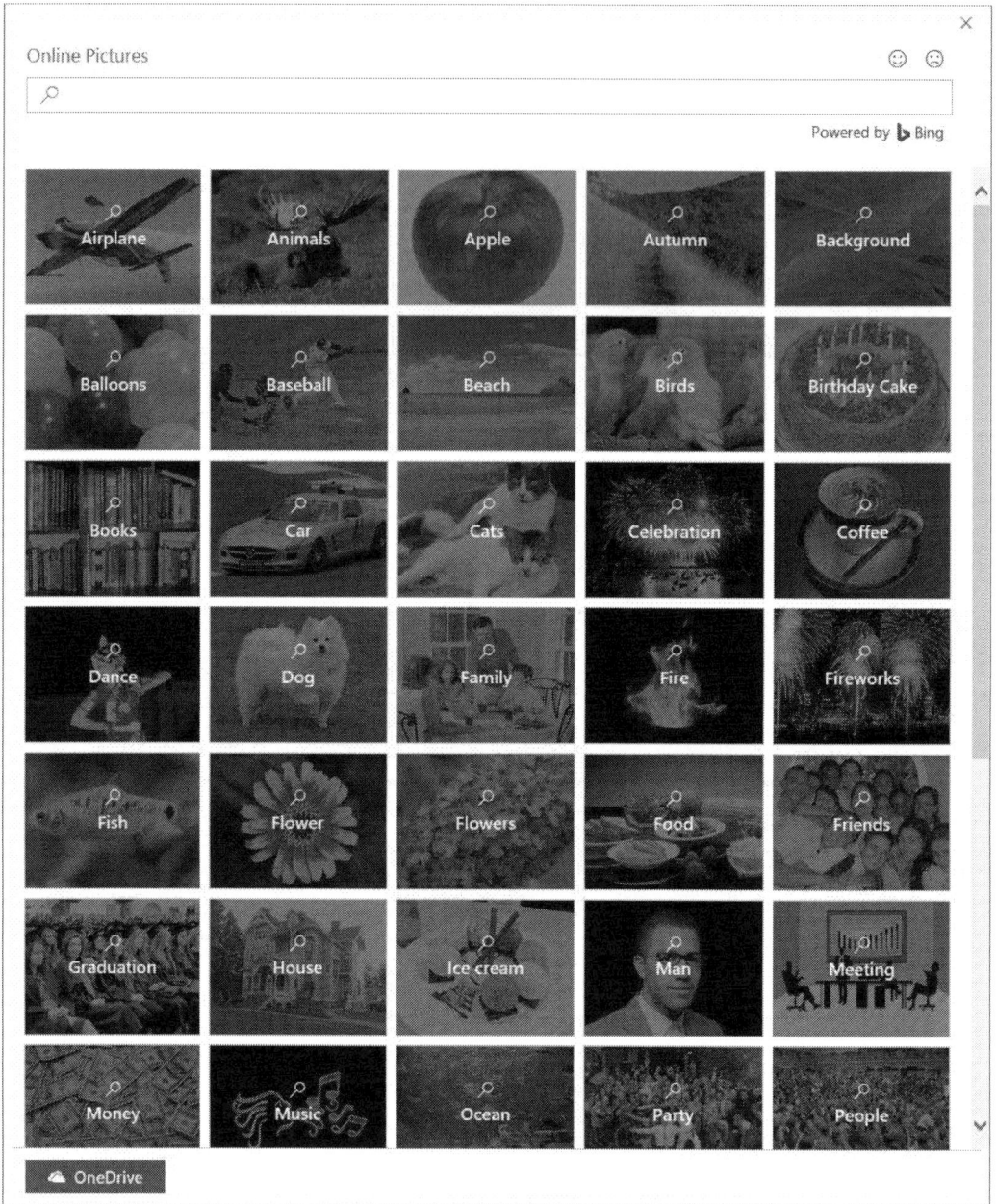

Figure 3.20

Shapes are another commonly used object that you can insert into your publications. There are many types to choose from and once you insert a particular shape you can then format it to make it look the way you like. I will be going over formatting shapes and images in Chapter 5.

Figure 3.21 shows all the types of shapes that you can insert, and they are categorized making them easier to choose from.

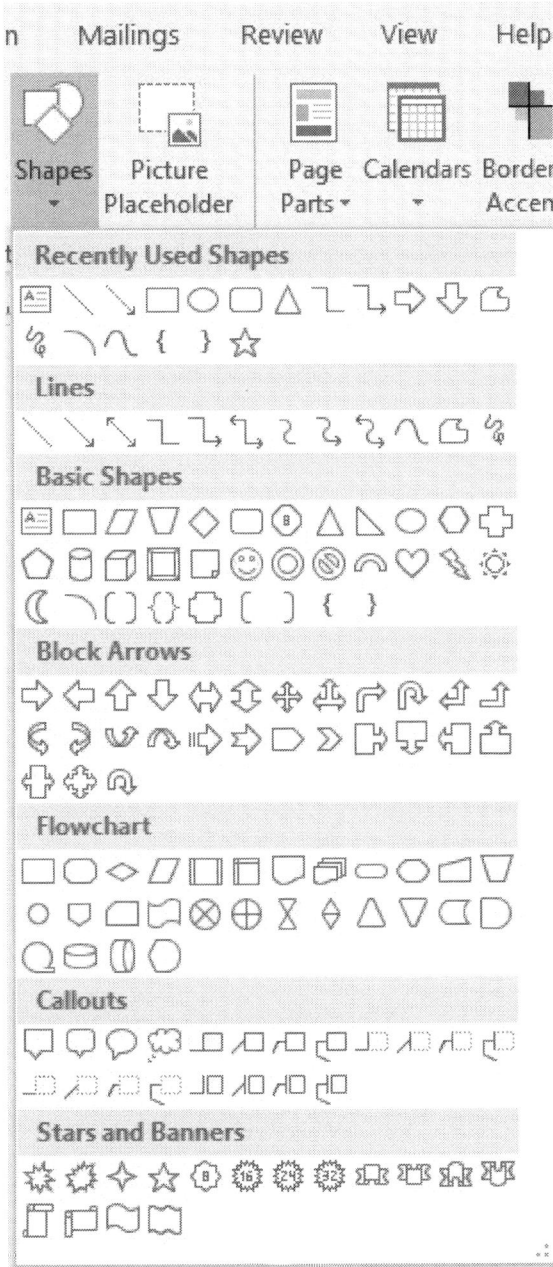

Figure 3.21

Finally, we have the *Picture Placeholder* option which allows you to reserve a spot in your publication for a picture that you can then go back to and add later. I don't really see the point of this, but I suppose if you want to add a spot for an image because you don't have it yet and don't want to put something else in its place it can be used for that. It might be easier than having to rearrange your text and images to add the picture later in case you forget.

Once you add the picture placeholder it will make a box that you can resize to fit the area that the picture will take. Then when you are ready to add your picture all you need to do is click on the picture icon in the middle of the box and find your file either from your computer or online and have it inserted into your publication.

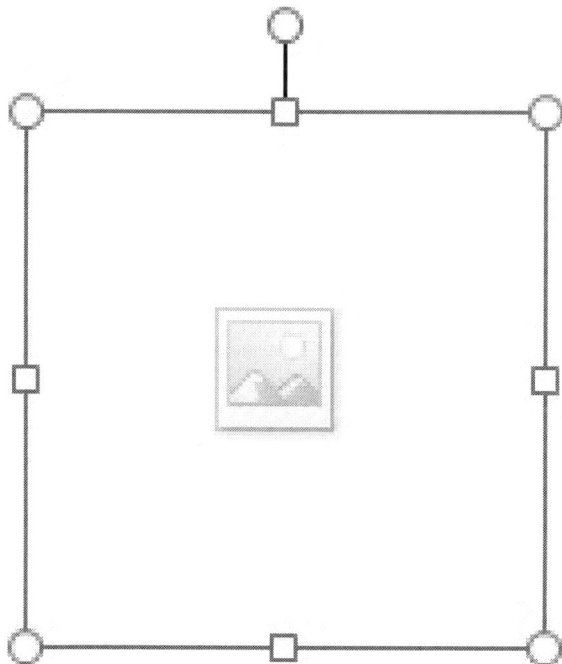

Figure 3.22

Building Blocks

The Building Blocks section has some very useful features that allow you to add some professional looking parts to your publication without a lot of work. And once you add one of these parts you can easily modify it to make it more unique and personalized.

The first option here is called *Page Parts* and these include many types of preconfigured items you can use within your publication. Figure 3.23 shows some of the Page Parts you can use such as accent boxes, reply forms, custom layouts and table of contents.

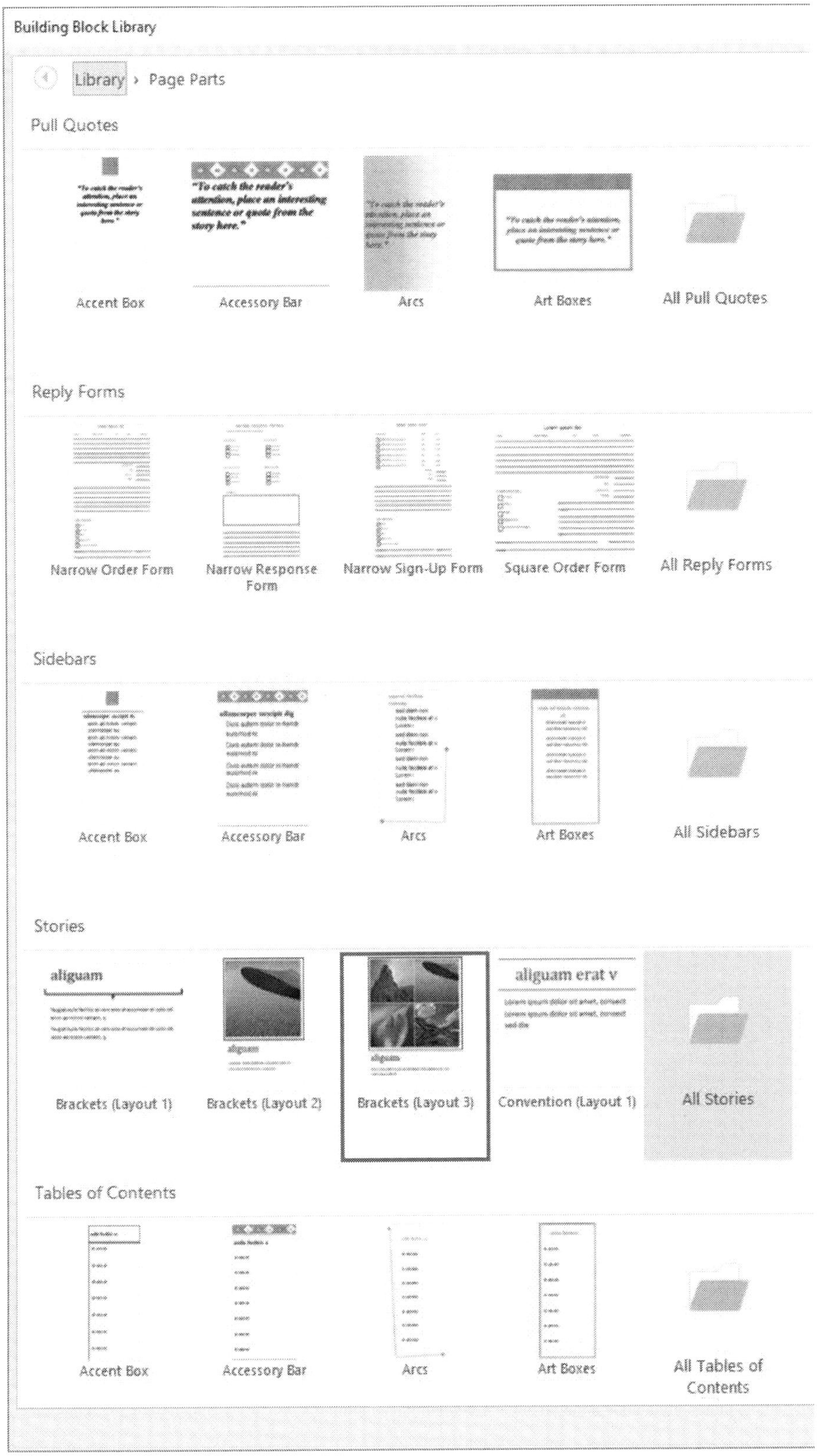
Building Block Library
Library › Page Parts
Pull Quotes
Accent Box
Accessory Bar
Arcs
Art Boxes
All Pull Quotes
Reply Forms
Narrow Order Form
Narrow Response Form
Narrow Sign-Up Form
Square Order Form
All Reply Forms
Sidebars
Accent Box
Accessory Bar
Arcs
Art Boxes
All Sidebars
Stories
Brackets (Layout 1)
Brackets (Layout 2)
Brackets (Layout 3)
Convention (Layout 1)
All Stories
Tables of Contents
Accent Box
Accessory Bar
Arcs
Art Boxes
All Tables of Contents

Figure 3.23

Once you add your Page Part all you need to do is highlight the text to change it or right click on a picture to change it to a different one or add some additional formatting.

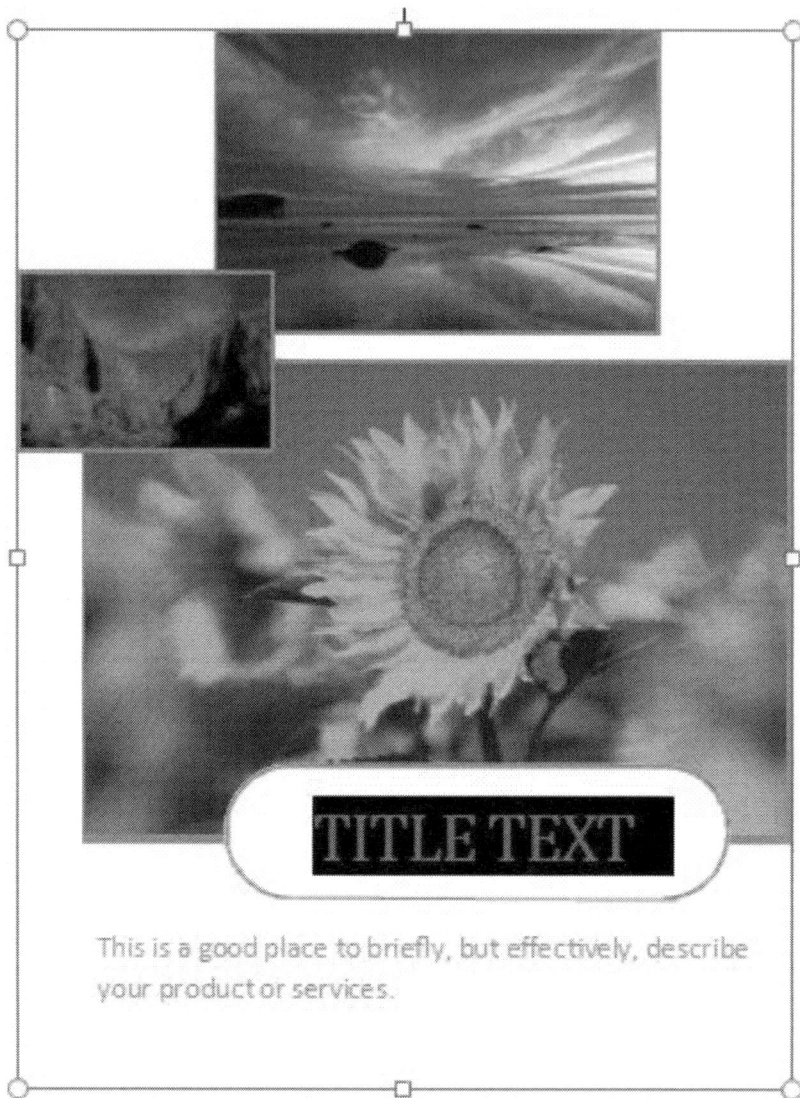

TITLE TEXT

This is a good place to briefly, but effectively, describe your product or services.

Figure 3.24

Inserting a *calendar* into your publication can come in handy and doing this is a very simple process. All you need to do is choose the style of calendar you want, and the month and year and you are ready to go. Once you insert the calendar you can then do things like change the font and colors.

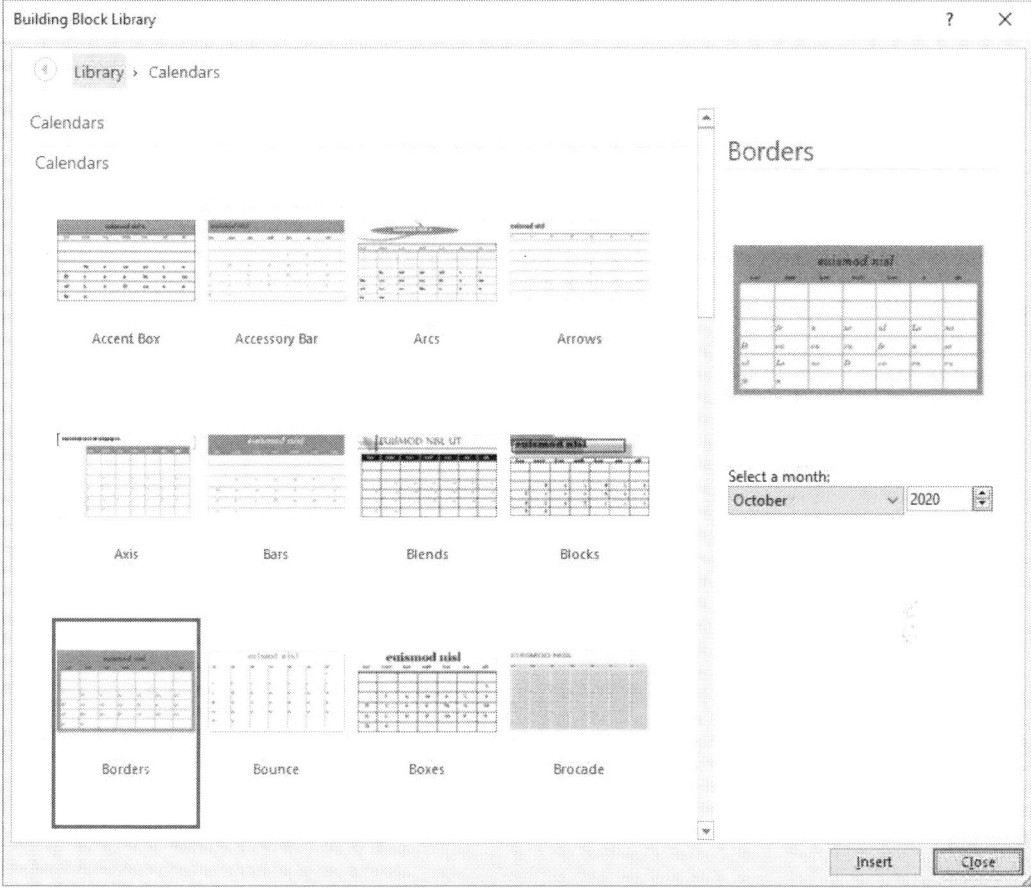

Figure 3.25

Figure 3.26

Borders are a quick and easy way to add some flair to your publication, especially if you use one of the built in designs rather than creating your own. Once you select the type of border you want to use, all you need to do is drag it to the proper size and shape to fit your publication.

Figure 3.27

Tip

When you use a predefined border in Publisher and insert it into your publication, it will tend to cover up your existing work and won't have an option to send it to the back like we say earlier for other objects. To get around this you can either insert the border first or select your other objects, go the Home tab and Arrange group and send them to the front.

Just an FYI, you can also insert a box into your publication and then format the line style, thickness and colors to make your own custom border. I will be going over formatting shapes in Chapter 5.

Another type of Building Block that you can insert is called an *Advertisement*. These are similar to Page Parts but are more geared towards promoting your products or services. Figure 3.28 shows some examples of the types of Advertisements you can insert. Once you insert an Advertisement you can then edit it just like you can with Page Parts.

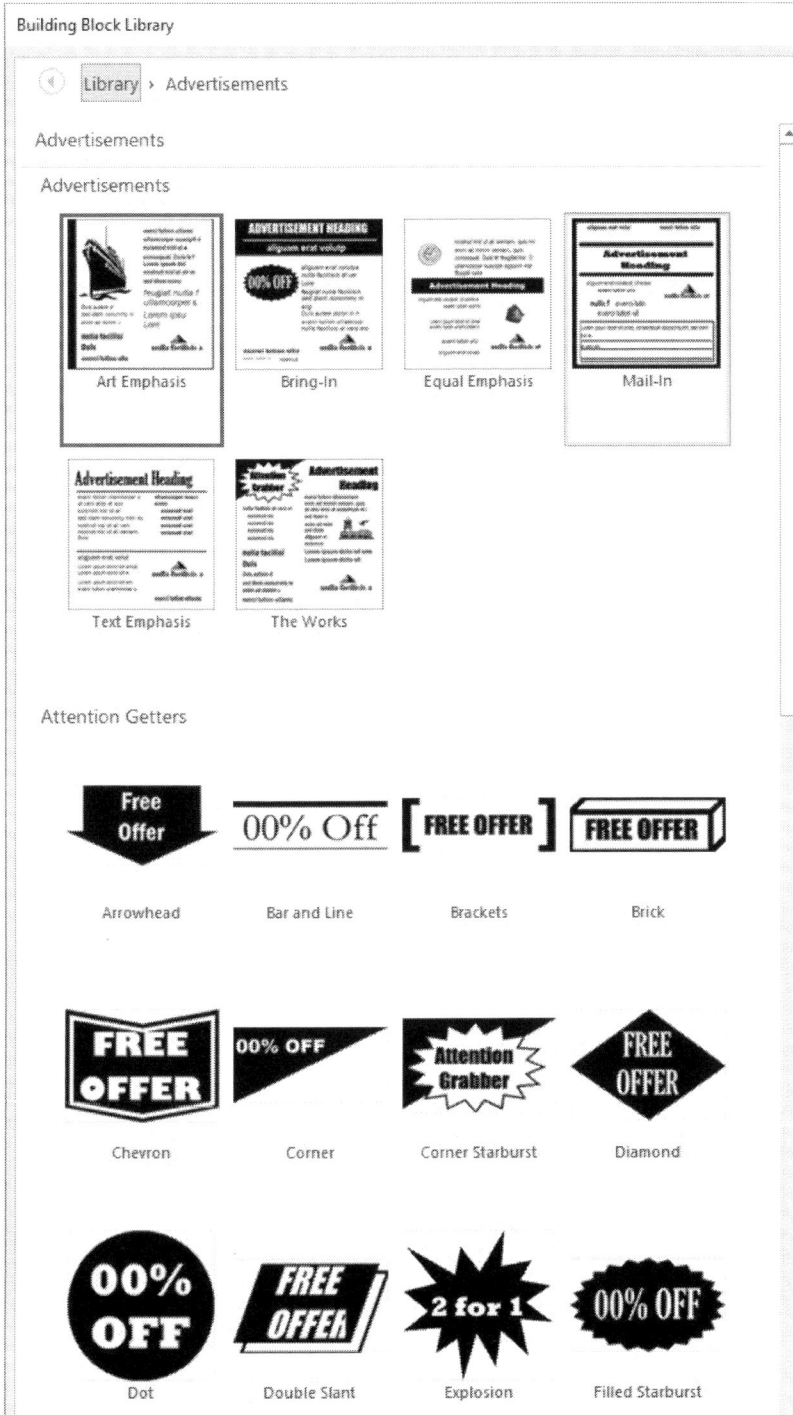

Figure 3.28

ADVERTISEMENT HEADING

Organization Name

00% OFF

List your hours or the time and date of your event.

Describe your location by landmark or area of town.

Describe your special offer, and tell readers to bring in the ad to qualify.

Tel: 555 555 5555   **Organization**

Expiration Date: 00/00/00

Figure 3.29

Text

The Text group has a variety of text related items you can add to your publication. There are various text related activities you can perform from this group.

- **Text Box** – This choice lets you add text within a box that you can move around the screen and place on top of images. You can then format the text in the box any way you like and also format the text box itself to add a box around the text if you like.

- **Business Information** – If you plan on adding things like your business name, address and phone number to your publications you can store that information in Publisher, and then have it easily placed into your documents. If you choose the *Edit Business Information Set* option then you can fill in the details about your business and every time you insert a Business Information graphic into a publication it will fill in the details for you.

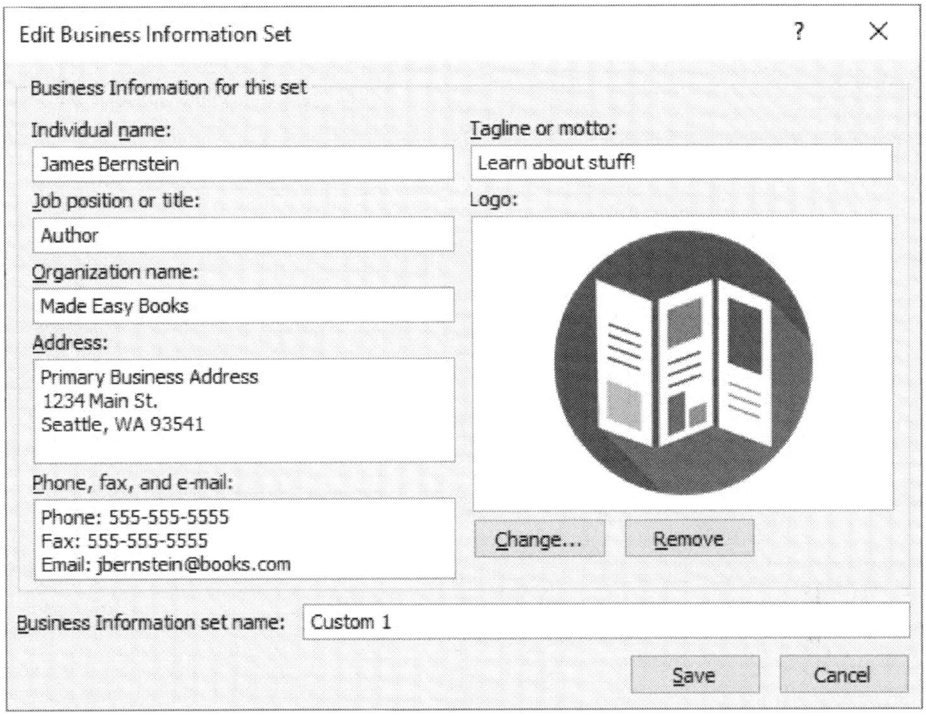

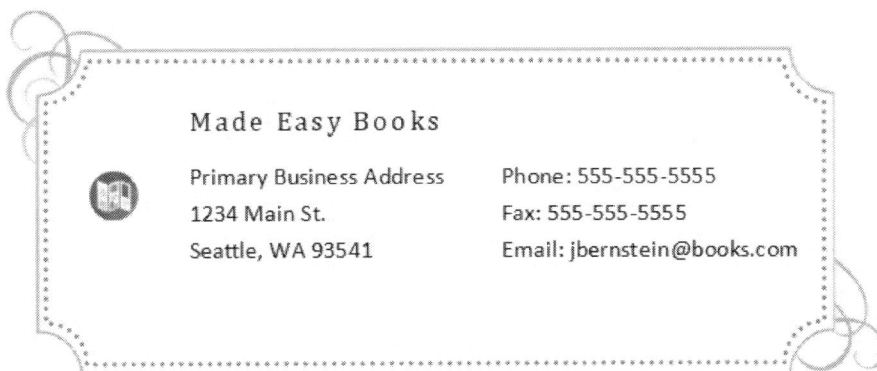

Figure 3.30

Figure 3.31

- **Word Art** – WordArt has been around for some time, but it is still a cool way to add some flash to your slides. All you need to do is click on a WordArt style you like and start typing. Then you can drag your new text box around the screen and place it wherever you want on your slide, as shown below.

- **Insert File** – Here you can insert various pre-existing files such as Word, text, and other Publisher files which will then be displayed in your publication, so you don't have to add the information from scratch.

- **Symbol** – These are used when you need to add a specific kind of character to your document such as ©™ π. Equations can be inserted as well if you are the smart type that has a use for that!

- **Date & Time** – If you would like the current date and time placed on your slides you can add it from here.

- **Object** – Another feature of the Text group includes the ability to embed (insert) other types of documents such as Word files or PDFs within your primary document so they can be opened right off the page itself.

Links

If you have ever used a web browser to go online then you should be familiar with the concept of links. Links consist of text or images that you can click on to take you to another page on a website, another website altogether or even another part of your publication. Publisher has two types of links that you can use within your publication.

- **Hyperlink** – The hyperlink option is used to create a link to things such as a particular website, place within the publication, or an email address. Think of it as the same type of link you sometimes get in your emails where you can click on it and it will take you somewhere else. All you need to do is select the text or object you want to act as your link and click the *Link* button and then choose the type of link you wish to create and fill in the details.

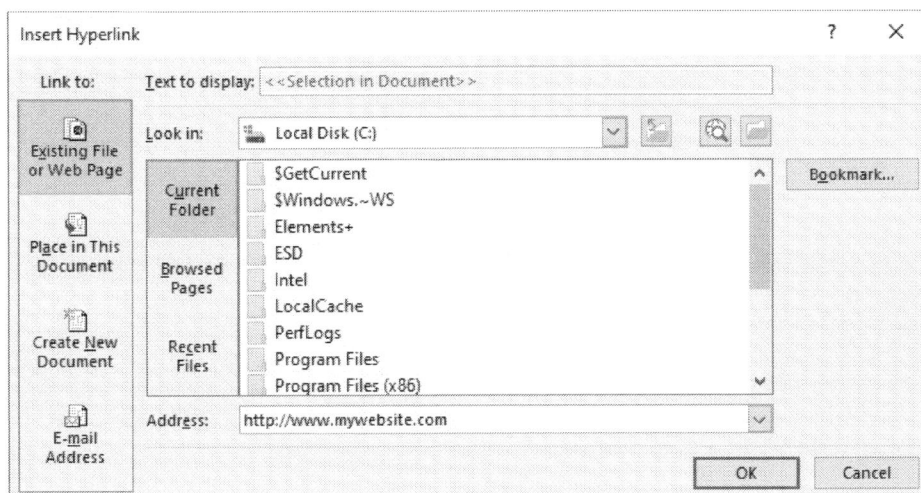

Figure 3.32

- **Bookmark** – Bookmarks are used to mark a place that you want to find again easily in the future. After you create a bookmark and click on where you want the bookmark to reside in the publication, you can go back to your bookmarks, choose the one you want, and it will take you back to that same spot in the publication. Bookmarks can be created on text or other objects.

Header & Footer – These are used to display information in publications with multiple pages and are shown on either the top or bottom of the page.

- **Header** – Headers are shown on the top of the page and can contain things such as the publication's name or title.

- **Footer** – Footers are on the bottom of the page and are commonly used for things like references and anything else you want to put there, including information you can put in a header.

- **Page Number** – Publisher can automatically number your pages for you as you add more, and you can select the style and placement of the page numbers from here.

Page Design Tab
Once you get some information into your publication you might start second guessing your design and the Page Design tab is where you can go to try out some new ideas on your existing work. Of course you can always start here too when creating a new publication if that's the way you like to work.

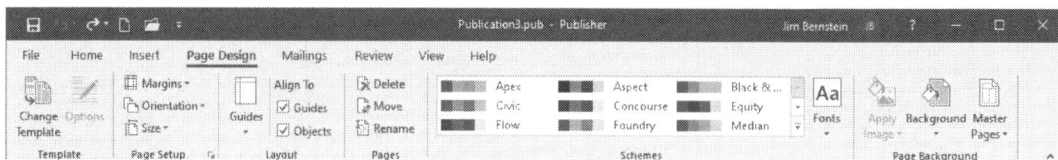

Figure 3.33

The Page Design tab has its own set of groups that are specific to formatting how your overall page will look so I will go over those groups now.

Template
Templates are used to apply an overall look and feel to your publication in regards to text, colors, graphics and page layout. There are many templates to choose from so if you didn't pick one when you started your work, you can apply one from here.

If you already have a template applied and want to change it then you can click on the *Change Template* button to choose a new one that you like better. When you do this you will be prompted to either apply that template to your current publication or create a new publication using your text and graphics.

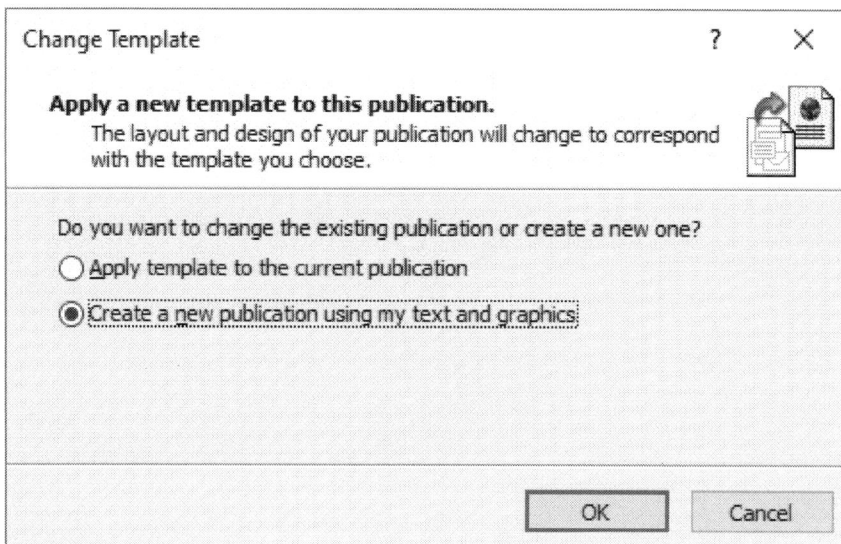

Figure 3.34

This process is hit and miss depending on how you have your publication configured when you apply the new template. For example, I applied a new template to my flyer publication, and it didn't work out so well since Publisher was unable to add many of my objects to this new template. Figure 3.35 shows the box I got to the right of the screen telling me which objects it was not able to add. You will have the option of adding these objects back manually though, but it means extra work for you since you will have to redo their placement in your publication.

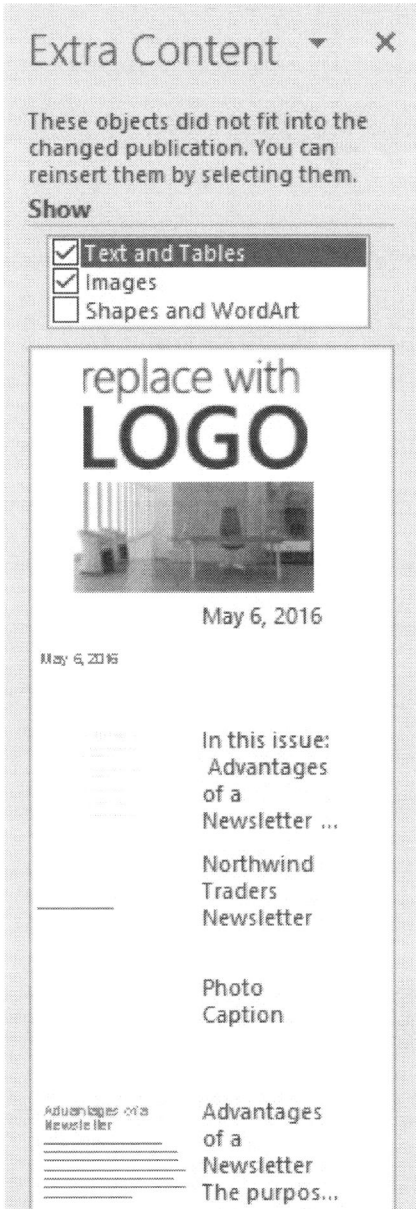

Figure 3.35

Page Setup

This group is one that you will commonly use to change the way your page is initially set up in regards to paper size, margins and so on.

- **Margins** – Margins are the amount of white space between the edge of the page and the text or graphics on the page. There are built-in margins you can choose from, or you can create your own custom margins. This will apply to the entire publication unless you tell Publisher otherwise.

- **Orientation** – There are two choices for orientation, and they are portrait (which is where the page is up and down the long way) and landscape (which the page is longer from left to right).

- **Size** – The default size for Publisher documents is 8.5x11 (letter), but you can choose from one of the many built-in sizes or create your own custom size. This will apply to the entire publication unless you tell Publisher otherwise. Keep in mind when changing the size of your publication that if you want to print it, you will have to have that size paper at hand, otherwise it won't print correctly.

Layout

When working on publications it's important to make sure that things are aligned properly so that when you go to print your publication, everything looks correct and fits together as a whole and using guides can help you accomplish this.

Guides are lines that appear in your publication that help you align your objects yet don't appear when you go to print your final work. They are used to keep things in line with each other just in case your eyes are not working as good as you think they are! Publisher has many built in guide configurations to choose from as you can see in figure 3.36.

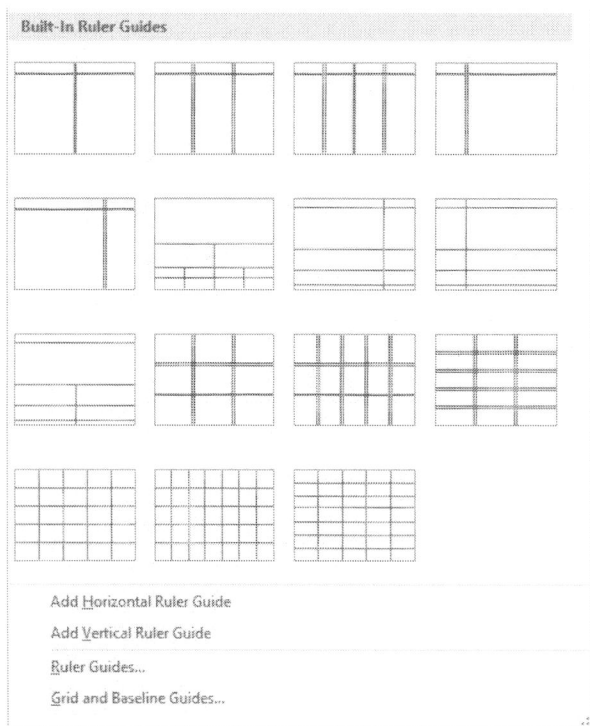

Figure 3.36

You can use one of these built in guide configurations or add individual horizontal and vertical guide lines to create your own setup.

If you want to enter in the exact location on the page where you want the guide lines to be you can use the *Ruler Guide* option and enter in the position for one or more guide lines.

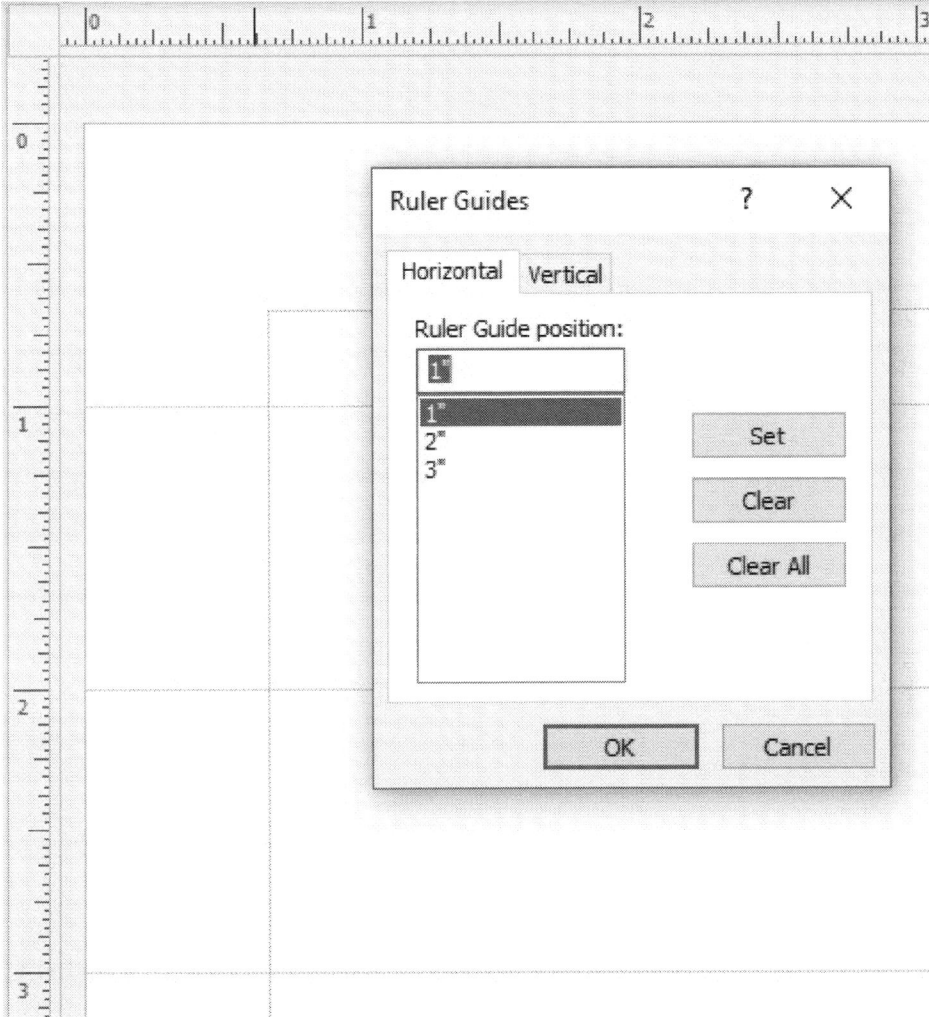

Figure 3.37

The *Layout Guides* option allows you to create a custom grid and guide configuration all from one spot if you know exactly where you want your guide lines to be placed.

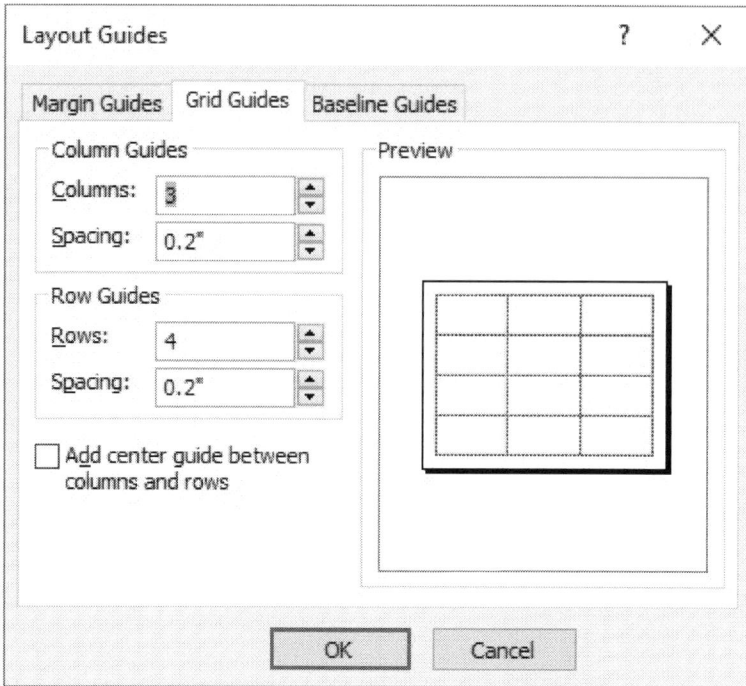

Figure 3.38

The best way to see how this all works is to play around with them and try out some of the other options. You can always remove the lines if you decide you don't need them. Or better yet, start a new blank publication and add some guide lines there.

The *Align to Guides* and *Align to Objects* checkboxes force your objects to either align themselves with the guide lines you have created or to align themselves to other objects relative to their position on the page. If you find that objects are getting aligned where you don't want them to be you can try to uncheck one or both boxes and see how that works for you.

Pages

The Pages group should be pretty easy to figure out and I have gone over the options here when I discussed the Pages Pane. To summarize, you can do things such as delete specific pages from your publication, rename one or more pages and move pages around to reorder them within your work.

Schemes

Schemes are designed to change the color scheme of your publication but will only work on certain items. They are not like templates where they can affect everything on the page to give it a completely new look but rather change the color combinations used for things like filled in shapes, text colors, calendar colors and so on. So if you are not happy with the overall color design of your work then you can easily apply one of the schemes to change the appearance of your entire publication. To the right of the color schemes is the *Fonts* button which will let you change the overall theme of your text by replacing the fonts (typestyles) within your publication.

Tip

One thing to keep in mind when working in Publisher is that the Undo option is your friend. If you make a change and want to revert it all you need to do is click the Undo button (left arrow in the Quick Launch Bar) as many times as needed to go back a step. You can also press Ctrl-Z on your keyboard to do the same thing (Command-Z for Mac). There is also an option for Redo (Ctrl-Y).

Page Background

If you don't want to stick with a plain white background for your publication then you can easily change that from the *Page Background* group of the Page Design tab.

The first thing you can do from here is make one of the existing images on your page be the background image for that page. Figure 3.39 shows a simple page with some text and a picture of a dog. Then I clicked on the picture of the dog and went to the *Apply Image* button and choose the *Fill* option and the results are shown in figure 3.40.

Dogs (Canis lupus familiaris) are domesticated mammals, not natural wild animals. They were originally bred from wolves. They have been bred by humans for a long time, and were the first animals ever to be domesticated. ...  **Today, some dogs are used as pets, others are used to help humans do their work.**

Figure 3.39

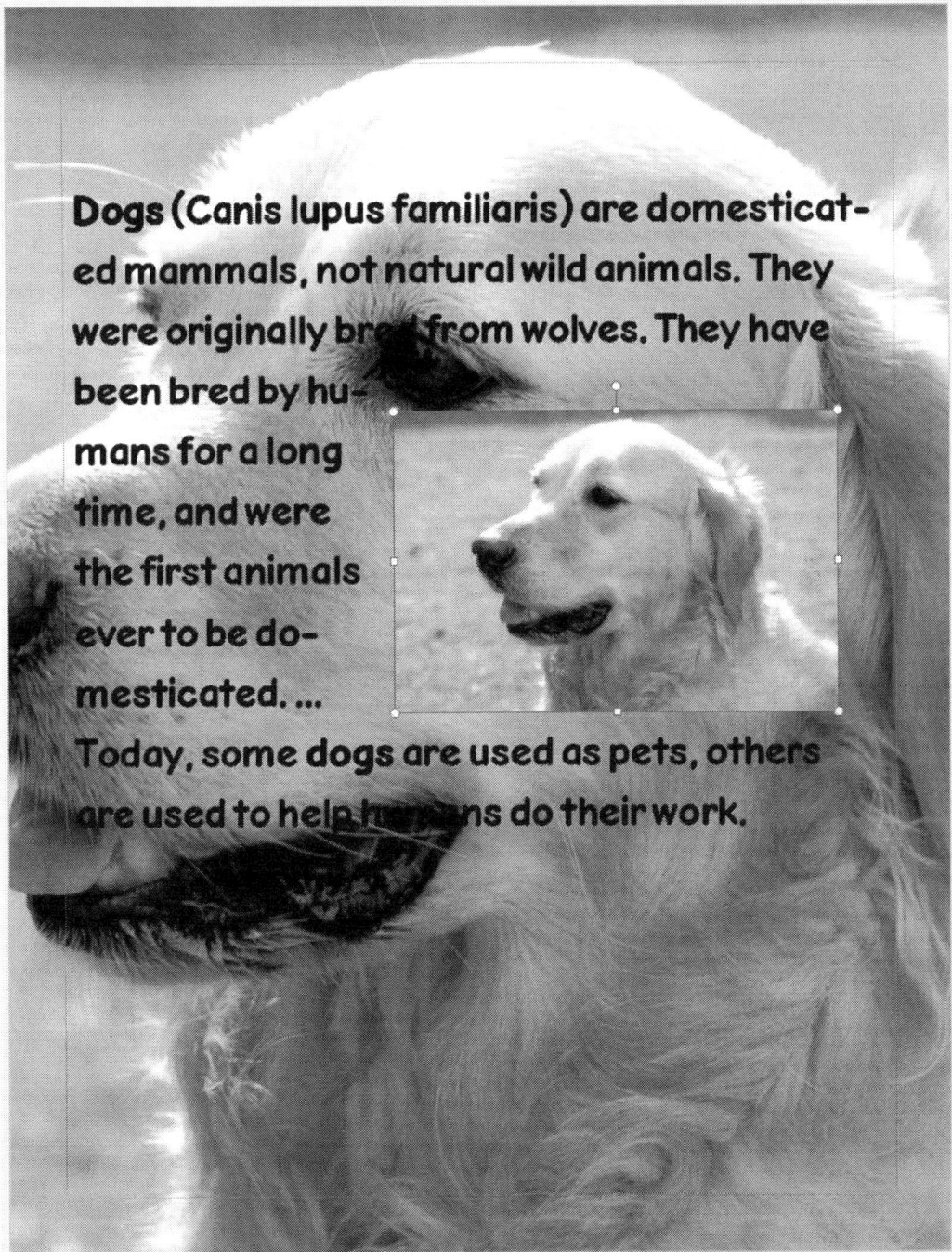

Figure 3.40

If you would rather not use an image for your background but instead use something a little more subtle then you can apply things like solid colors, gradients and patterns as your background. Figure 3.41 shows the same page with a gradient background applied as an example.

Figure 3.41

If you click on *More Backgrounds* under the Background options you will be able to create your own custom colors, gradients and patterns as well as use images that you have stored on your computer or online.

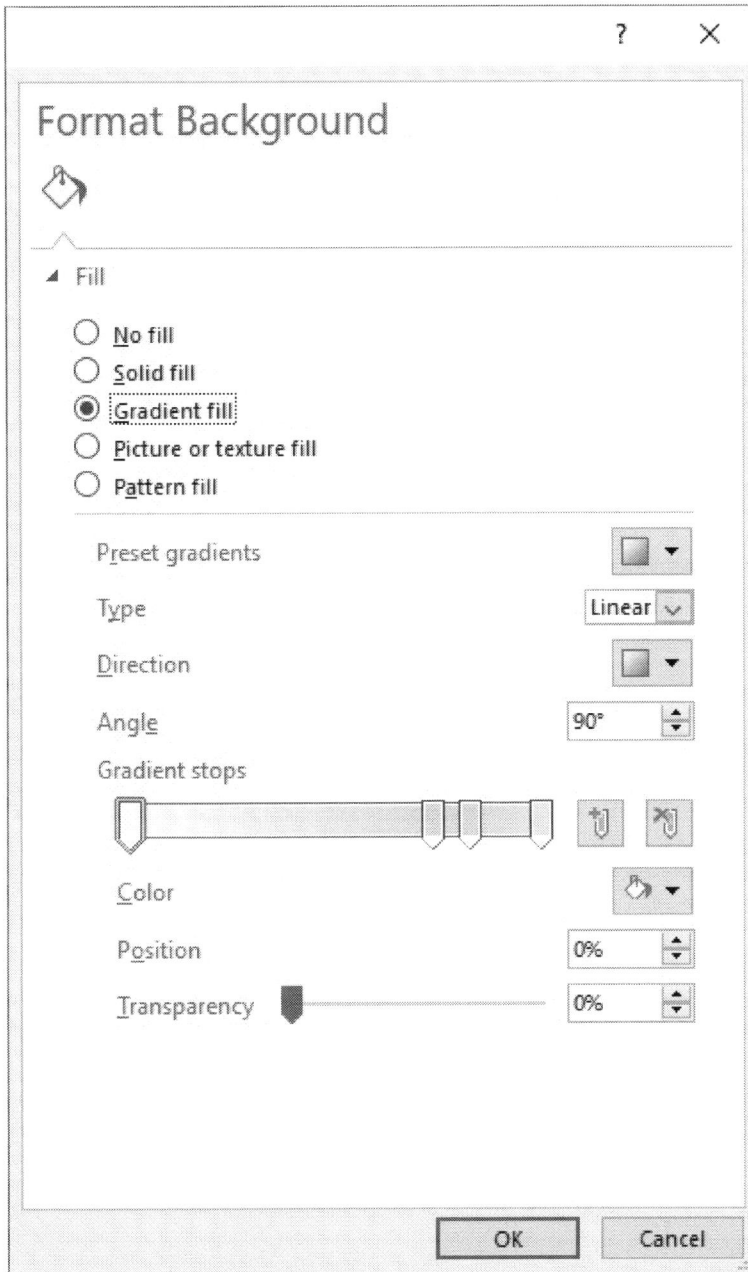

Figure 3.42

Master Pages contain settings and attributes that apply to all of the pages in your Publication and I will be discussing these in Chapter 5.

Mailings Tab

A big part of creating publications such as newsletters, for example, is to be able to easily mail them out to a group of people without having to do a lot of manual work.

This is where the Mailings tab comes into play. Here you can do things such as create *Mail Merge* and *Email Merge* lists that allow you to create mailing lists quickly and easily. I will be going over the Mail Merge and Email Merge process in Chapter 5 so I will not go into too much detail until then.

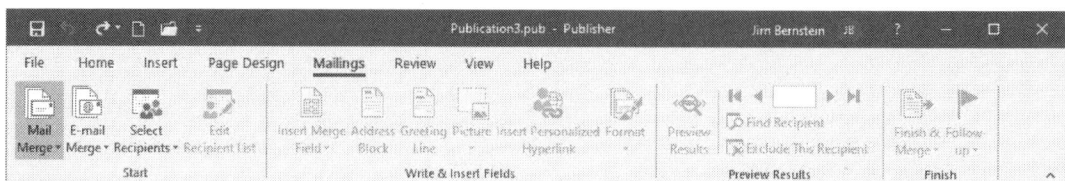
Figure 3.43

Review Tab

There aren't too many things you can do from the Review tab besides check your spelling or use the thesaurus, but there are a couple of cool features that I really like.

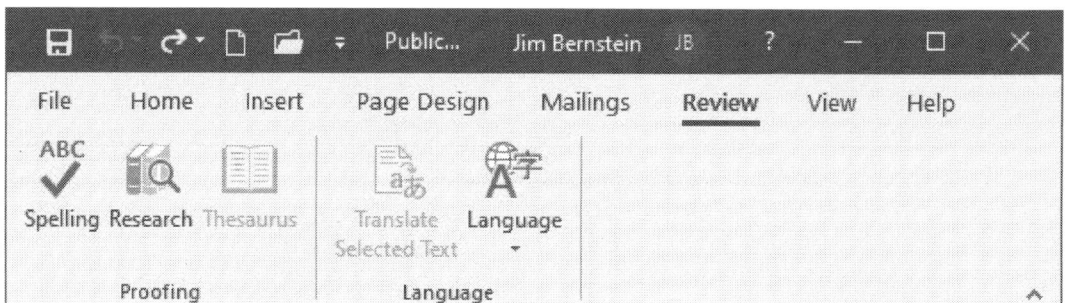
Figure 3.44

One of those features is the *Research* button. You can highlight some text within your publication, click the Research button, and Publisher will research that text for you online using the Encarta Dictionary or the thesaurus (figure 3.45). It will then show you results that you can use within your publication.

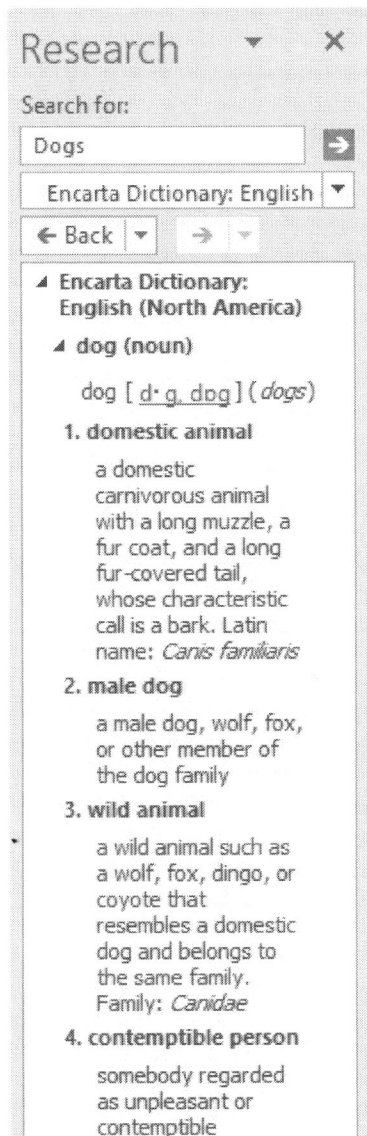

Figure 3.45

The other feature I like is the *Translate Selected Text* button. You can use this by highlighting the text you want to translate and then choose a *from* and *to* language to have Publisher give you the translated text (figure 3.46). Then you can have the translated text inserted directly into your publication, or you can have it copied to the clipboard to use elsewhere.

The *Language* button also deserves a little attention because if you are using more than one language in your publication, you can choose another one from this area to be used for proofing. You can also get to the Publisher Language options by clicking on *Language Preferences*.

Figure 3.46

View Tab

The View tab is important because it is used to change the way you see your publication making it easier to work with.

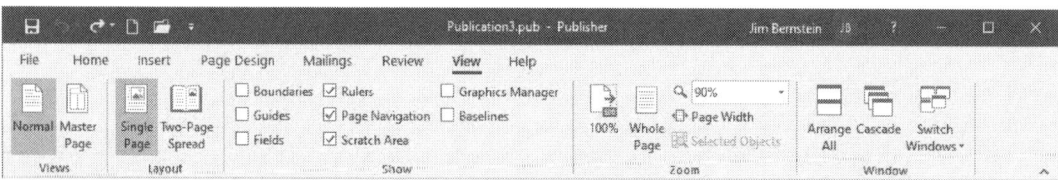

Figure 3.47

Now I would like to go over all of the groups in the View tab.

Views

There are two main views you can choose from in the View group and they are *Normal* and *Master Page*. Most of the time you will be working with the Normal view because the Master Page view is meant to be used to make changes that will affect every page in your publication. I will be covering the Master Page in Chapter 5.

Layout

The layout will determine how your pages are displayed on the screen and unless you are working on a publication that is going to be bound or folded for printing purposes then you will most likely be using the *Single Page* view.

Show

This grouping will allow you to show the ruler at the top of the page as well as gridlines across the body of the page in case you need them to help with the alignment of text and images.

The *Navigation Pane* checkbox is used to toggle the Pages Pane on the left side of the screen on and off.

The *Scratch Area* checkbox enables or disables the Scratch area which can be used to hold text, graphics and images off to the side of your publication in case you want to add them later. Items in this area won't show up when you print your file.

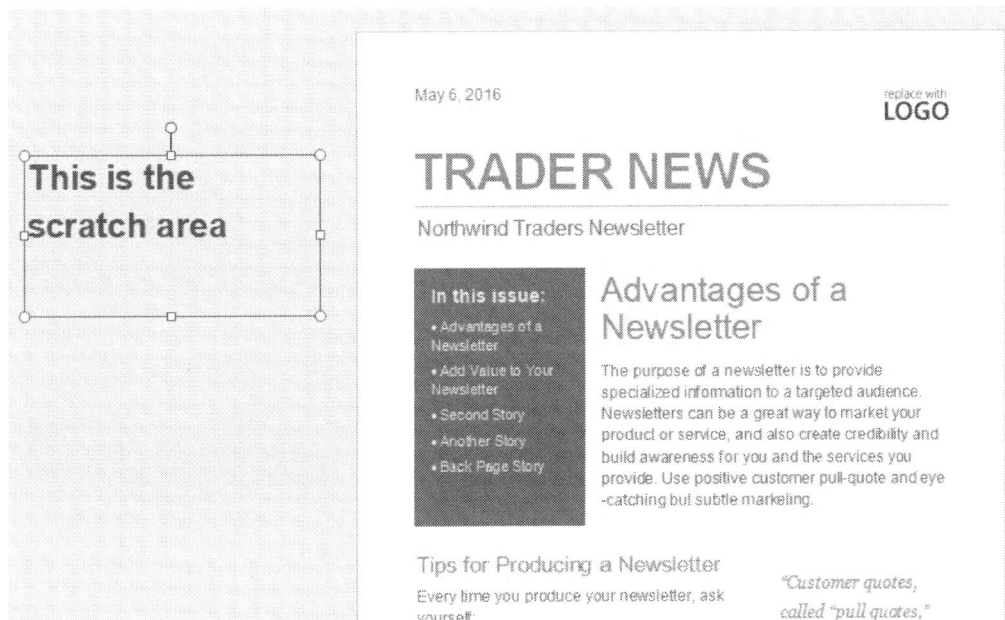

Figure 3.48

If you enable the *Graphics Manager* it will open a pane to the right of the screen that shows the details about all the images you have on the page. From here you can then do things such as save the image to your hard drive, replace the image or show details about an image as shown in figure 3.50.

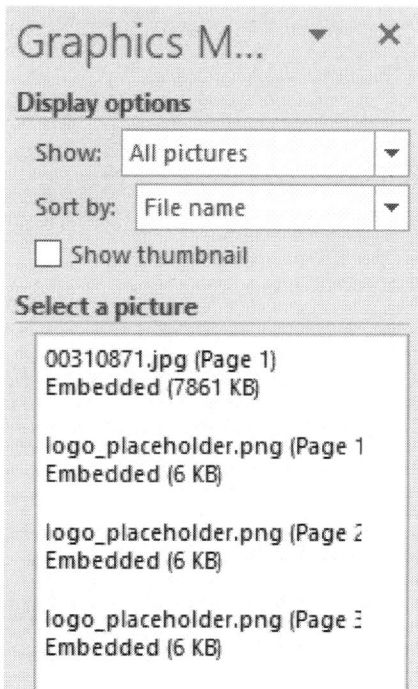

Figure 3.49

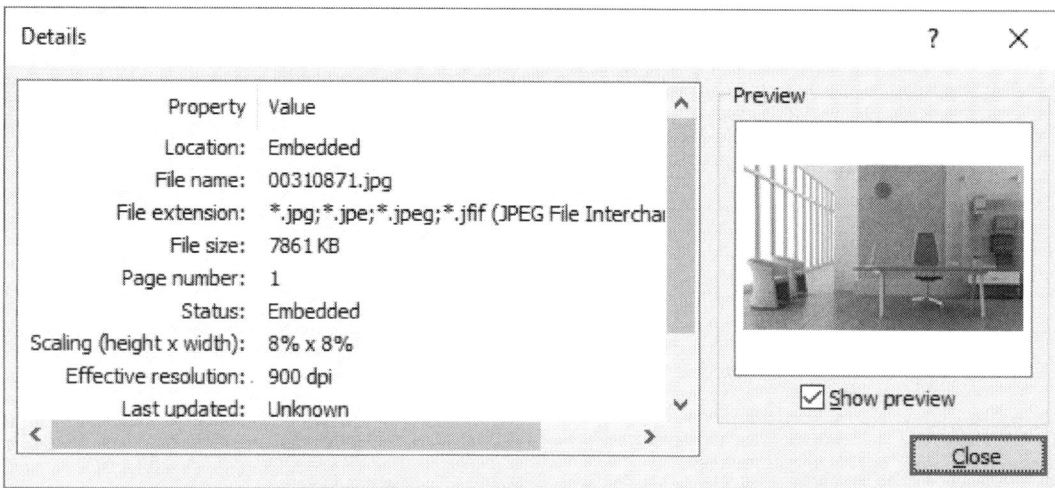

Figure 3.50

The Baselines checkbox will show the default baseline guides in your publication. Baseline guides allow you to align text lines across multiple columns.

Figure 3.51

Zoom
This group has tools you can use to zoom in and out of your publication to make things easier to see and work on. There is also a zoom slider at the lower left of the screen that will let you easily zoom in and out.

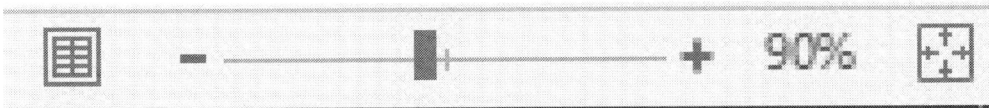

Figure 3.52

In the Zoom group there is a button called *Selected Objects,* and what that does is makes whatever object you have selected take up the whole screen so you can get a better look at it. To reduce it back to normal, simply click a smaller zoom percentage from the zoom box above.

Window
The Window group allows you to change the views when you have more than one document open. You have several views to choose from:

- **Arrange All** – This view will arrange all the documents on your screen so you can see all of them. If you have too many documents open at one time, this view doesn't do a lot of good.

- **Cascade** – This view will arrange your windows with an overlapping cascade from top to bottom.

- **Switch Windows** – If you have multiple publications open, you can click on this button to switch back and forth between them.

Help Tab

I will just spend a little time on the Help tab because it should be obvious as to what it does. If you need help on how to do something within Publisher you can come to this tab and see if you can find what you are looking for. There is only one group here and it only has a few options within that group.

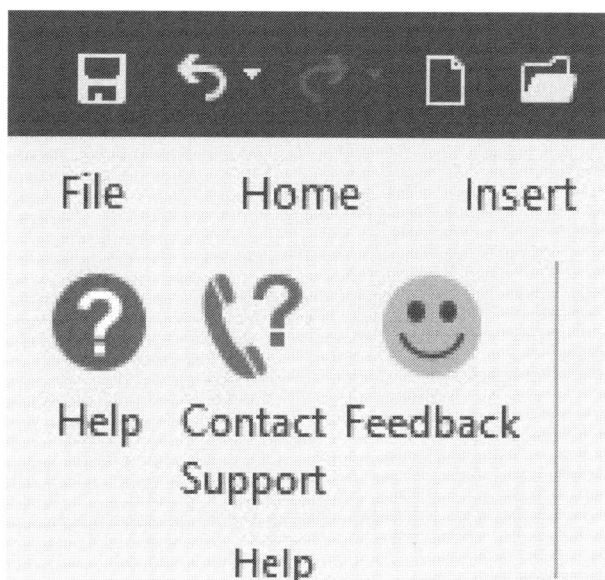

Figure 3.53

- **Help** – Here you can type in questions you are looking for an answer for or type in the name of a feature to see if you can find help to show you what it does or how to use it.

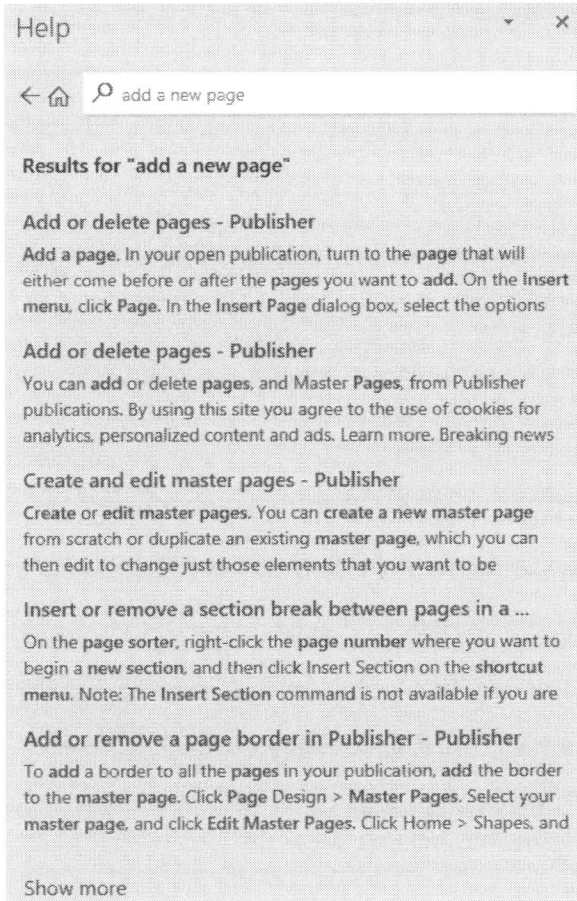

Figure 3.54

- **Contact Support** – This option is similar to the regular help option where you can type in what you want help with. The main difference is that it will bring up other support options that you can choose from such as a live chat. Just be careful when using this option so you don't end up paying for someone to answer a question for you.

- **Feedback** – If you want to voice your option and let Microsoft know what you think then you can leave some feedback or offer up a suggestion on how to improve their software. Your guess is as good as mine as to whether or not they actually read these!

Chapter 4 - Creating a New Publication

Now that you have an idea of what all the items in the Ribbon do (hopefully), it's time to start a new publication and get your ideas on paper, digital paper that is. Once we get a publication type decided on and created then the next step will be to format it and make it look professional which I will go over in the next chapter.

Choosing a Publication Type

The first thing you need to do when starting a new Publisher file, of course, is to decide on what type of publication you want to create. This is important because you should decide on things such as your paper size before you begin otherwise you will be doing a lot of rearranging later on if you decide to change its size.

When creating a publication you have the option to start from scratch with a blank file or use one of the supplied template files to help get you started on a design. You can also go online and download other templates if the supplied versions are not what you are looking for. Just be careful where you download them from and make sure it's a trustworthy website.

When you first open Publisher you will see something similar to figure 4.1 where you have a list of recently opened files if you have already used Publisher, otherwise there will be now recent files shown.

For newer versions of Office and Office 365, you usually sign in with a Microsoft account that will keep track of all of your recent documents and also link your Office programs to your OneDrive account. So if you sign out of your Microsoft account within Publisher or any Office program, your list of recent files and connection to your OneDrive storage will be removed until you sign back in.

There will also be options to choose various blank file types of various sizes if you plan on starting from scratch. If you click on *More Blank Page Sizes* you will be taken to another screen with many different sizes and other blank publication types as seen in figure 4.2.

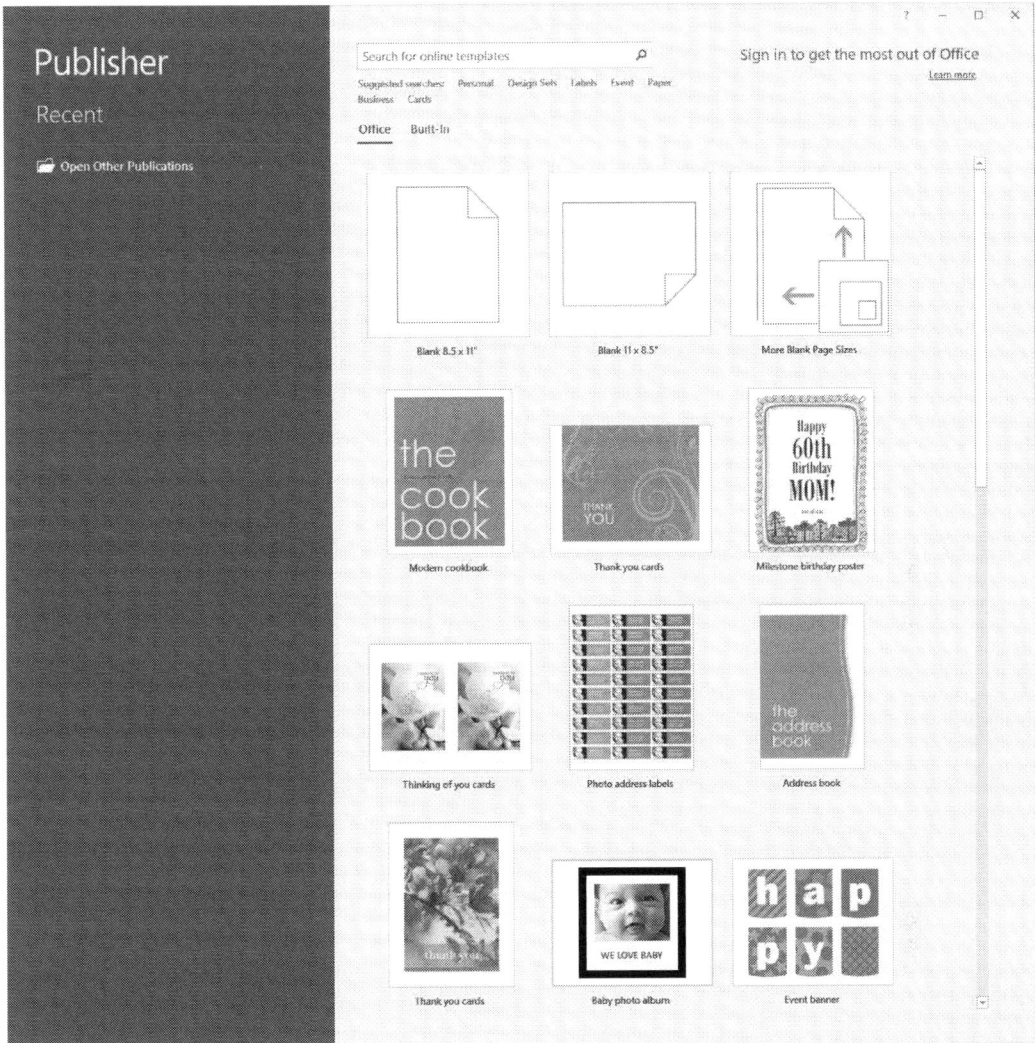

Figure 4.1

If you look closely at figure 4.2 you will see there is a *Custom* section where you can create a new file with your own specific paper size in case you can't find what you are looking for with one of the built in files.

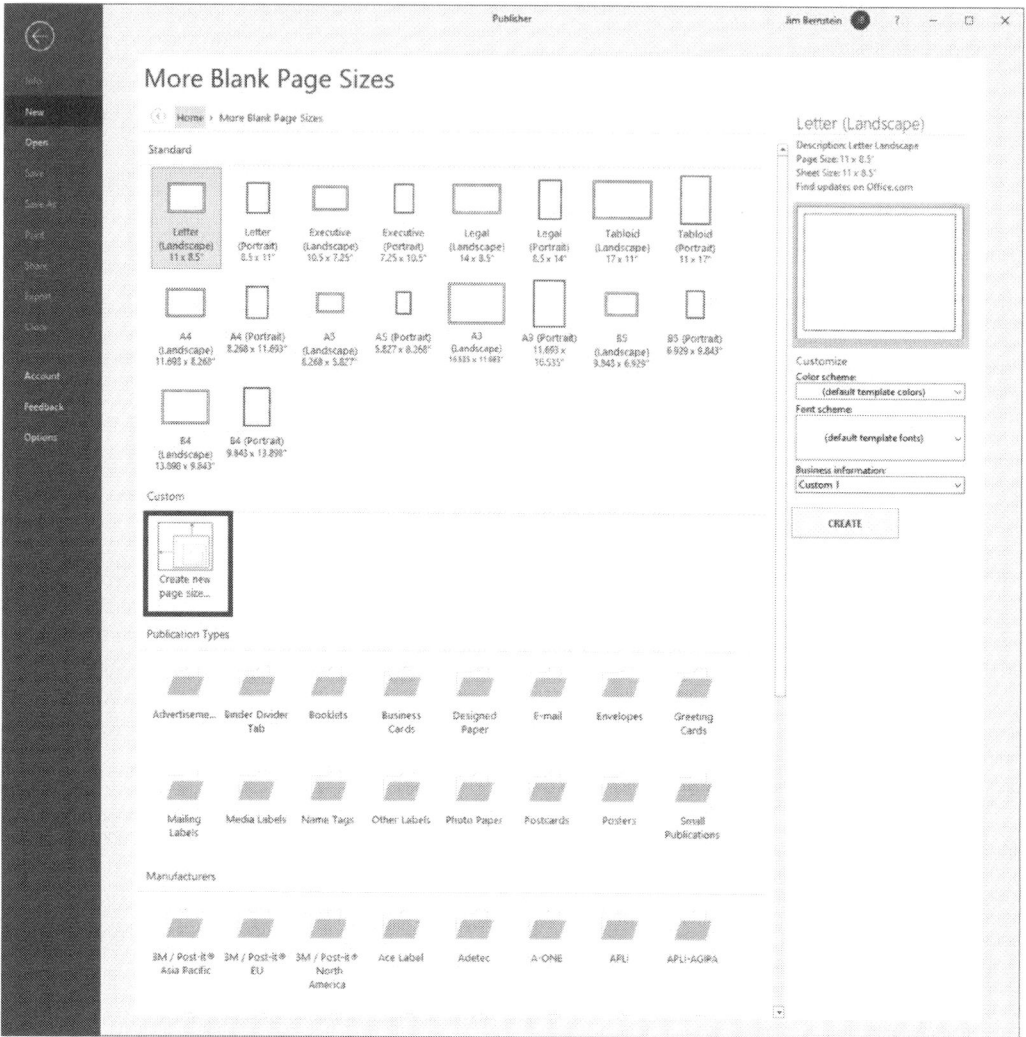

Figure 4.2

If you would rather start with a predesigned template file to save yourself a little work then you can choose from one of the available templates as you can see back in figure 4.1. If you click on *Built-In* you will get some template categories to help you narrow down your search for the right type of template.

Office   Built-In

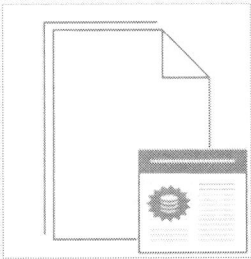
Advertisements

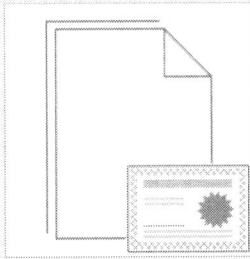
Award Certificates

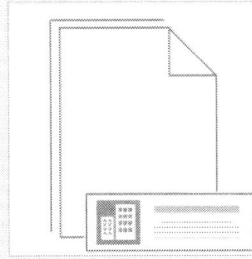
Banners

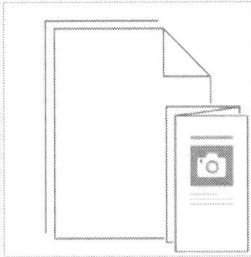
Brochures

Business Cards

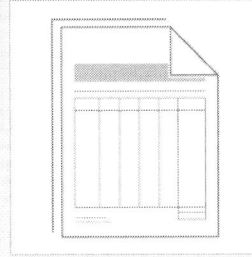
Business Forms

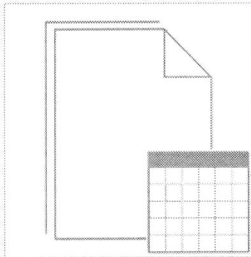
Calendars

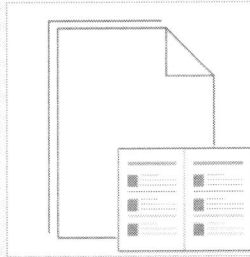
Catalogs

E-mail

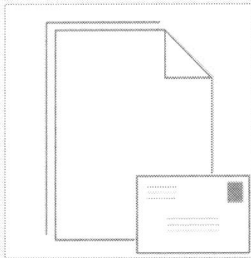
Envelopes

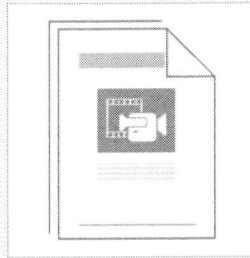
Flyers

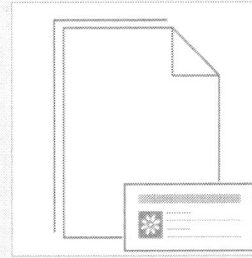
Gift Certificates

Figure 4.3

If you still can't find what you are looking for then you can try the search option at the top of the page and enter in the type of template you are looking for.

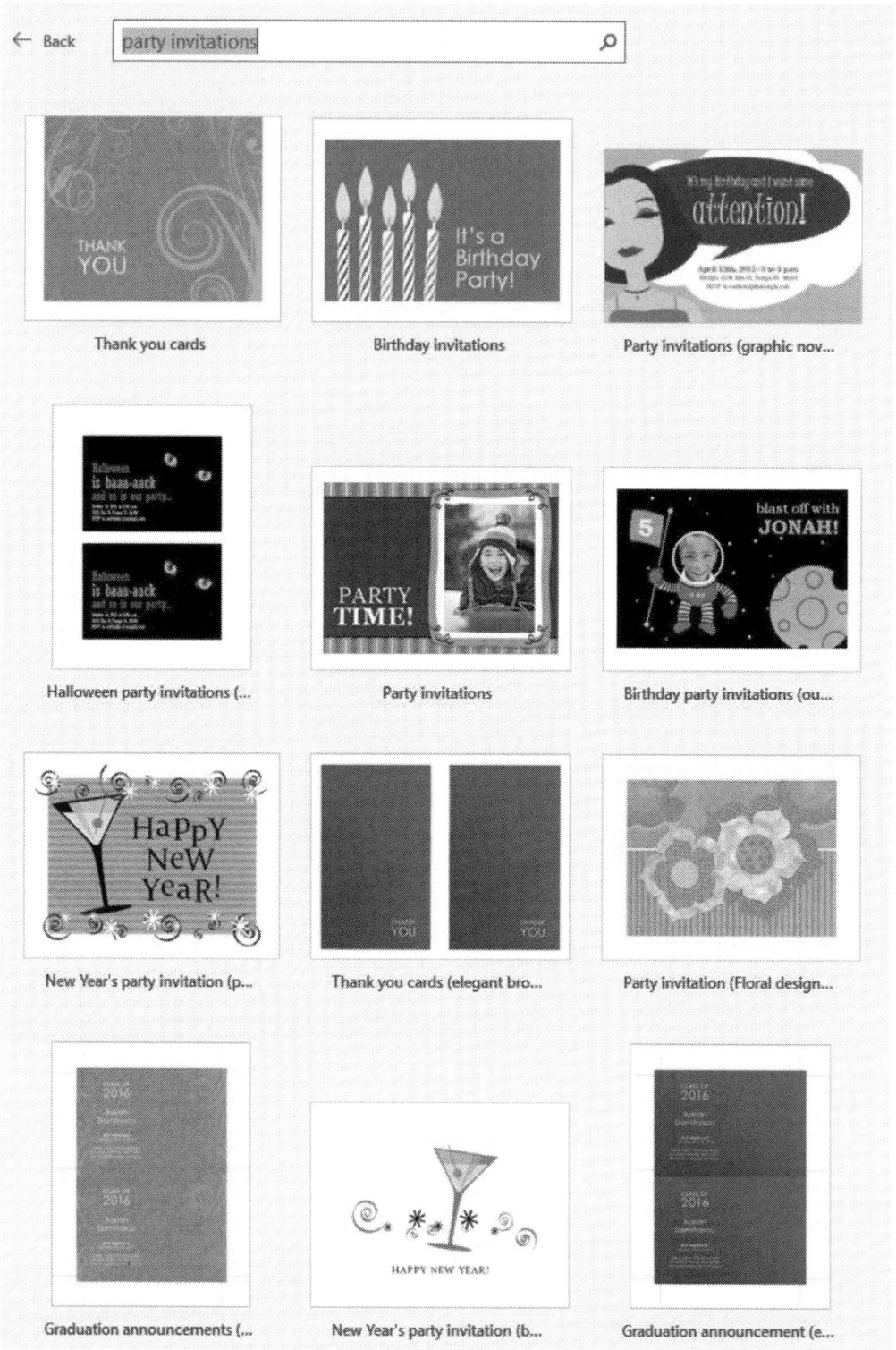

← Back   party invitations   🔍

Thank you cards

Birthday invitations

Party invitations (graphic nov...

Halloween party invitations (...

Party invitations

Birthday party invitations (ou...

New Year's party invitation (p...

Thank you cards (elegant bro...

Party invitation (Floral design...

Graduation announcements (...

New Year's party invitation (b...

Graduation announcement (e...

Figure 4.4

For my example, I want to create a dog calendar and will do so from scratch just to help show you the steps required to add the features you would already have provided for you in the template file. This will by no means be a super professional looking publication but rather a lesson on how to create your file and add text and graphics to it.

To begin I will choose a blank 8.5x11" paper size file and Publisher will create the file with one page to start with.

Figure 4.5

The Pages Pane

Since I will be creating a calendar I will need a page for each month of the year so that means I need 11 more pages. I have already discussed the Pages Pane, but I will now use it again to add more pages to my publication. The big question is do I want to add all 11 pages now or wait until I get some text and graphics on my first page in case I can copy the first page with the information on it 11 times to save myself some work.

What I think I will do is add the calendar part of the publication to my first page and then copy it 11 times, so I don't need to repeat that step over and over. Then when I add the text and graphics I will do that separately for each page since each month will have unique text and images.

To add my calendar I will use a calendar *Building Block* from the *Insert* tab. I will choose the Blends style calendar and start it at January 2020 since that will be the first month of my calendar.

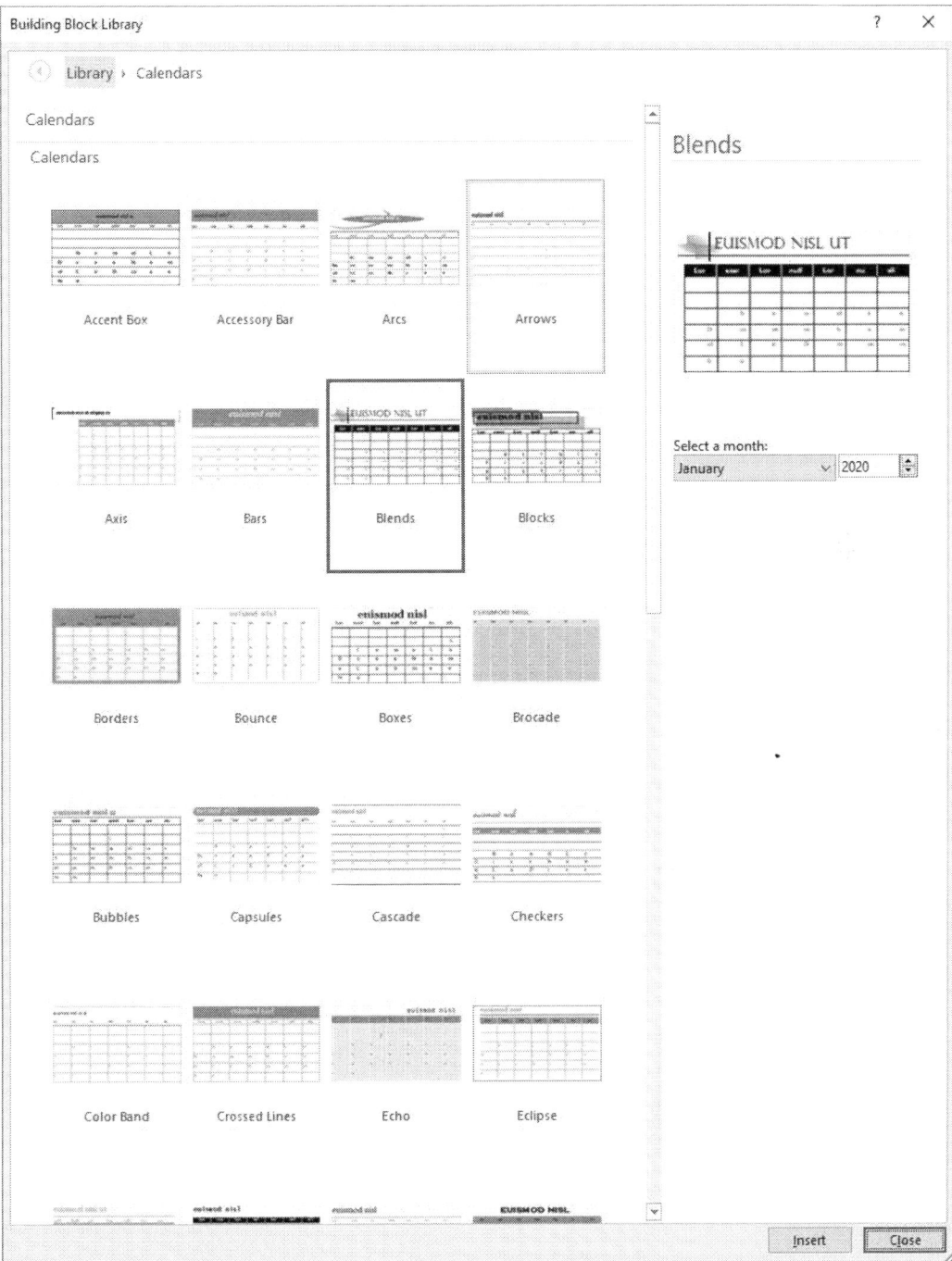

Figure 4.6

As you can see in figure 4.7, Publisher inserts the calendar in the middle of the page and it's not really the right size or in the right position so that will take a little adjustment on my part so I will drag the calendar to where I want it to go and also resize it to make it better fit the page. I will go into more detail about how to do these types of adjustments in the next chapter on formatting.

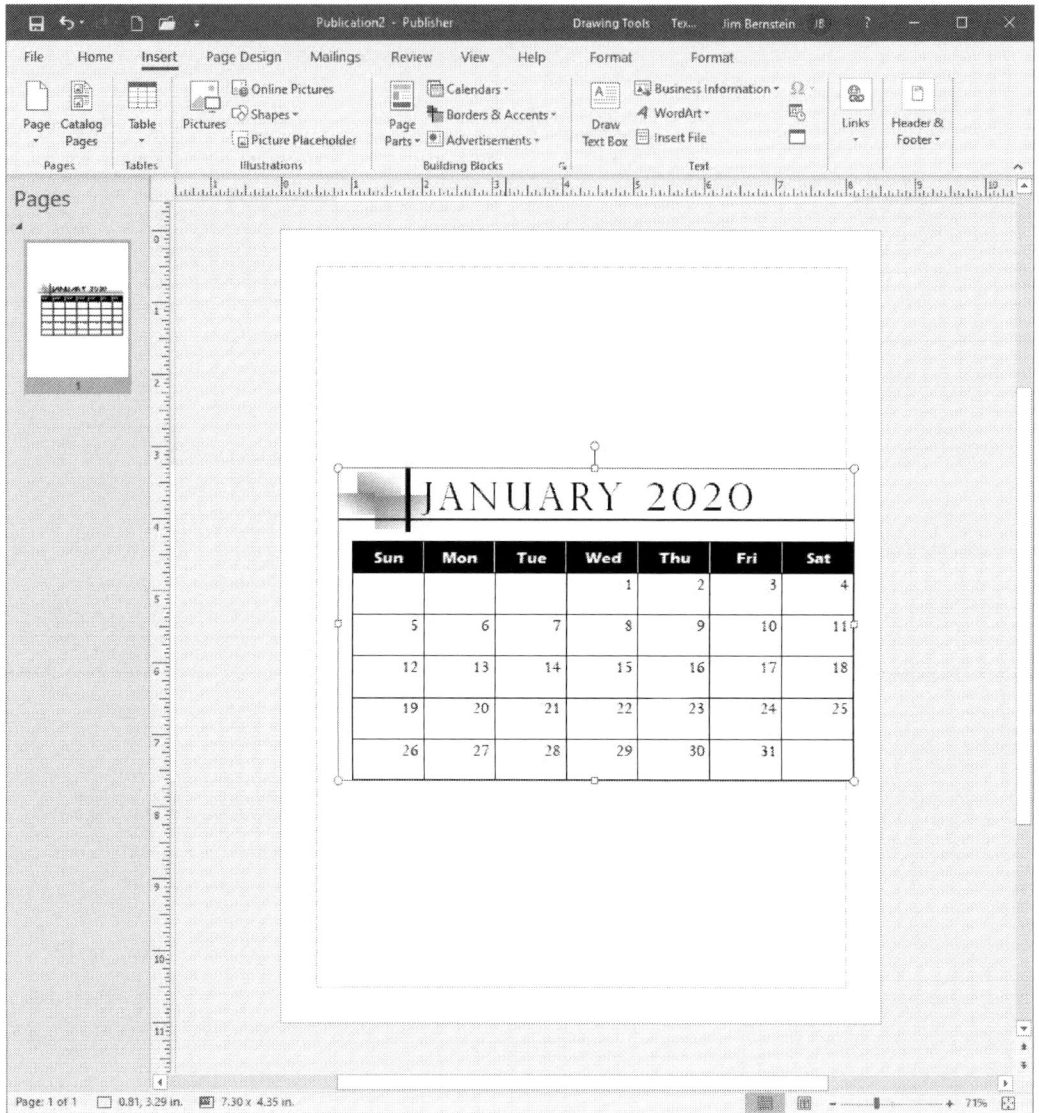

Figure 4.7

After making my adjustments things look a lot better as shown in figure 4.8.

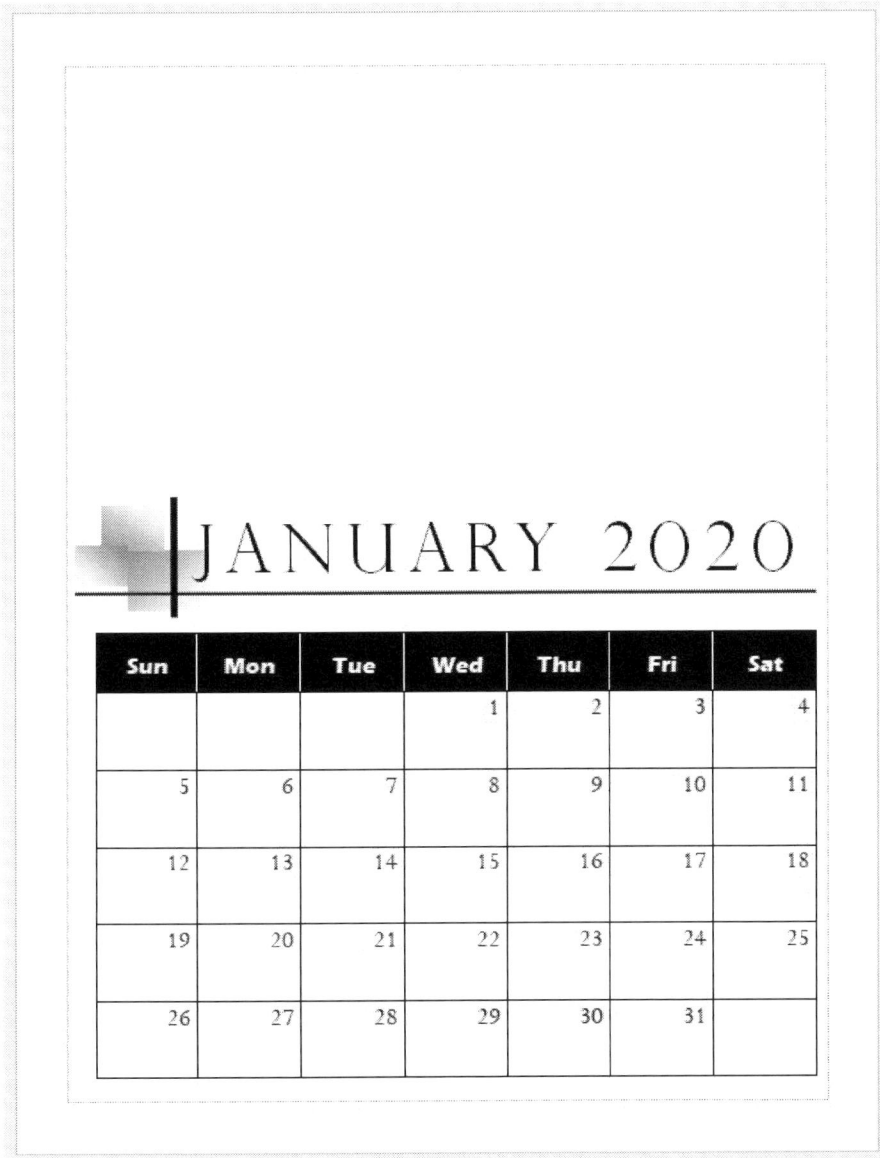

Figure 4.8

Now I want to duplicate what I have on this page 11 more times to get my full 12 month calendar pages in place. One way to do this is to right click on my page and choose *Insert Duplicate Page* and do this 11 times which I suppose wouldn't be too bad. But rather than do that I can go to the Insert tab, click on the down arrow below Page and choose *Insert Page*. Then I can enter in 11 for the number of pages and choose the *After current page* and *Duplicate all objects* on page 1 options to do the same thing all in one step.

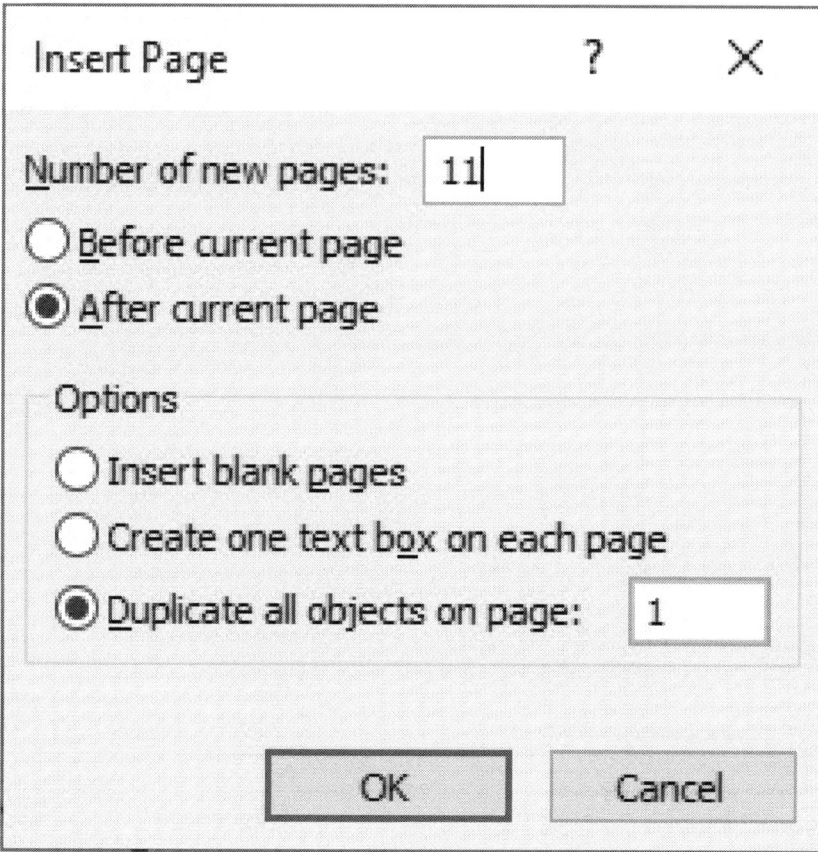

Insert Page   ?   ✕

Number of new pages: 11|

◯ Before current page

◉ After current page

Options

◯ Insert blank pages

◯ Create one text box on each page

◉ Duplicate all objects on page: 1

OK   Cancel

Figure 4.9

Now you can see that I have my 12 pages and they all have the same calendar on them. You might think I just need to go edit the calendar month name for each page, so I have one for each month of the year.

Tip

If you want to place a calendar Building Block onto your page that is for a different month and\or year then you will need to choose the *More Calendars* option otherwise Publisher will use the current month and year for the calendar that it inserts into your publication.

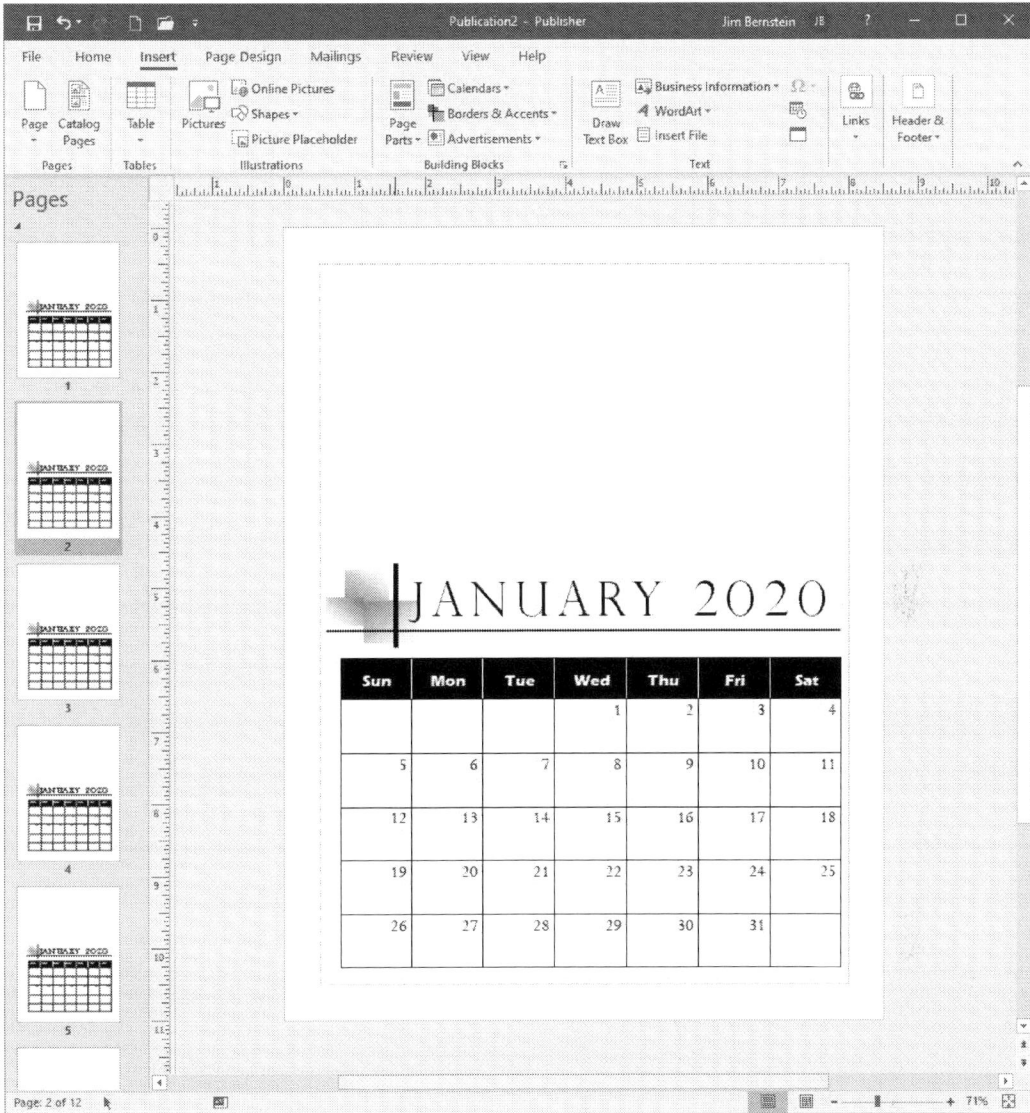

Figure 4.10

But if you think about it, that won't work because then I would have the same calendar days of the week for each month which is not accurate. Therefore I will need to go to each page and insert a new calendar with the correct year and month. This is something to think about when creating calendars! Also, keep in mind that you can use a calendar template and enter the start and end months and choose to have one month per page and Publisher will do all the work for you rather than have to do it manually like I ended up having to do.

Inserting Text

The next step in my dog calendar creating will be to add a different dog related fact or saying at the top of the page for each month of the year. To do this I will need to add a text box which will then allow me to type in some text within that text box.

To do this I will need to go to the *Insert* tab and then click on *Draw Text Box* and use my mouse to draw a box where I want to place the text (figure 4.11). You don't need to worry about getting the size and position exact because you can easily change things around after you enter in your text.

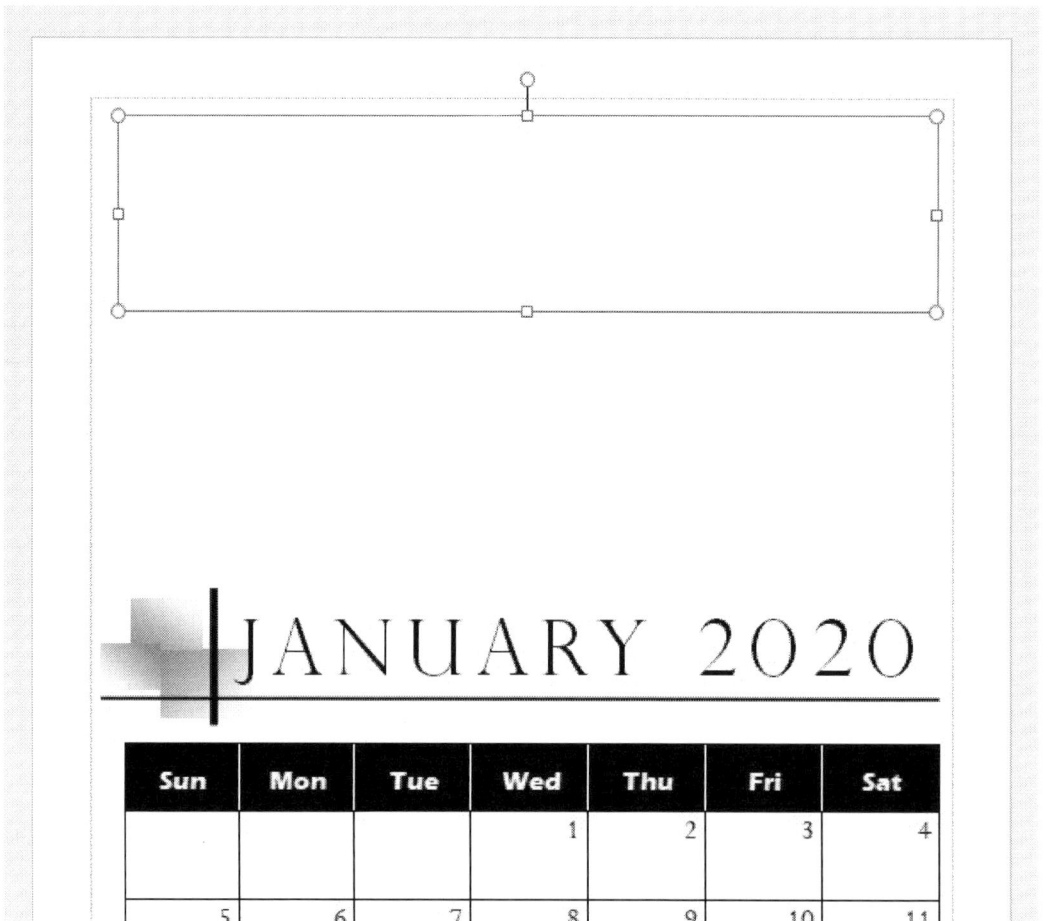

Sun	Mon	Tue	Wed	Thu	Fri	Sat
			1	2	3	4
5	6	7	8	9	10	11

Figure 4.11

Now that I have my text box I can easily type in my text, or in my case paste in my text from a website I found that has interesting facts about dogs. Figure 4.12 shows the results. If things don't look exactly as you like then they can easily be changed, and I will be going over formatting text in the next chapter. For example,

I don't like how the word temperatures is hyphenated in my text box.

Also, notice how the box around the text disappears when you click off of it because most of the time you don't want a box around your text but if you do then it's very easy to add one.

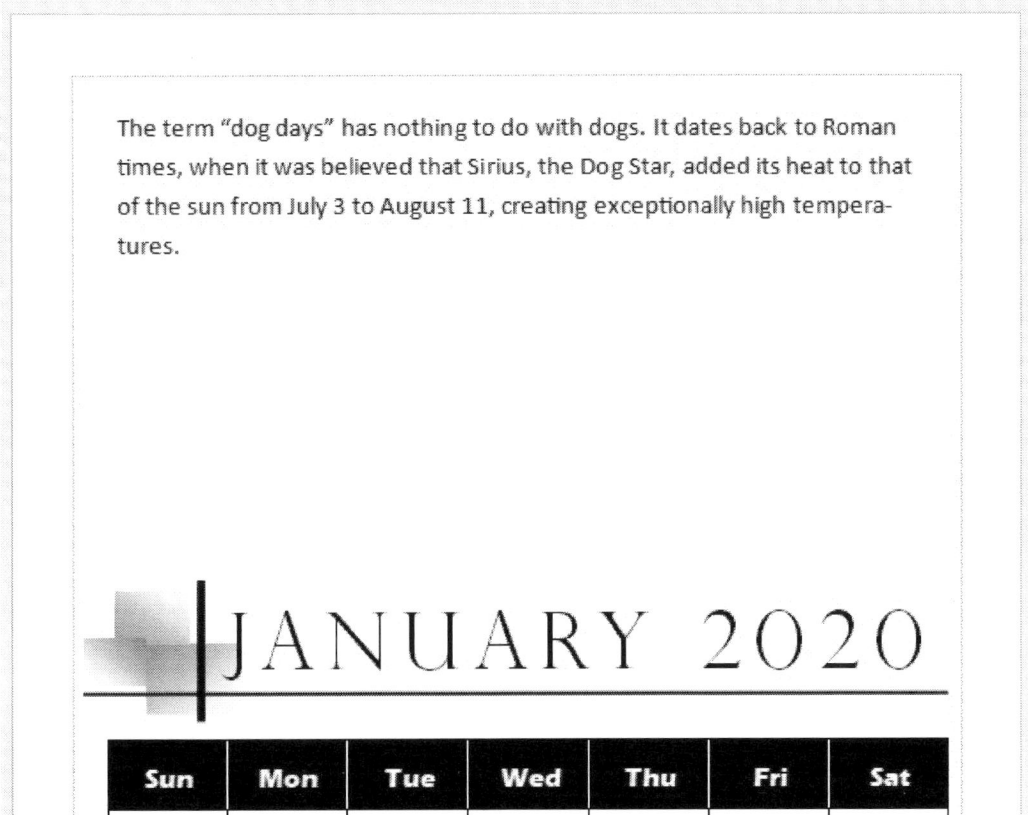

The term "dog days" has nothing to do with dogs. It dates back to Roman times, when it was believed that Sirius, the Dog Star, added its heat to that of the sun from July 3 to August 11, creating exceptionally high temperatures.

JANUARY 2020

Sun	Mon	Tue	Wed	Thu	Fri	Sat

Figure 4.12

Inserting Images

Now that I have my text at the top of my calendar I will now insert my first dog picture below the text and above the calendar itself. To do this I will once again go to the Insert tab and then click on the *Pictures* button to insert a picture from the hard drive on my computer. To do this process you will need to know where you have your picture stored on your local computer.

As you can see in figure 4.13, Publisher just placed the image in a random spot on the page and kept it the default size rather than try to make it fit in the space that I want it to go.

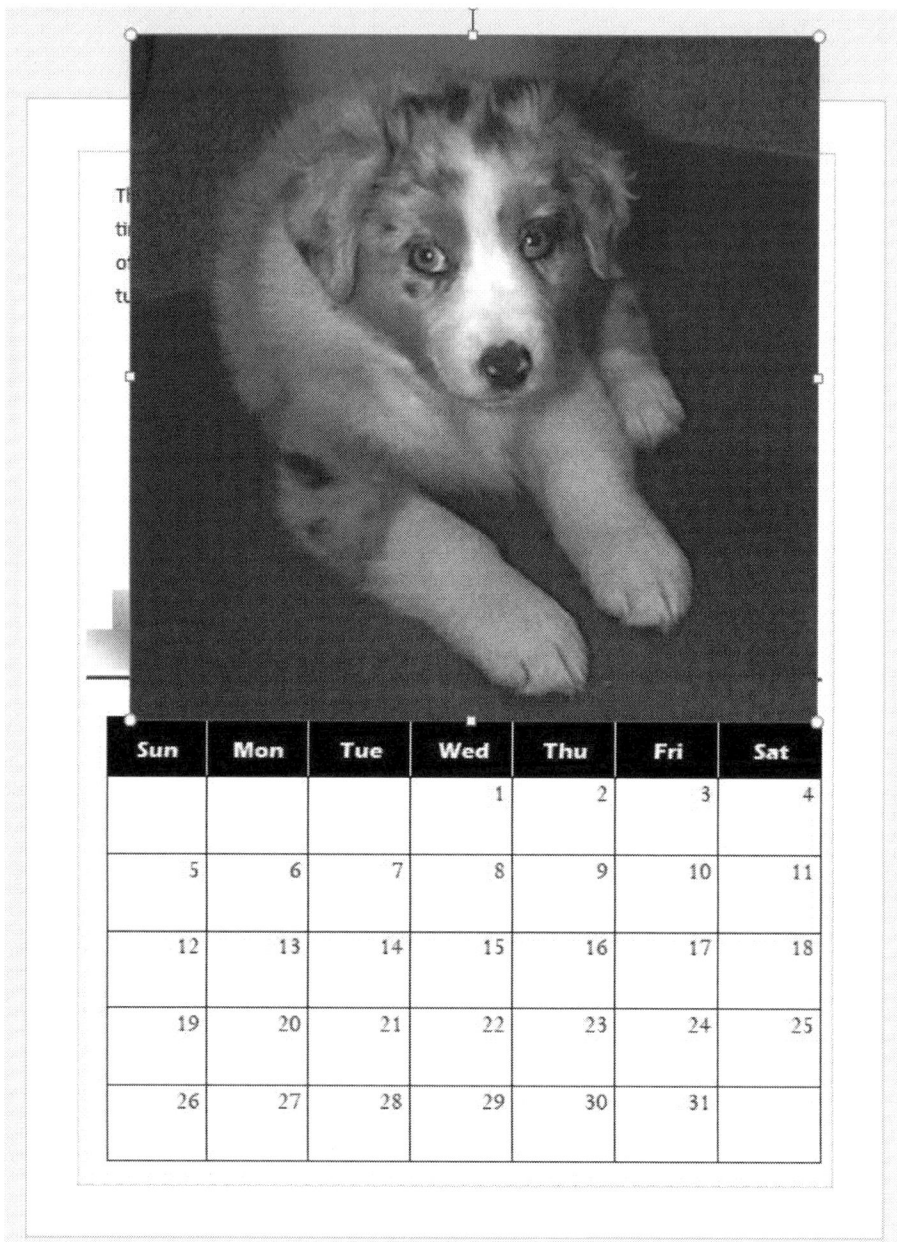

Figure 4.13

I will now resize the picture so it fits in the spot where I want it to go. Once again, I will be going over formatting pictures in the next chapter. The results are shown in figure 4.14 and I think I might want to change how the text and image go together when I get to the point where I do my final formatting.

The term "dog days" has nothing to do with dogs. It dates back to Roman times, when it was believed that Sirius, the Dog Star, added its heat to that of the sun from July 3 to August 11, creating exceptionally high temperatures.

JANUARY 2020

Sun	Mon	Tue	Wed	Thu	Fri	Sat
			1	2	3	4
5	6	7	8	9	10	11
12	13	14	15	16	17	18
19	20	21	22	23	24	25
26	27	28	29	30	31	

Figure 4.14

For February's calendar, I want to go online to find a picture of a Husky to use as my image so to do that I will go back to the Insert tab and this time choose the *Online Pictures* option and type in *husky*. As you can see, I get many results and once I find the one I like all I need to do is click on it to put a checkmark in the box and then click on the *Insert* button.

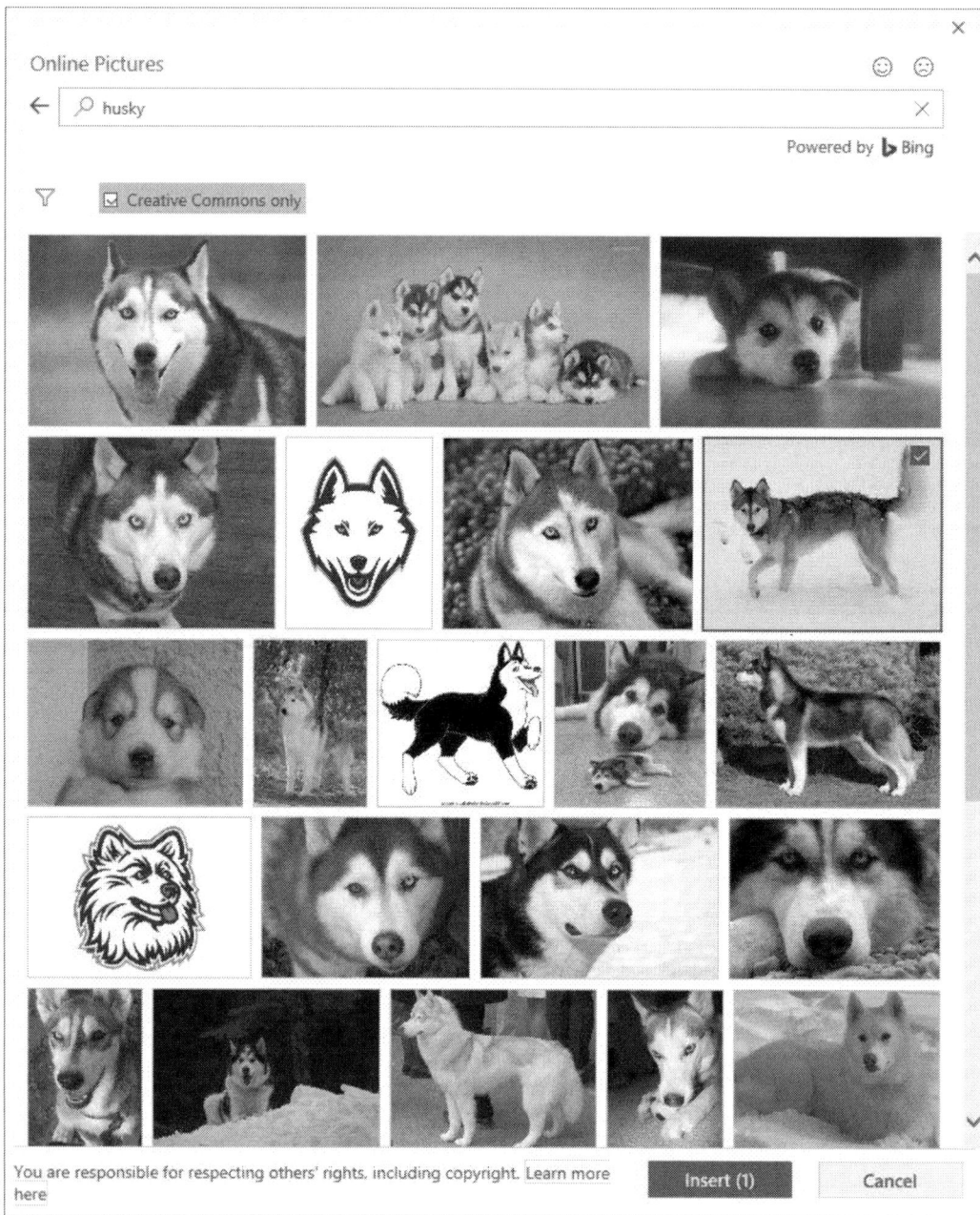

Figure 4.15

Then I can simply drag the image where I want it to be on the page and resize it to make it fit in the space I have for it. I left room above the image for my text which I will add later.

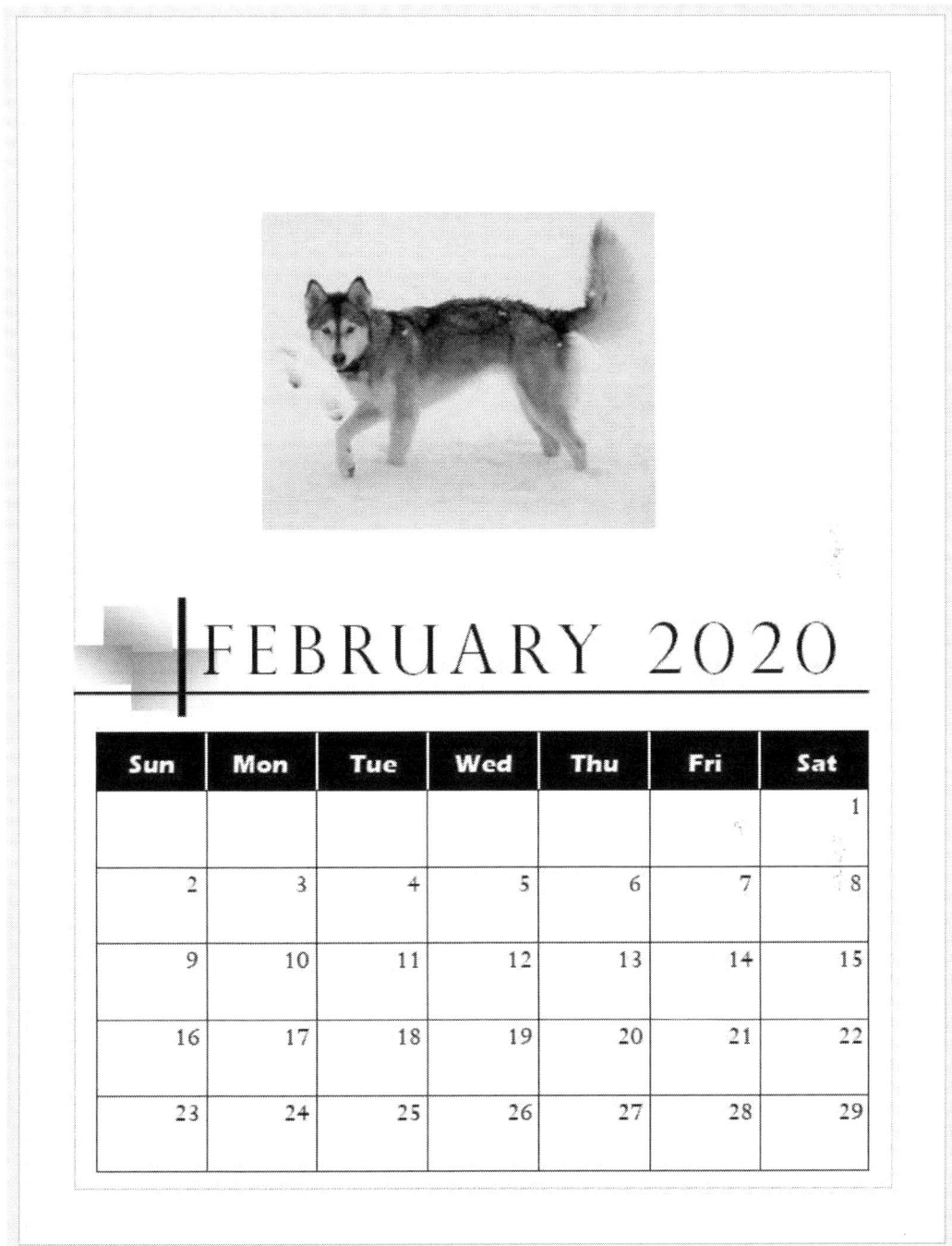

Sun	Mon	Tue	Wed	Thu	Fri	Sat
						1
2	3	4	5	6	7	8
9	10	11	12	13	14	15
16	17	18	19	20	21	22
23	24	25	26	27	28	29

Figure 4.16

I don't know what dog picture I will be using for March so what I did was insert a *Picture Placeholder* from the Insert tab and dragged its size to fill the approximate space of where I want it to go. Then I added my text above it, and by having the placeholder it gave me an idea of what kind of space I had for my text.

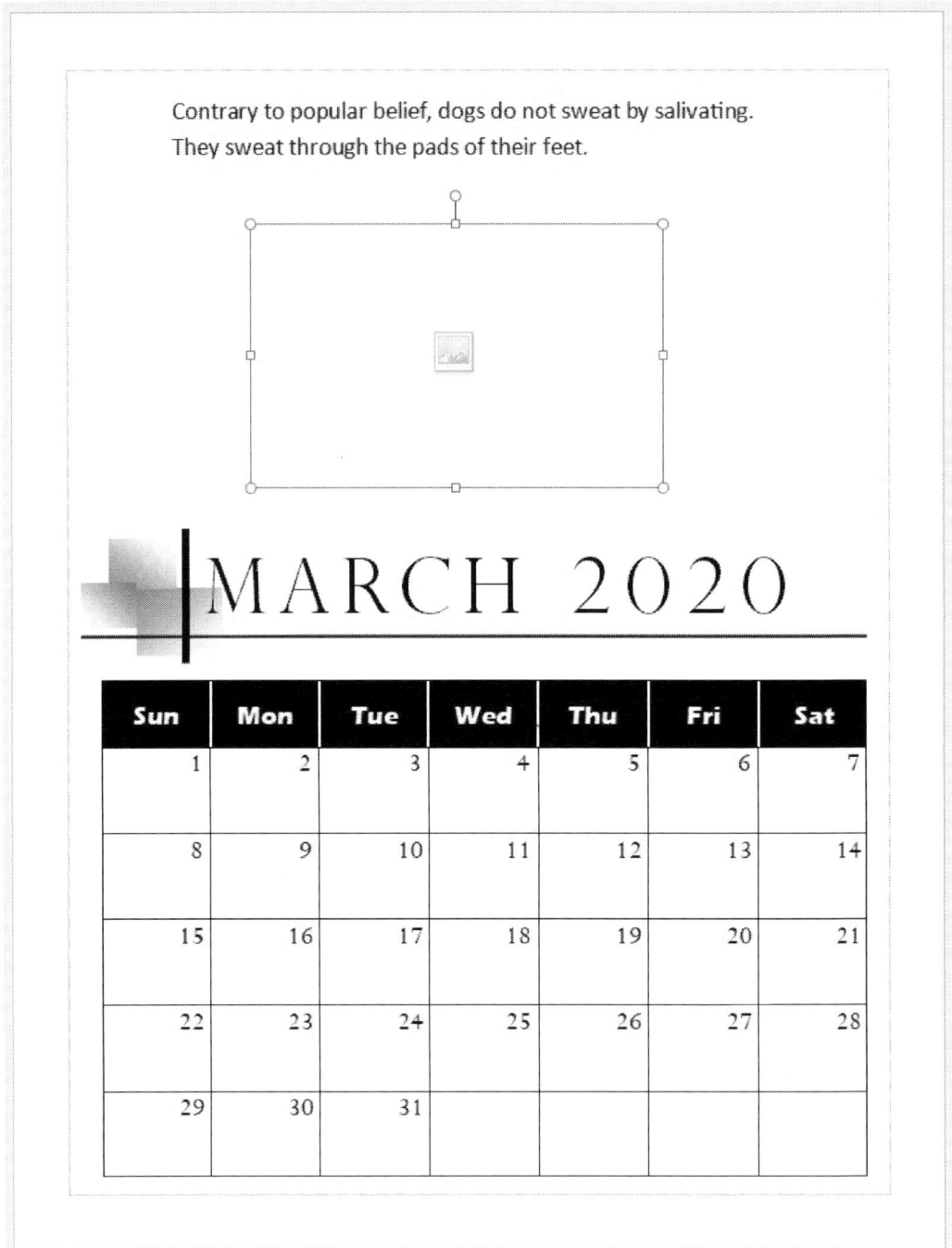

Contrary to popular belief, dogs do not sweat by salivating.
They sweat through the pads of their feet.

MARCH 2020

Sun	Mon	Tue	Wed	Thu	Fri	Sat
1	2	3	4	5	6	7
8	9	10	11	12	13	14
15	16	17	18	19	20	21
22	23	24	25	26	27	28
29	30	31				

Figure 4.17

Then I can insert the rest of my dog fact text and images for the rest of the months to finish things out.

Schemes

I talked about schemes in the last chapter and once again what they do is change the color scheme for certain aspects of your publication. If you don't have anything that is really colored on your page then changing the scheme won't really do anything. If I apply a scheme to my publication the only thing that gets changed is the color of the design at the top of the calendar.

Figure 4.18

In order to illustrate how schemes work, I will first make some changes to my publication that can then be modified by adding a scheme. To begin with, I will use my mouse to highlight all of the days in my calendar. The whole calendar is technically a table with the days being cells in that table.

Once I have everything highlighted I will right click anywhere on my calendar and choose the *Format Table* option. Then I will change the fill color from No Fill to blue and click OK (figure 4.19).

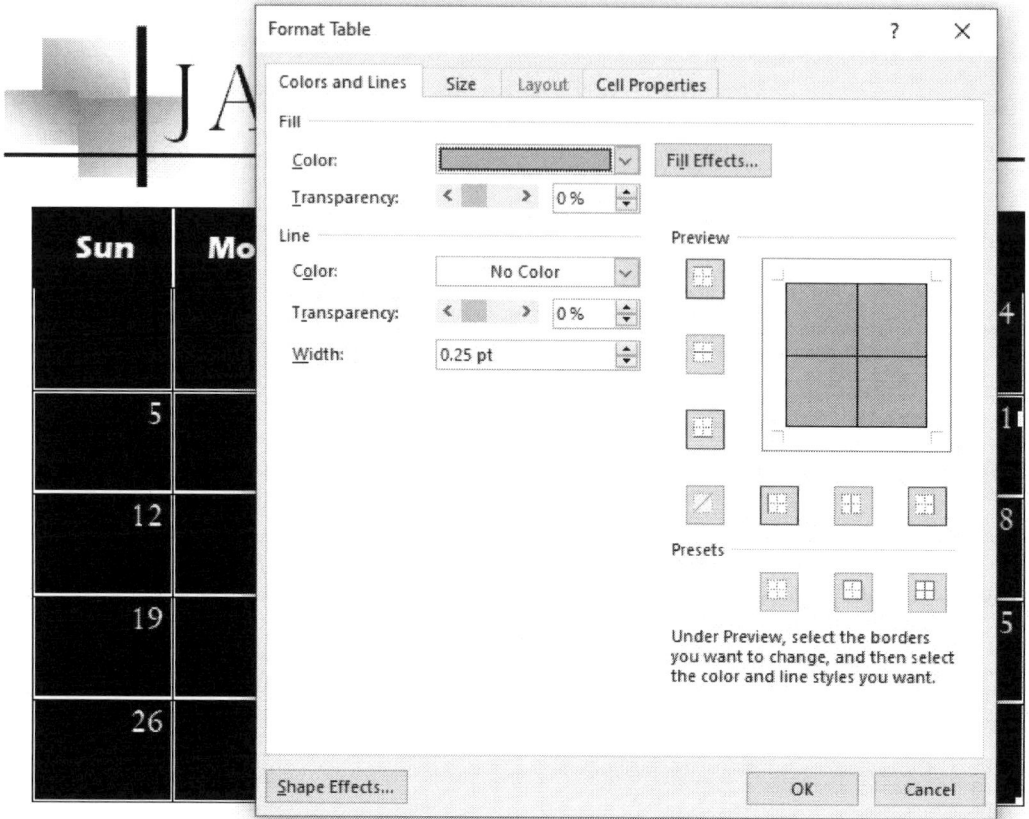

Figure 4.19

Figure 4.20 now shows my table with the days of the month filled in blue. If you are reading the paperback version of this book then you will obviously not be able to see the exact color changes and will have to take my word for it!

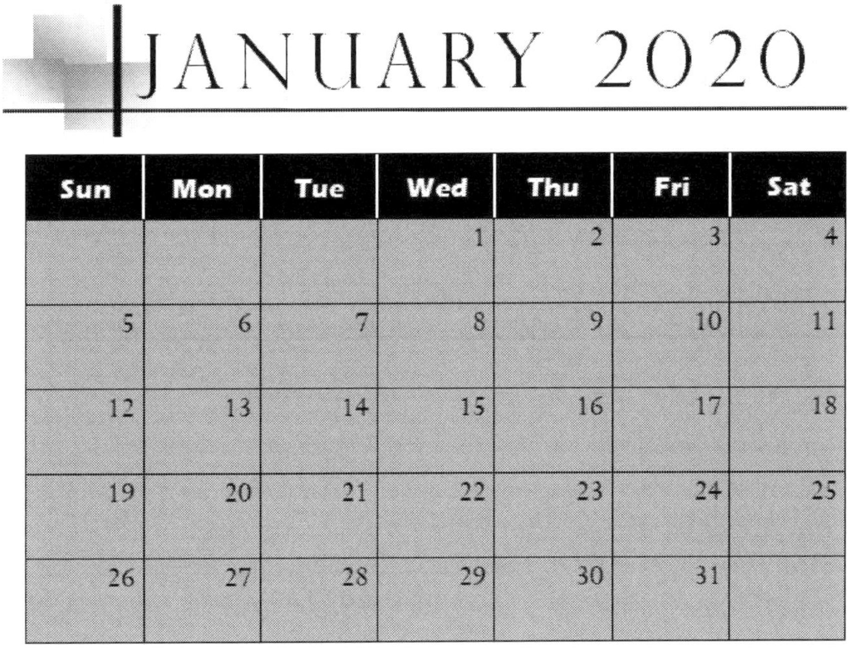

JANUARY 2020

Sun	Mon	Tue	Wed	Thu	Fri	Sat
			1	2	3	4
5	6	7	8	9	10	11
12	13	14	15	16	17	18
19	20	21	22	23	24	25
26	27	28	29	30	31	

Figure 4.20

Now I will choose a scheme that has some red and yellow to it in order to drastically change the way my calendar looks. The scheme changed the colors of the cells as well as the colors of the boxes in the title design.

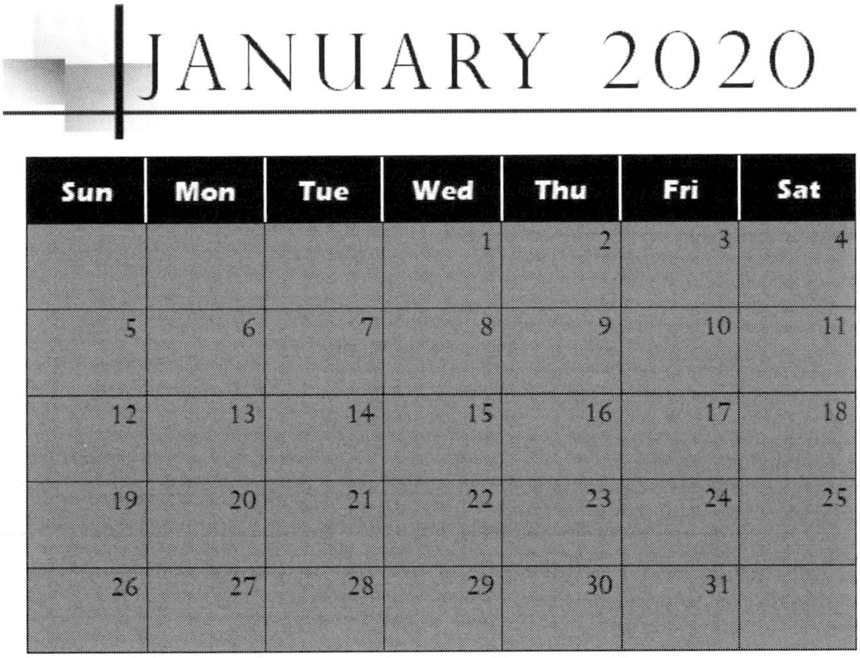

JANUARY 2020

Sun	Mon	Tue	Wed	Thu	Fri	Sat
			1	2	3	4
5	6	7	8	9	10	11
12	13	14	15	16	17	18
19	20	21	22	23	24	25
26	27	28	29	30	31	

Figure 4.21

If you apply a scheme and decide you don't like it just remember that you can always undo the action just like anything else you do in Publisher. And if you have made other changes after changing the scheme and don't want to have to revert all those changes just to undo the scheme, you can select the *Office* scheme to go back to the default scheme.

Adding Shapes and Borders

Since many publications are used for things like promoting and event or your business, it's important to make them as eye catching as possible without overdoing it of course. Adding various shapes and even borders to your work can enhance its overall appearance and really make it stand out.

Publisher comes with many built in shapes that you can add to your publication and then format to make them look exactly the way you like. You can also insert shapes in the form of images you have on your computer or that you can find online, but you can't format them the way you can with a Publisher shape.

You will find these shapes under the *Insert* tab and in the *Illustrations* group. Once you click on the shape that you want to use all you need to do is draw it on the page where you would like it to go and when you release the mouse button your new shape will be there. If you don't like the size or position of the shape then all you need to do is click on it and either drag it to its new location or resize it. You can also change its shape and do things like stretch it out as well. Figure 4.22 shows that I inserted a speech bubble shape on my dog image.

The term "dog days" has nothing to do with dogs. It dates back to Roman times, when it was believed that Sirius, the Dog Star, added its heat to that of the sun from July 3 to August 11, creating exceptionally high temperatures.

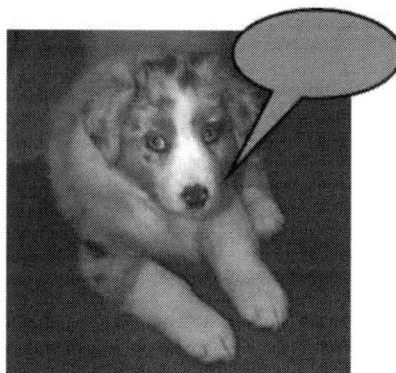

Figure 4.22

92

Once I get my shape looking the way I want it, I can then copy and paste it just like text if I want to duplicate it rather than have to create another one and try and manually make it look exactly the same. To do this simply select the shape and either go to the *Home* tab and choose *Copy* from the *Clipboard* group or right click the shape and choose Copy. Then you can choose *Paste* from the Clipboard group or right click and choose Paste. You can also use the keyboard shortcuts *Ctrl-C* for copy and *Ctrl-V* for paste.

You can add borders to your publication in a couple of different ways. You can either add a line based border to a shape or insert a predesigned border on to your page. And of course you can always add a border image from your computer or download one online.

Let's say I want to add a border around my dog image. To do so I can right click on it and choose *Format Picture*. Then all I need to do is adjust the settings on the *Colors and Lines* tab to suit my needs.

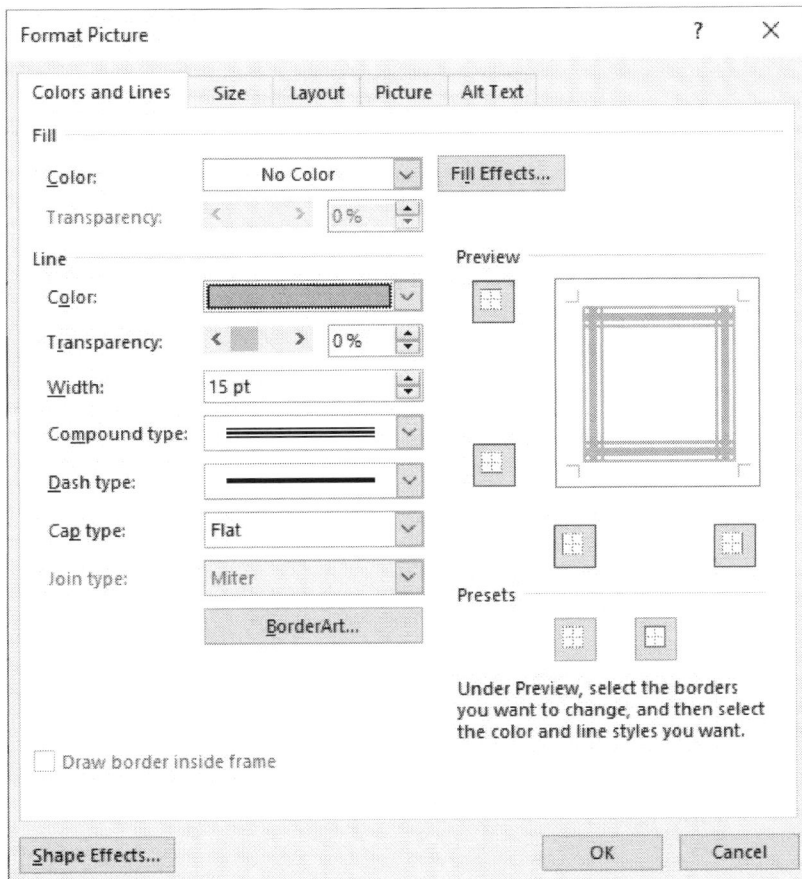

Figure 4.23

In my case, I am going to make the following changes to my line which is technically my border.

- Change the line color to blue
- Increase the width of the line to 10pt
- Change the compound type to be a thick line with 2 thinner lines on each side of it.

The results are shown in figure 4.24.

Figure 4.24

Another way to create a border is to add an actual border from the *Insert* tab and then the *Borders & Accents* tool under the *Building Blocks* group. As you can see there are some various built in borders that you can choose from in the Frames section. For my next example, I am going to use Border 6 and add it to the dog picture on the February calendar page.

Frames

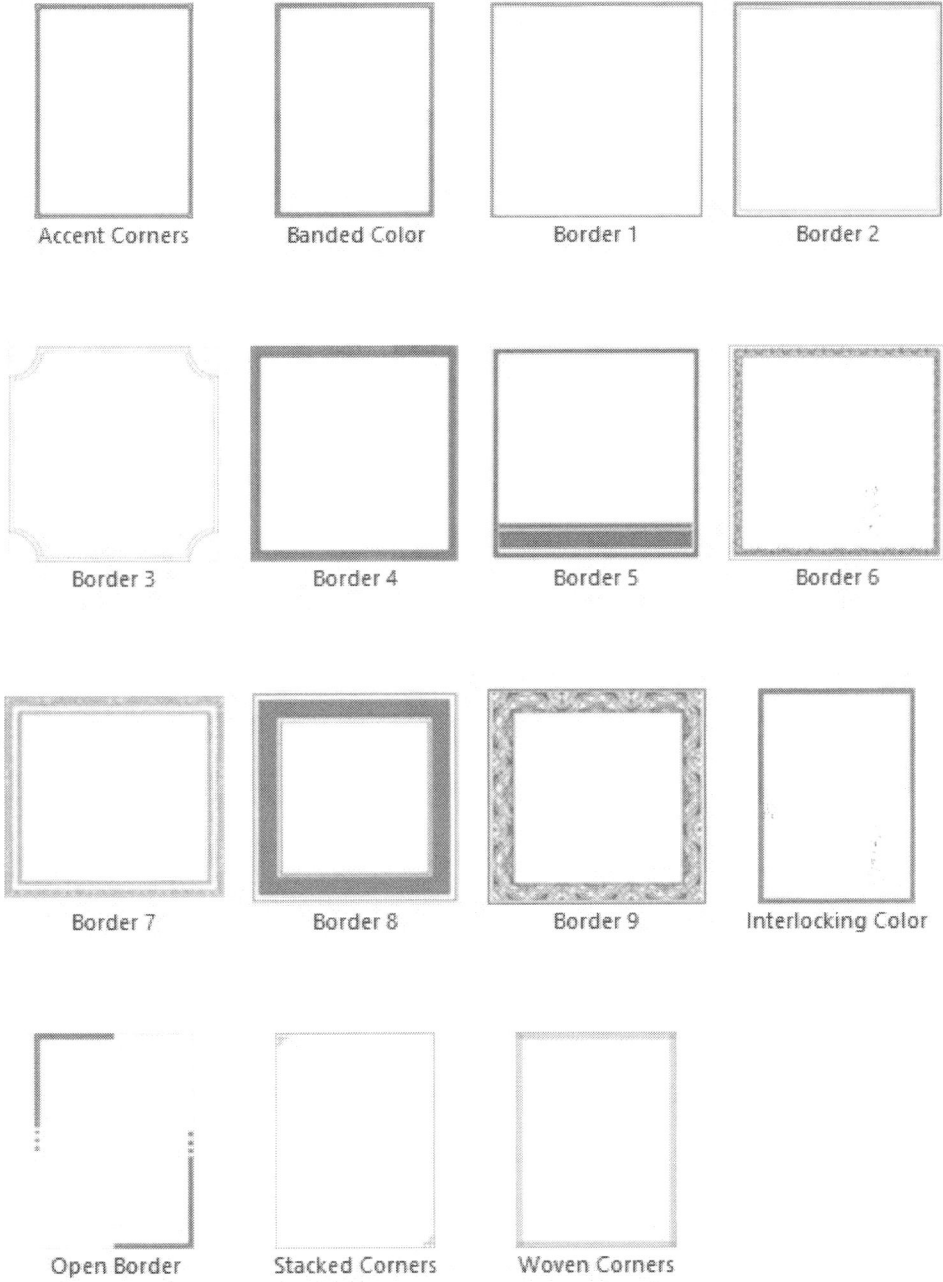

Figure 4.25

Once I choose the border it places it in the middle of the page, and you can see that it covers the dog image and that is not the look I am going for.

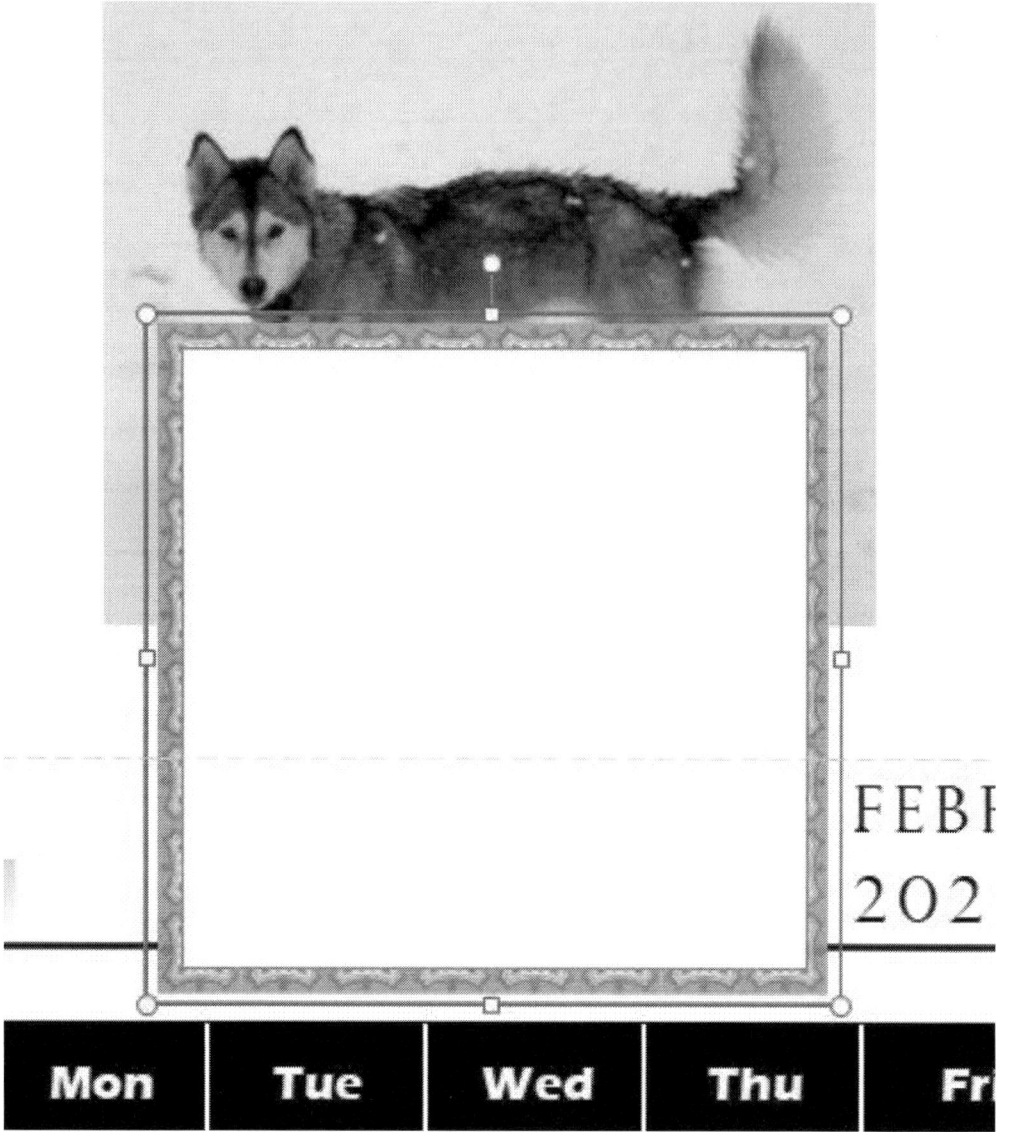

Figure 4.26

To get around this I will need to click on the dog picture to select it and then go to the *Home* menu and then to the *Arrange* group and use the *Bring to Front* option to have the dog picture brought in front of the frame graphic as shown in figure 4.27.

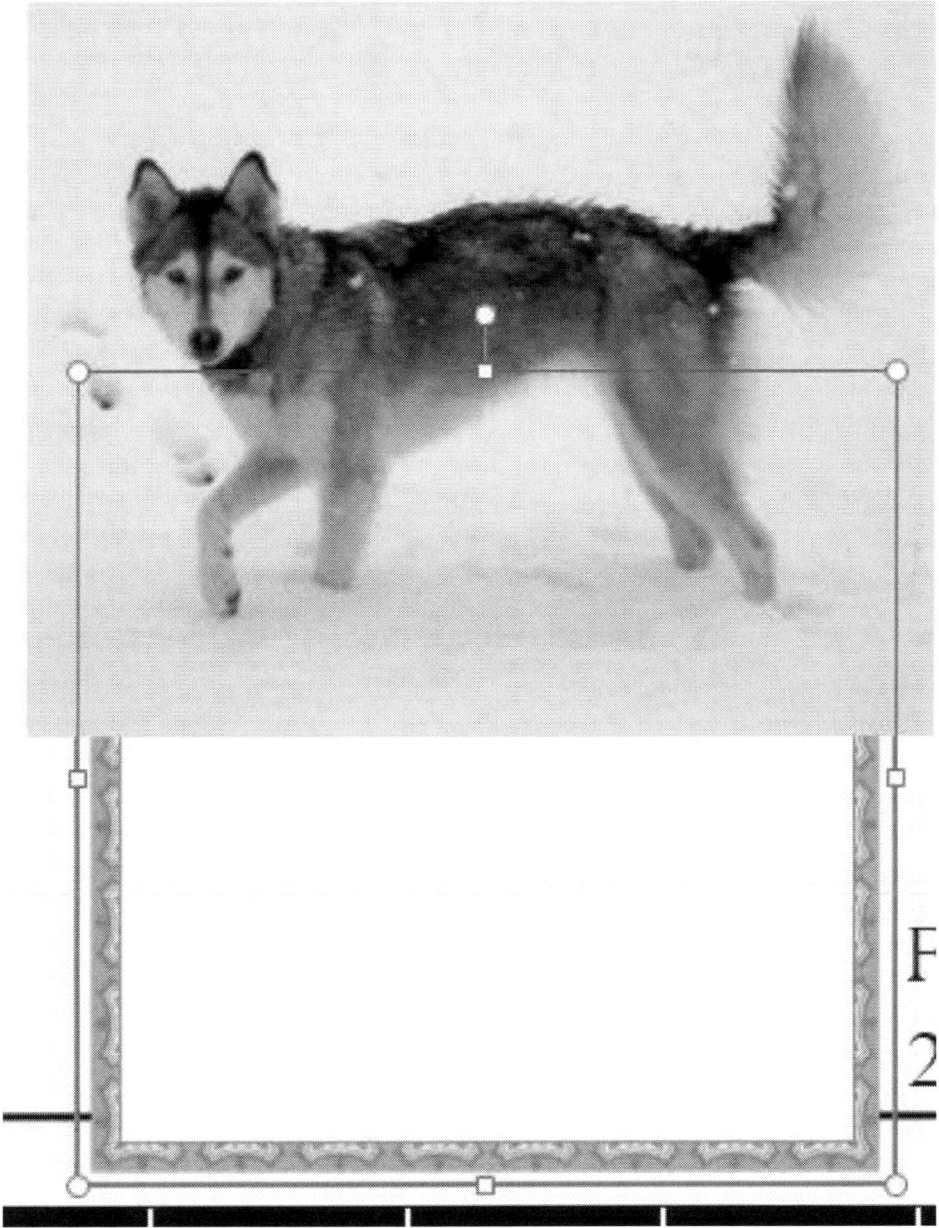

Figure 4.27

Now what I need to do is drag and resize the frame graphic so it fits around the edge of the dog photo to make it fit correctly as shown in figure 4.28.

Figure 4.28

Now I want to add a border to the page itself so it's not quite so plain looking. Rather than use another preconfigured border which will require me to bring all of my text and graphics to the front of it, I am going to add a border using the same method as I did for the January dog picture. But this time I won't be formatting a picture to create the border but rather formatting a shape to create the border.

To start with I will go to the *Insert* tab and then choose *Shapes* and then choose the rectangle shape. Then I will draw a rectangle around the page where I want my border to go. This will then create a rectangle shape that is filled in with a solid color which is not what I want. To fix this I will right click on the shape and choose *Format AutoShape*.

From here I will change the fill to *No Color* since I don't want to have all of my text and graphics covered up. For the border itself, I am going to use a preconfigured design by clicking the *BorderArt* button rather than make my own by configuring the line options like I did last time. For this border I will choose the Torn Paper design and then click on OK.

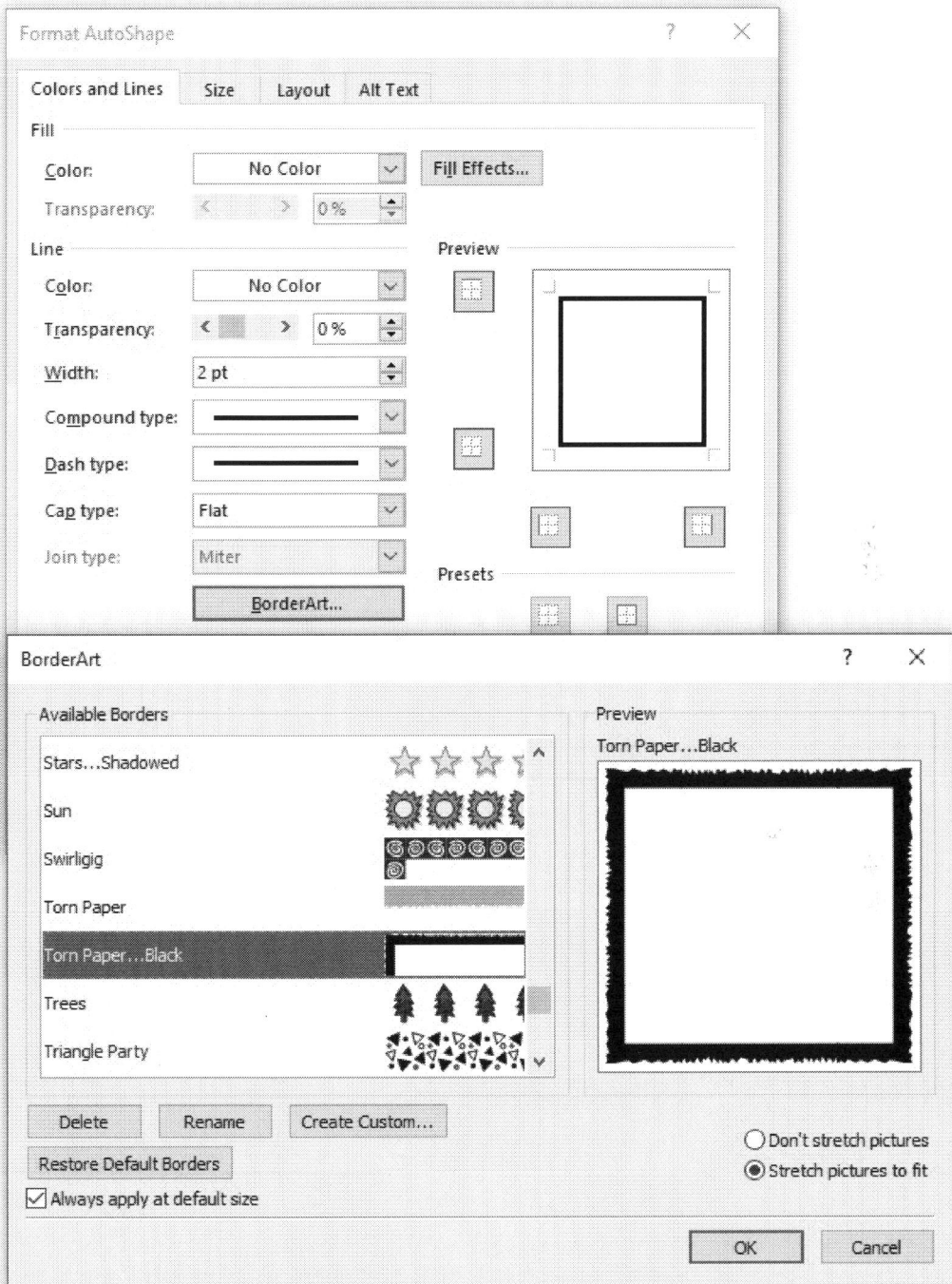

Figure 4.29

Figure 4.30 shows how my newly created border looks. I did have to send the rectangle shape to the back because it was covering some of my text and the calendar but that was an easy fix, and everything looks good.

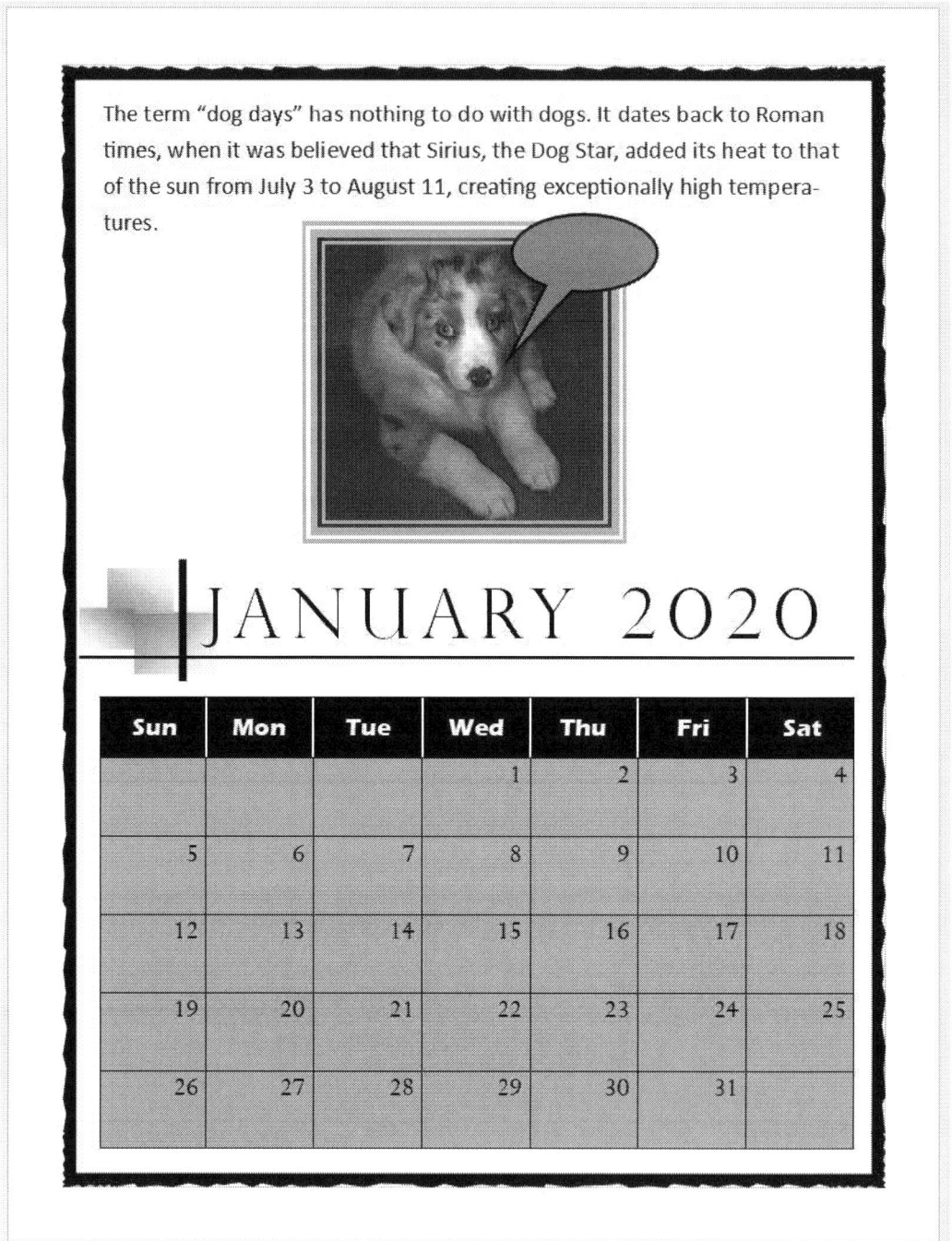

The term "dog days" has nothing to do with dogs. It dates back to Roman times, when it was believed that Sirius, the Dog Star, added its heat to that of the sun from July 3 to August 11, creating exceptionally high temperatures.

JANUARY 2020

Sun	Mon	Tue	Wed	Thu	Fri	Sat
			1	2	3	4
5	6	7	8	9	10	11
12	13	14	15	16	17	18
19	20	21	22	23	24	25
26	27	28	29	30	31	

Figure 4.30

Creating a Catalog

One potentially useful feature of Publisher is the ability to quickly create a product catalog from information that you manually enter about your products or from a listing of data that you already have, such as a spreadsheet. So if you sell multiple products and want a way to create a publication to display those products you can do so in Publisher.

The first thing to do before creating a catalog is to decide where your product information will be coming from. If you have a listing of all the product details in a spreadsheet or database then you can import that, otherwise you can add your product information manually within Publisher.

To start the process you will need to go to the *Insert* tab and then click on *Catalog Pages* under the *Pages* group. Publisher will then make a new group of pages and also create a Catalog Merge Area where you will insert the information about your products from your pre-created list or from a manually created list.

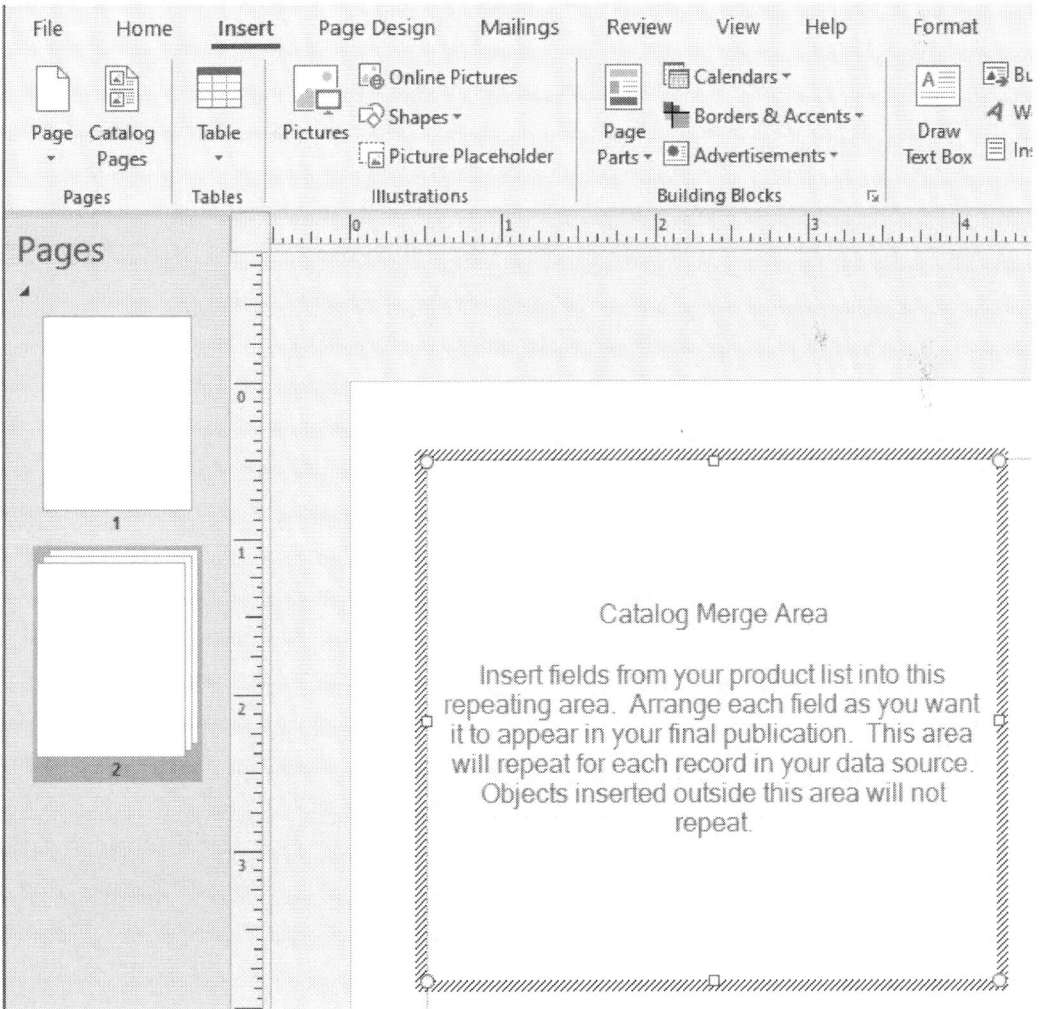

Figure 4.31

Now you should be taken to a *Catalog Tools* section with a *Format* tab where you can then add the product information to your catalog. Since I don't have any product data added to my catalog yet I will click on the *Add List* button.

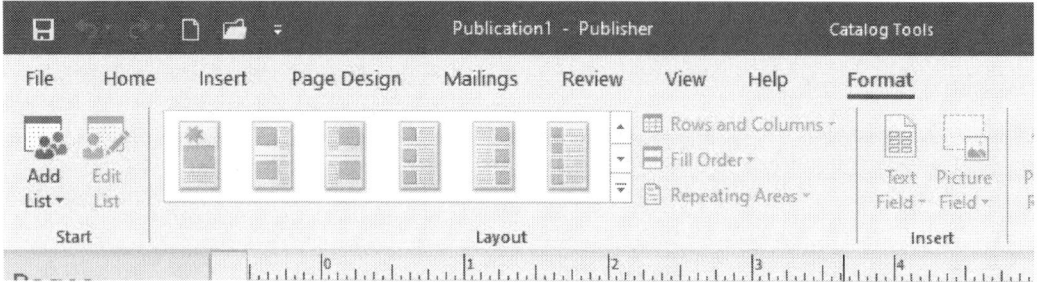

Figure 4.32

I am going to manually type in my product information since I don't have too many products since I'm only doing this as an example so I will choose the *Type a New List* option. I will then be presented with a *New Product List* box where I can enter in the information for my products. There are several pre-defined fields such as Product, Description, ID, Price and Picture as seen in figure 4.33.

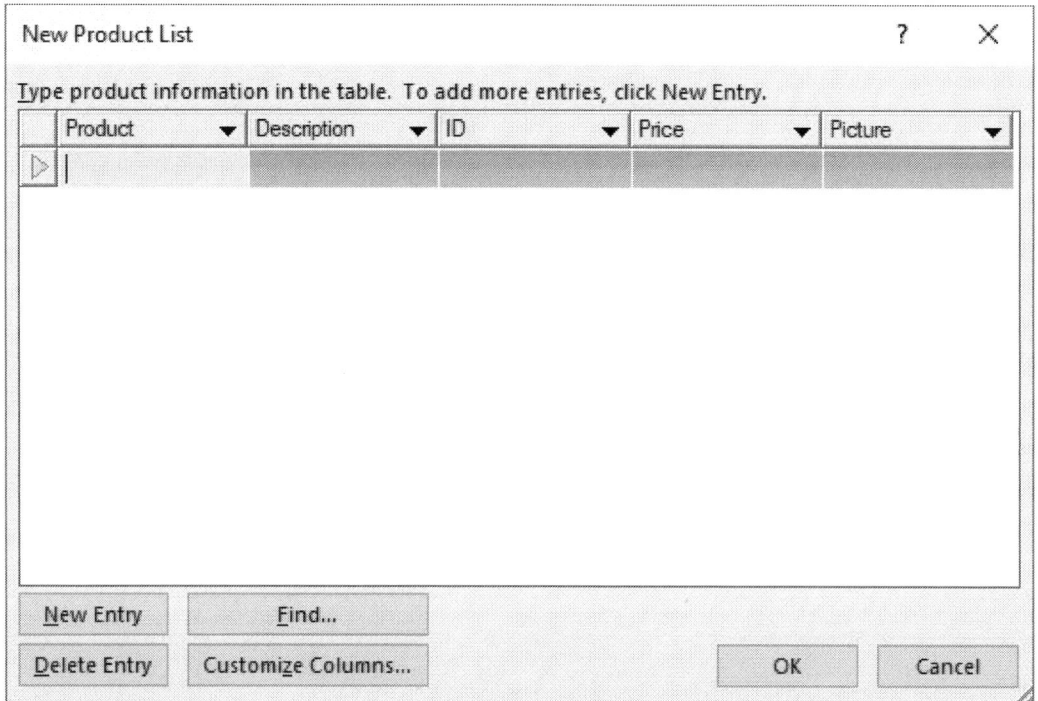

Figure 4.33

If you need to add, remove or rename fields from the ones here, you can click on the *Customize Columns* button and add, remove or rename them to suit your needs. I decided to remove the ID field and add a new field called Quantity. I could have also just renamed ID and called it Quantity.

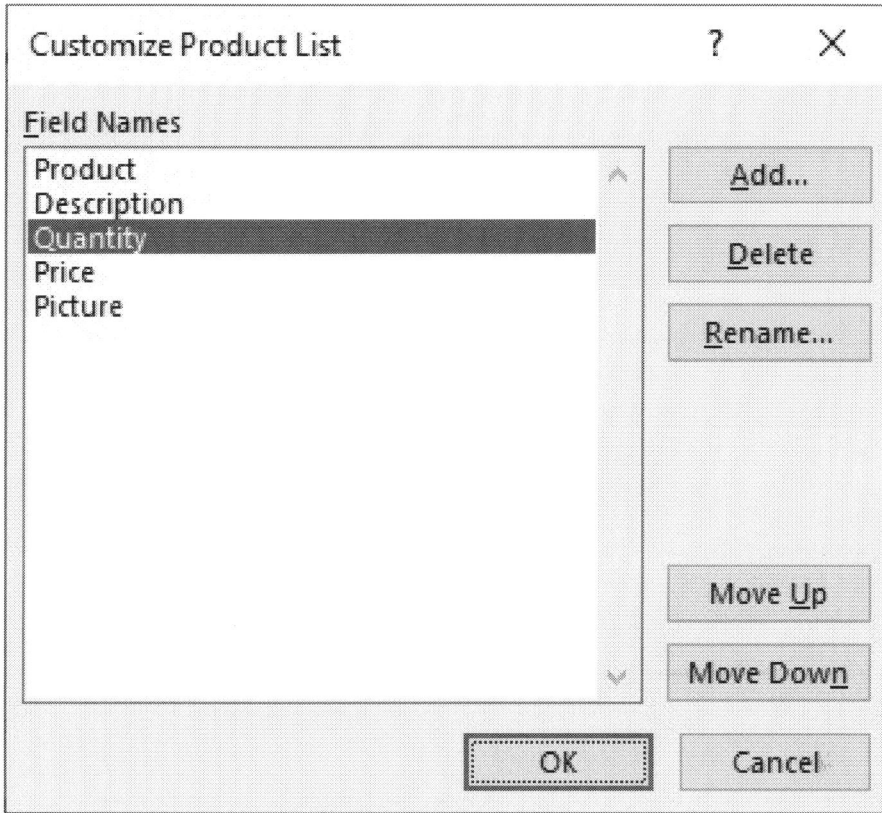

Figure 4.34

I will now enter the data into the fields within the New Product List box. I will click on the New Entry button when I need to add a line for another product. I will be making a product catalog for my make believe cookie business that I wish was real!

Figure 4.35 shows the six types of cookies that I will be adding to my catalog along with their description, quantity and price. The Picture field is left blank because I will be adding them later. Once I am done entering in my information I will click the *OK* button. If I need to edit this product list I can go back later and make changes.

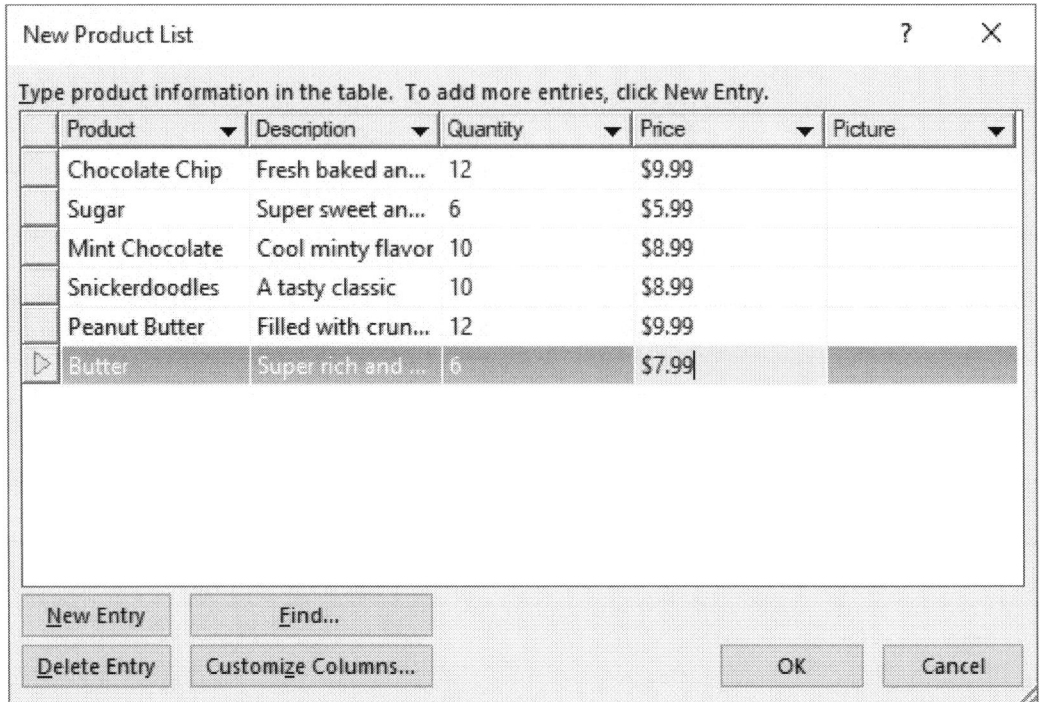

New Product List					? ✕

Type product information in the table. To add more entries, click New Entry.

	Product ▼	Description ▼	Quantity ▼	Price ▼	Picture ▼
	Chocolate Chip	Fresh baked an...	12	$9.99	
	Sugar	Super sweet an...	6	$5.99	
	Mint Chocolate	Cool minty flavor	10	$8.99	
	Snickerdoodles	A tasty classic	10	$8.99	
	Peanut Butter	Filled with crun...	12	$9.99	
▷	Butter	Super rich and ...	6	$7.99|	

New Entry	Find...		
Delete Entry	Customize Columns...	OK	Cancel

Figure 4.35

I will then be prompted to save this new list on my computer so it can be used later. I will use the default location to save my list and name it Cookies and click on the *Save* button.

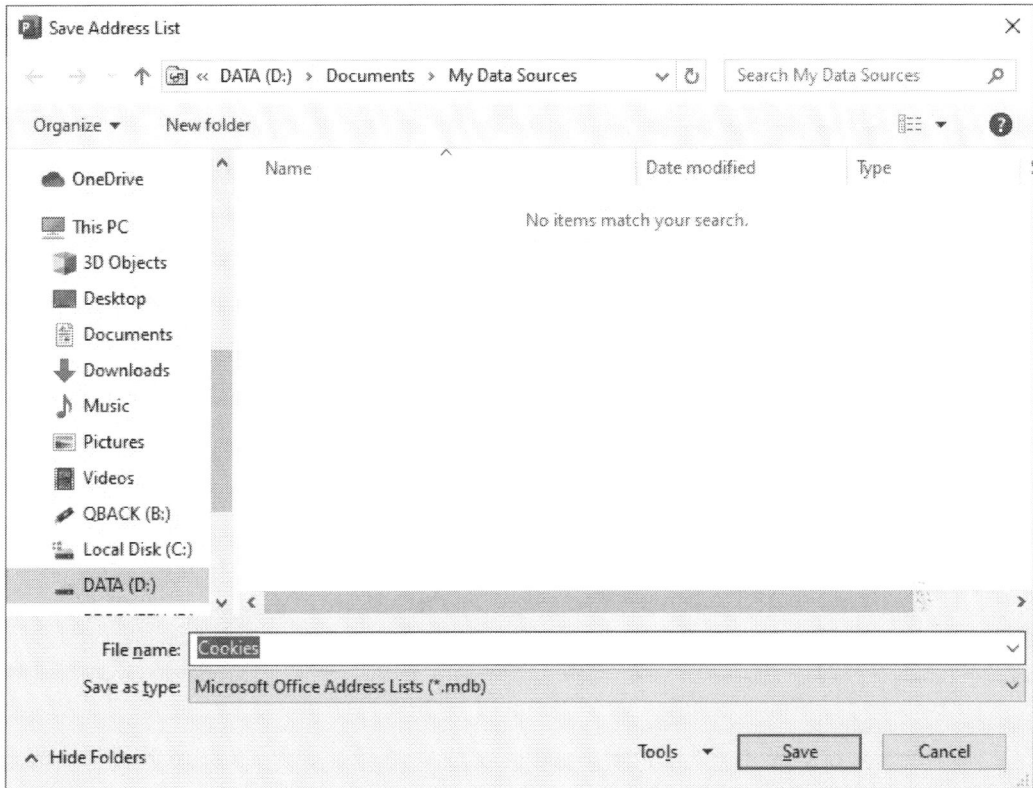

Figure 4.36

I will then be shown my list once again with the option to uncheck any products that I don't want to be included in my catalog (figure 4.37). I can also do things such as sort and filter my list but since mine is so small, there is no reason to do these things. I can also change my data source (Cookies file) and add more items to my list from existing lists or Outlook contacts.

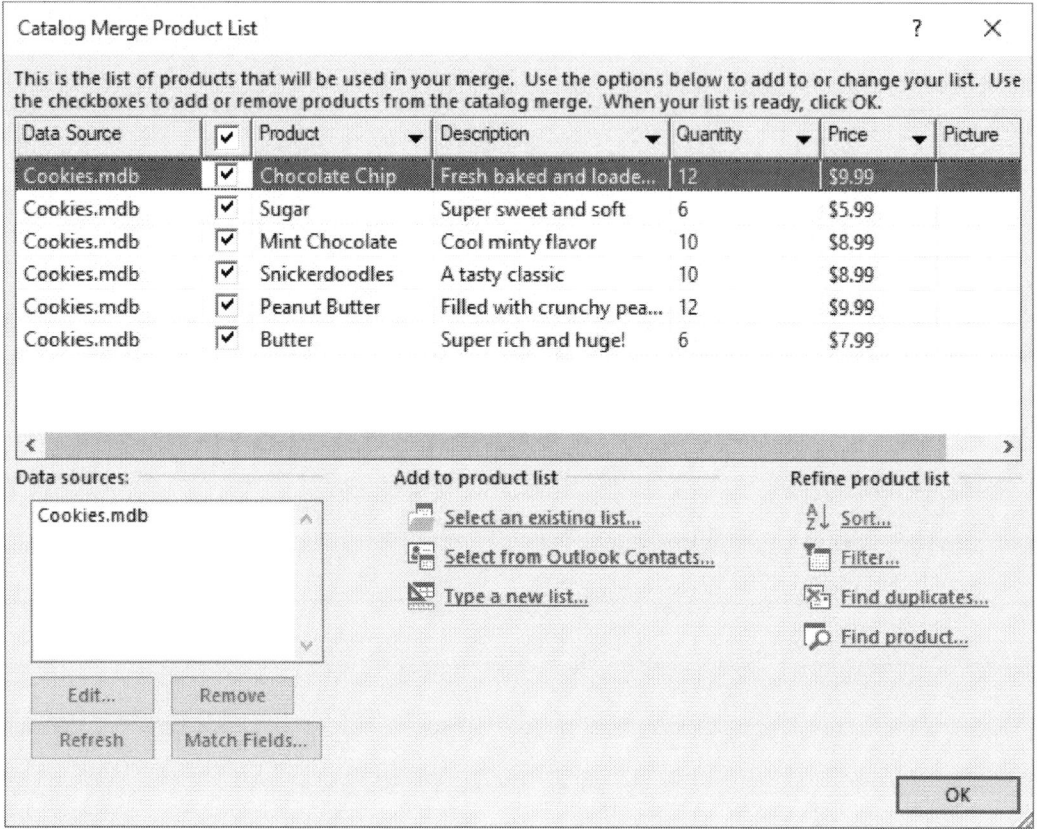
Figure 4.37

Now that I have my data list created I can see that all the tools in the Ribbon for the Format tab are active and I can begin to create my catalog.

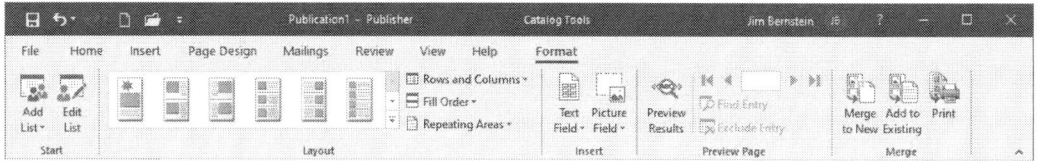
Figure 4.38

Under the *Layout* group, I am going to choose the *3 entries, picture on the left* layout by clicking on the corresponding icon. Publisher will then add that layout type to my page as seen in figure 4.39.

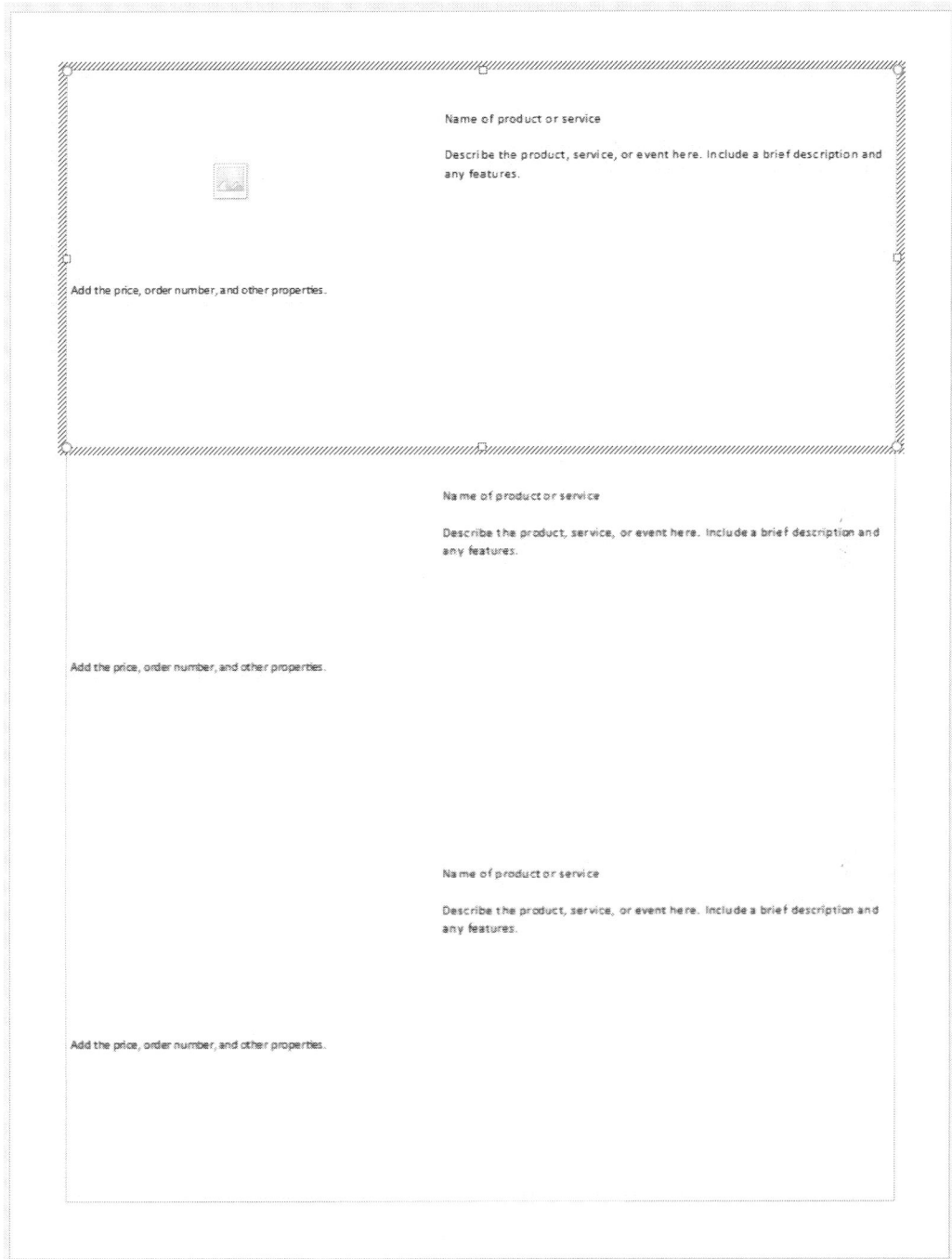

Name of product or service

Describe the product, service, or event here. Include a brief description and any features.

Add the price, order number, and other properties.

Name of product or service

Describe the product, service, or event here. Include a brief description and any features.

Add the price, order number, and other properties.

Name of product or service

Describe the product, service, or event here. Include a brief description and any features.

Add the price, order number, and other properties.

Figure 4.39

It might not look like much now but that's because I haven't added my data or pictures or even formatted the text from the default tiny font. To start I am going to add my data fields to the appropriate part on the page. So I will highlight the sentence that says *Name of product or service* in the top box and then click on the Text Field button and then click on Product (figure 4.40).

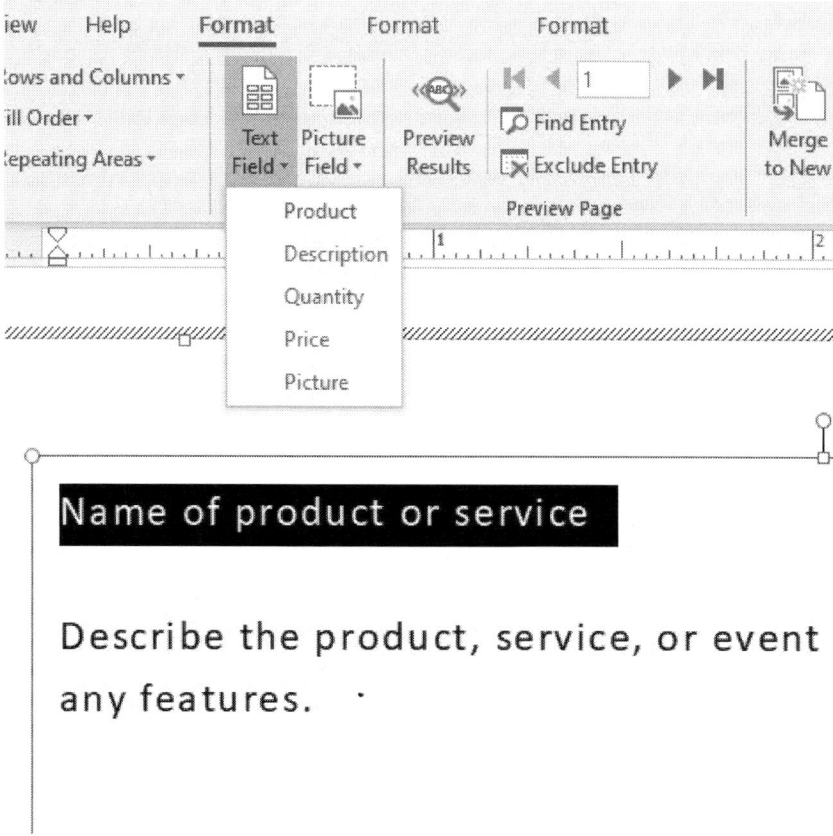

Figure 4.40

Then the field changes to the word *Product* indicating that it is now a product list field that can be populated with data from my product list.

Figure 4.41

I will now do the same for the Description, Quantity, Price and Picture fields and the results can be seen in figure 4.42.

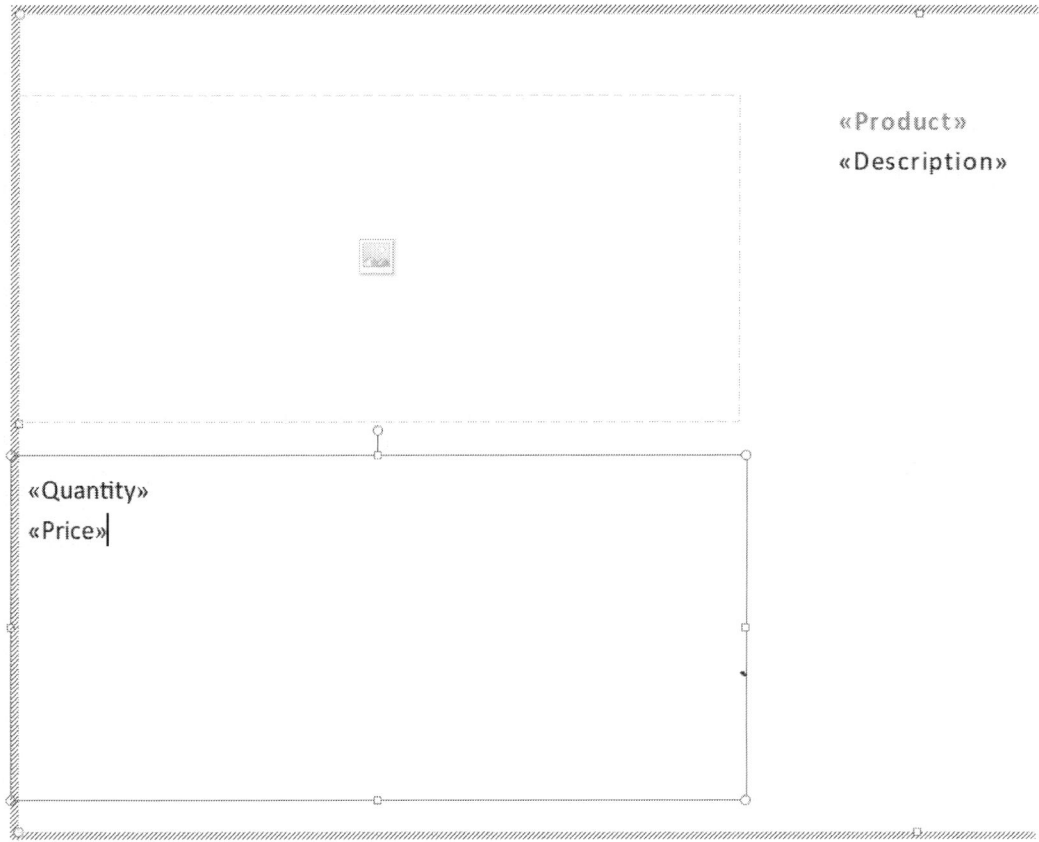

«Product»
«Description»

«Quantity»
«Price»

Figure 4.42

Now I can see that the fields on my catalog page have been updated with the information from my product list to match. The type is still way too small and needs to be spruced up a bit to make it look a little more exciting.

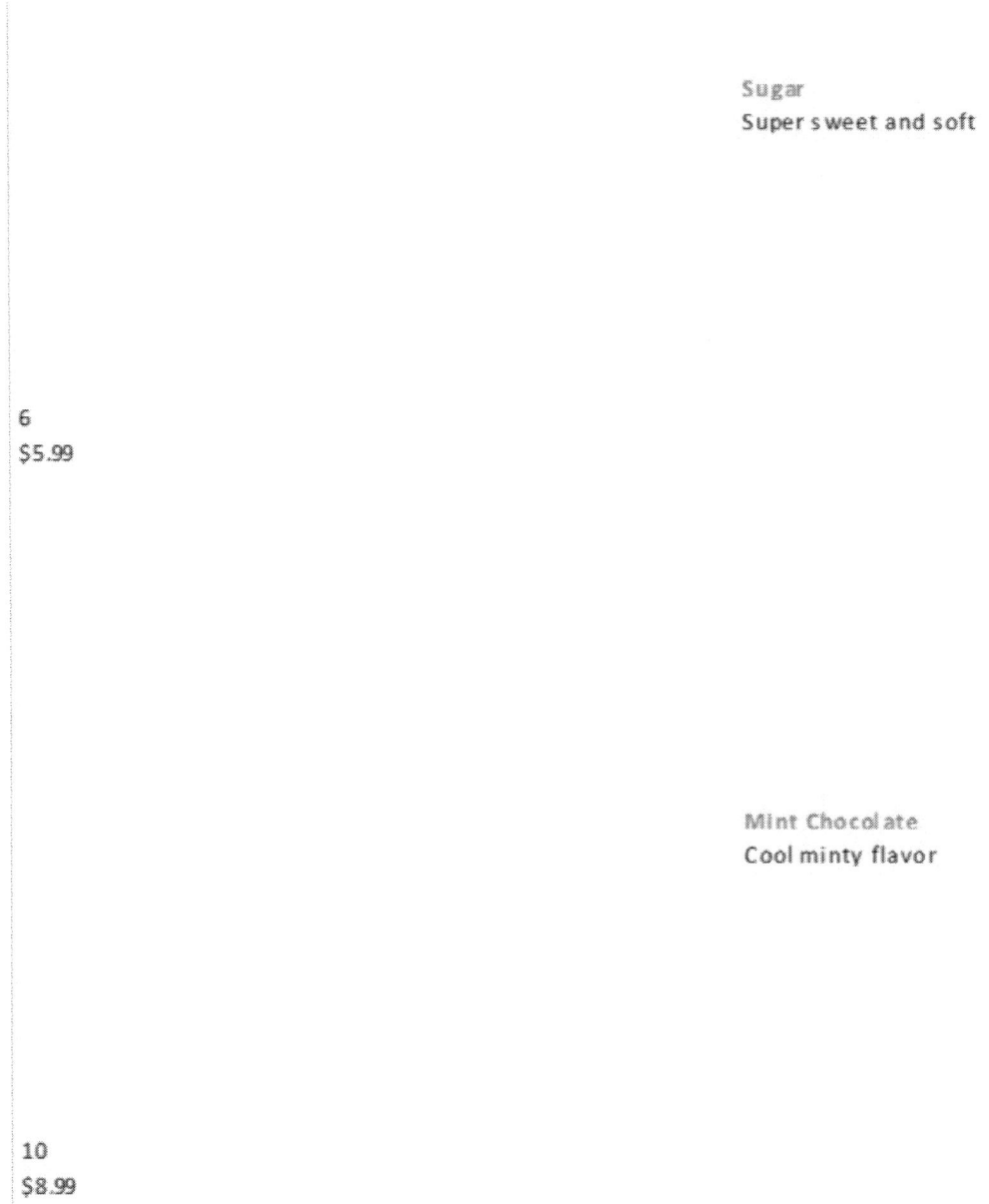

Sugar
Super sweet and soft

6
$5.99

Mint Chocolate
Cool minty flavor

10
$8.99

Figure 4.43

If I change the type on the first box of the layout where it shows the field names then it will apply those same changes to all of the other text in that same field in all of the other boxes.

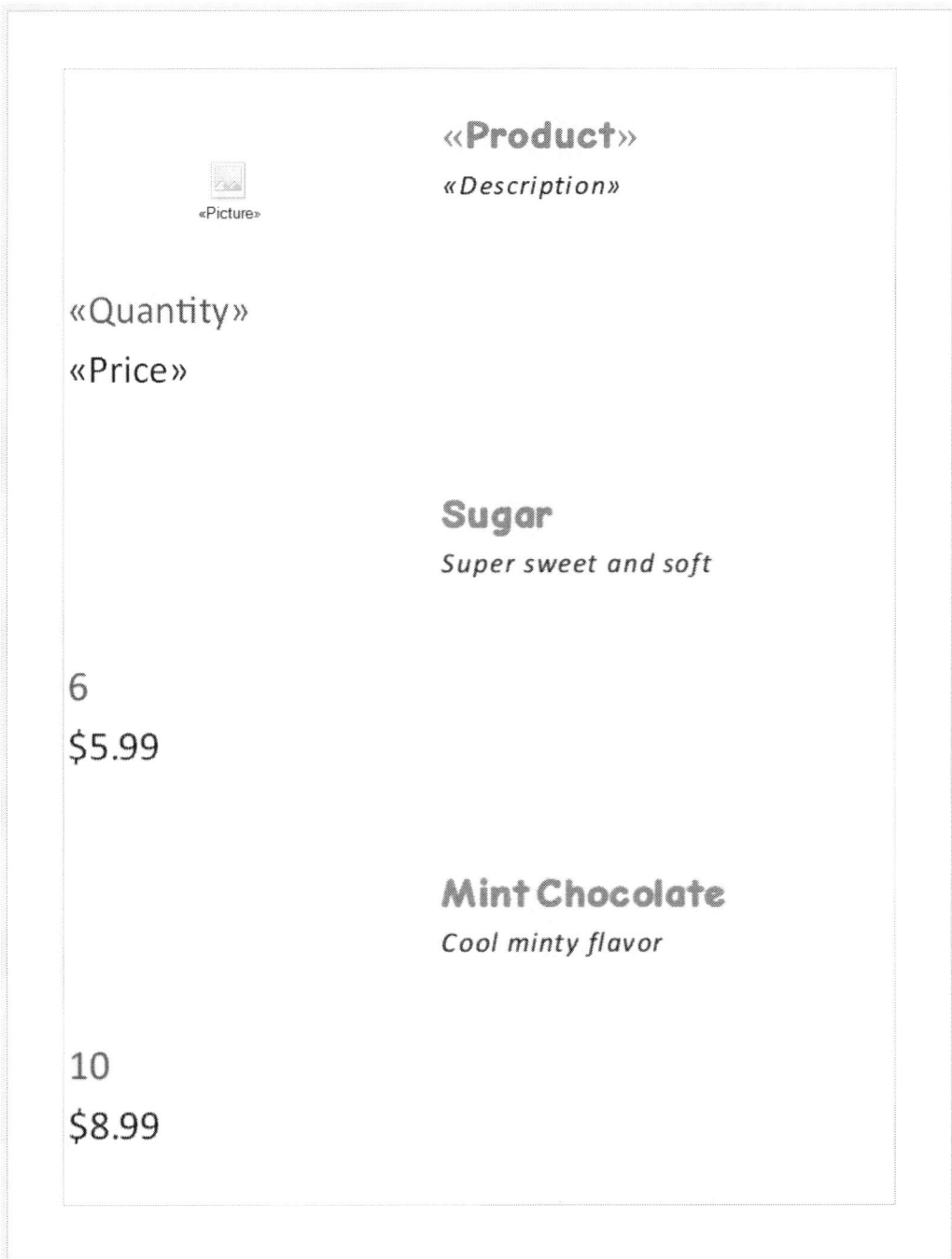

«**Product**»

«*Description*»

«Picture»

«Quantity»

«Price»

Sugar

Super sweet and soft

6

$5.99

Mint Chocolate

Cool minty flavor

10

$8.99

Figure 4.44

Now that I have my text looking the way I want, it's time to create the actual catalog so I can then finish the formatting to make it look presentable. I have three choices as to how I want to do this, and they are *Merge to New* which will create a new publication with my data, *Add to Existing* which will use the same publication file and just add to it, or I can just *Print* out the catalog right to my printer.

From the Merge group, I am going with the Merge to New option to have a new Publisher file created with my data.

Figure 4.45

To add the pictures to each cookie type I simply click on the picture icon and then choose the appropriate option as to where my cookie pictures are located.

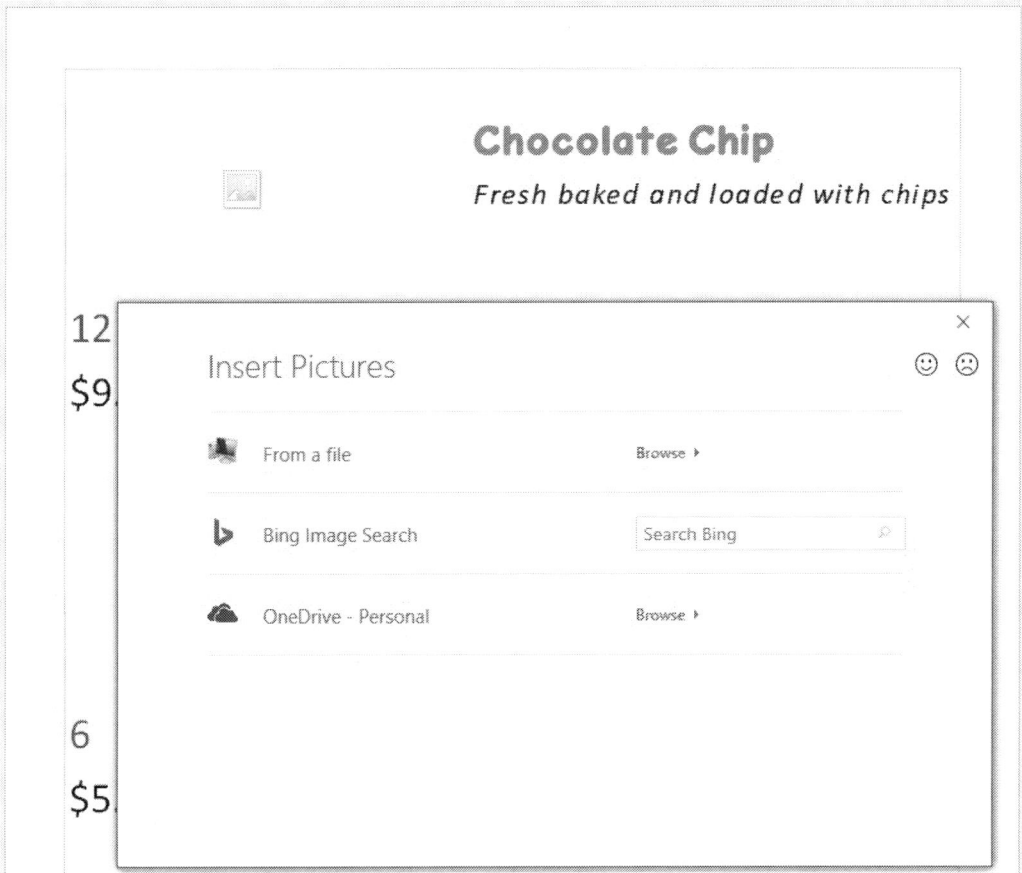

Figure 4.46

Then after a little formatting, I now have my cookie catalog Publisher file with three cookies per sheet (I will be going over formatting in the next chapter).

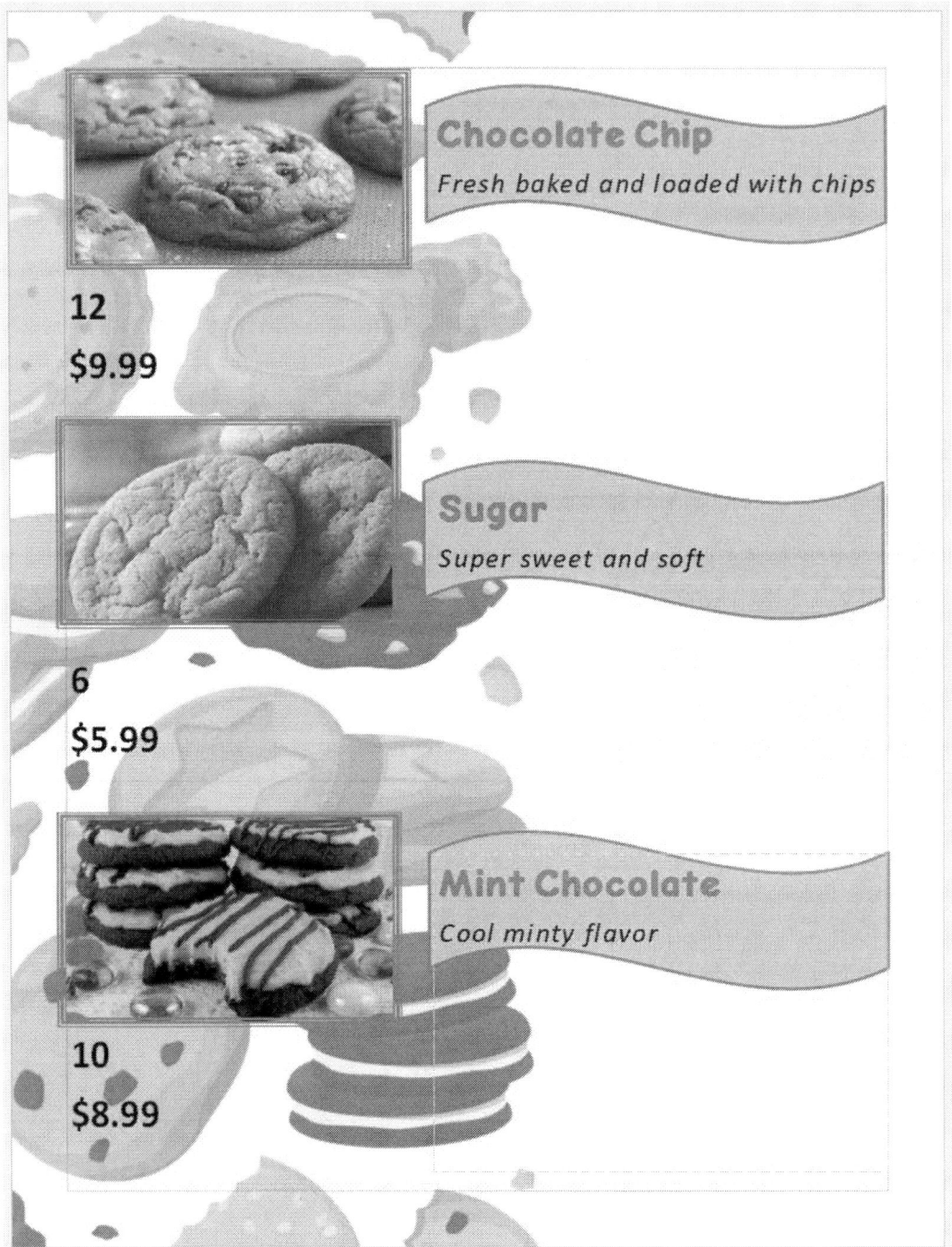

Chocolate Chip
Fresh baked and loaded with chips

12
$9.99

Sugar
Super sweet and soft

6
$5.99

Mint Chocolate
Cool minty flavor

10
$8.99

Figure 4.47

Chapter 5 - Formatting Your Publication

After you get all of your text, pictures, tables, shapes and so on into your publication you should take a little time to format your work to help give it that eye catching, professional look. Publisher allows you to easily format these types of objects without too much work on your end which is nice.

In this chapter, I will be going over some easy ways to make your work stand out that you can do with a few easy steps.

Tip: When formatting your publication keep in mind how it will look when its printed out vs. how it looks on the screen. Depending on what type of printer you will be using, things might not look as nice or clear on paper as they do on your monitor. Plus graphics and pictures will use up a lot of ink so be sure you don't run out in the middle of printing something important!

Page Layout
Setting up your page layout should really be done at the beginning of creating your publication but there might come a time when you need to make some adjustments here to make things fit better on the page or to accommodate changes in how your publication will be printed.

For most of your page setup duties you will go to the *Page Design* tab and then the *Page Setup* group. Here you have options to change the page margins, page orientation and size.

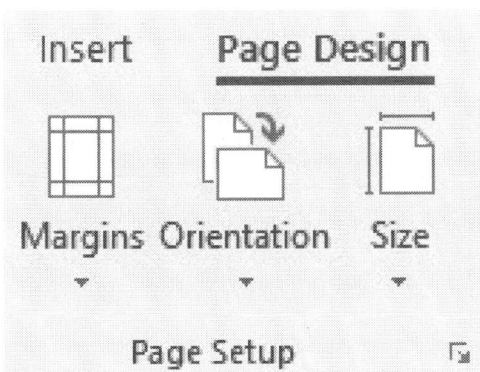

Figure 5.1

If you click on the arrow at the lower right side of the group you will see additional *Page Setup* options that can do many of the same things the other buttons do.

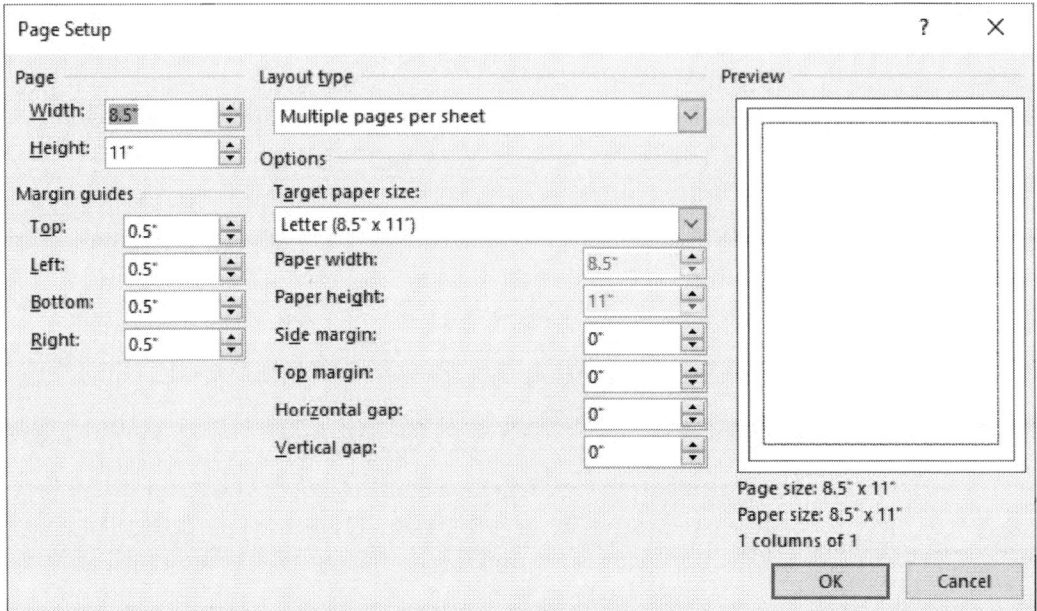

Figure 5.2

- **Margins** – Page margins are used to tell Publisher where the edge of the printable area of the page is. So if you want a half inch of white space around the edge of your page you can change the top, bottom, left and right margins to .5. You can also have different margins for each side of the page if you like. Be careful not to make your margins too small otherwise when you go to print, part of your page might get cut off.

- **Orientation** – This option lets you choose whether the page is set up portrait (tall) or landscape (wide) and what you choose will depend on the type of publication you are working on.

- **Size** – If you change your mind as to what size you want your publication to be then you can change that here. Publisher has all of the standard sizes such as 8.5x11, 8.5x14, 11x17 and so on preconfigured but you can also type in your own custom size if you like.

Master Pages

Master Pages are used to apply formatting that you want to apply to all of the pages in your publication. Microsoft PowerPoint has a similar feature that is used to apply formatting to all of the slides within a presentation.

To edit the Master Page you will need to go to the *Page Design* tab and then to the *Page Background* group and click on *Master Pages*. Then click on *Edit Master Pages* from the dropdown menu.

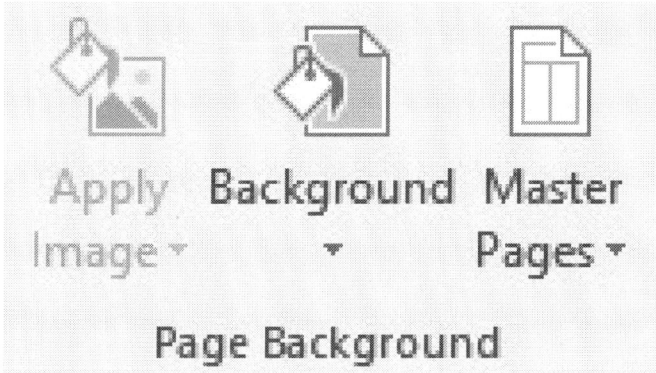

Figure 5.3

Then you will be shown a blank "master page" that you can edit the way you like. In my example, I gave it a marble background, changed the page margins, added a pattered bar to the top of the page and then changed the default font to something a little more exciting (figure 5.3).

After you make the desired changes to the Master Page you need to click on the *Close Master Page* button on the new Master Page tab that appears while you are making your changes.

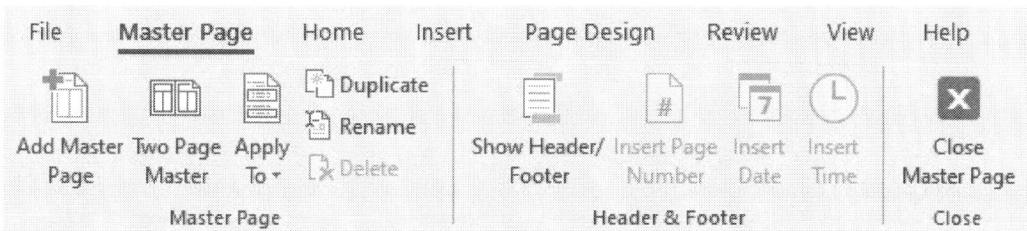

Figure 5.4

Figure 5.5

Now when I go back to my publication (my dog calendar file in this case) I can see that these changes have been applied to every page within my file.

Figure 5.6

Using Guide Lines and Grid Lines

When you are creating a publication that has a lot of objects that need to be aligned perfectly for the sake of appearances and printing, then this is where guide lines and grid lines will help you out. These types of lines can be placed on a page to help you align your objects, yet they will not show up when you print your publication.

Let's say you plan on creating some business cards that will be printed out and then cut down to size. When making business cards they are usually created with many cards on a single sheet and then that sheet is cut down to size. Figure 5.7 shows a single 2x3.5 inch standard size business card on an 8.5x11 inch page. Obviously, if I wanted to print out 500 business cards it would be quite wasteful to print this sheet 500 times and then have to cut out the single card 500 times as well.

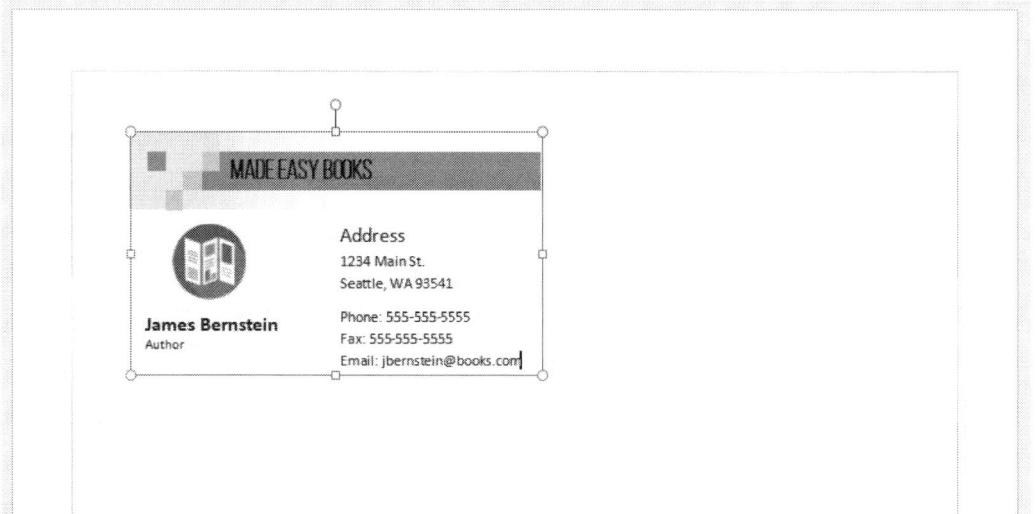

Figure 5.7

The proper way to do this would be to fit as many cards on the page as I can and have them be aligned so I can cut them with the least amount of cuts. To make sure they are all lined up correctly I will use some guide lines on my page. One way I could go about this would be to create horizontal and vertical lines and use the ruler to try and make a grid for my cards and hope that I have things set up correctly. You can create gridlines by going to *Guides* and then choosing *add horizontal or add vertical ruler guide* or simply drag a new guide out from the ruler on the top or bottom of the page.

I used this method and ended up with some guide lines as shown in figure 5.8. Then I can just copy and paste my business card and align them within my guide lines as shown in figure 5.9.

Figure 5.8

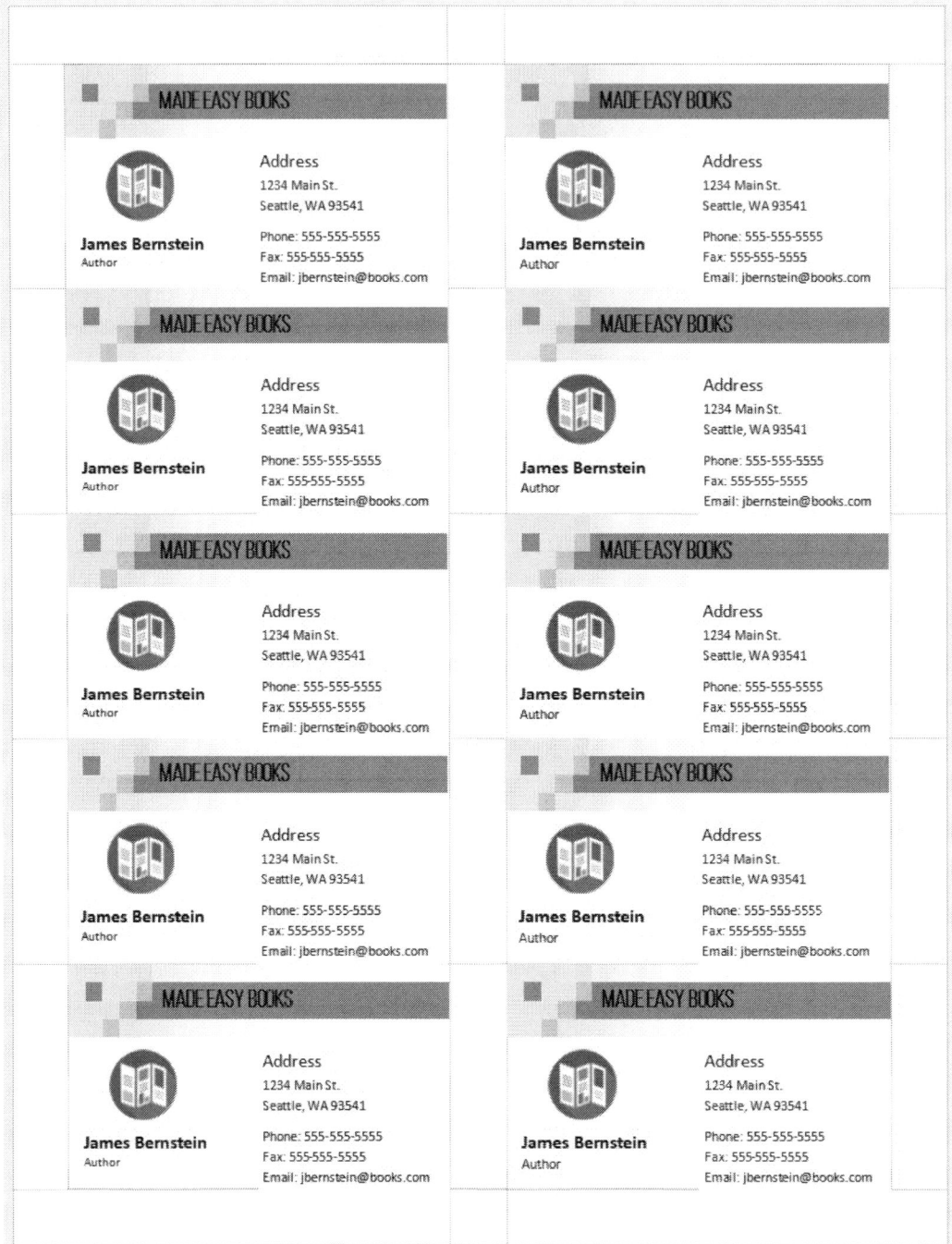

Figure 5.9

Another method I can use to accomplish this would be to go to the *Page Design* tab, then the *Layout* group and click on the *Guides* button. Since none of the built in guide layouts work for me I will then click on the *Grids and Baseline Guides* option and enter in the measurements manually as seen in figure 5.11.

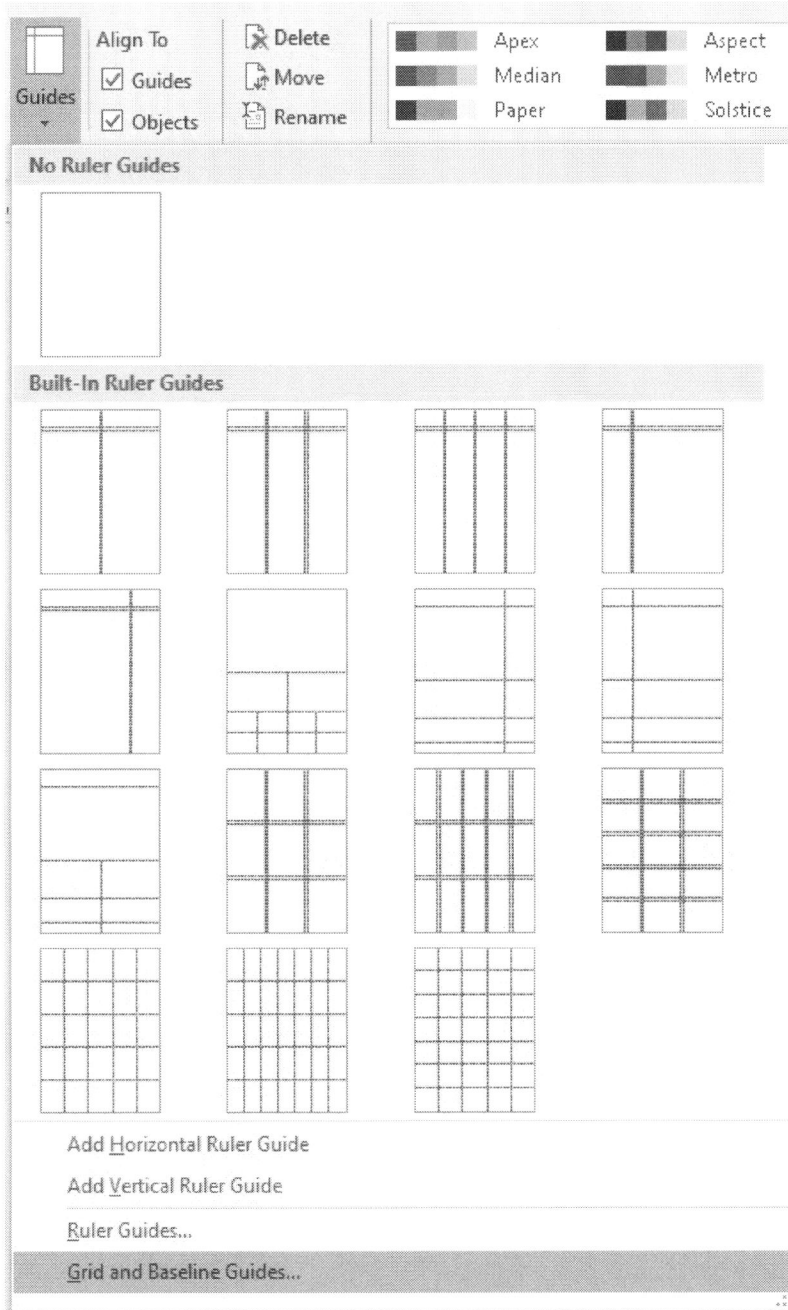

Figure 5.10

Then I will click on the *Grid Guides* tab and enter in the number of columns and rows I want and also the spacing between them. If I try and enter in more columns or rows than will fit with my spacing choice, Publisher will tell me that I need to change one of my measurements to make things fit.

To make boxes that are 3.5" by 2", I can fit three columns and five rows on the sheet in between my margins. The Spacing section tells Publisher how much space you want in between each column or guide. Keep in mind that you might have to adjust the guide lines by dragging them if things don't line up exactly the way you like.

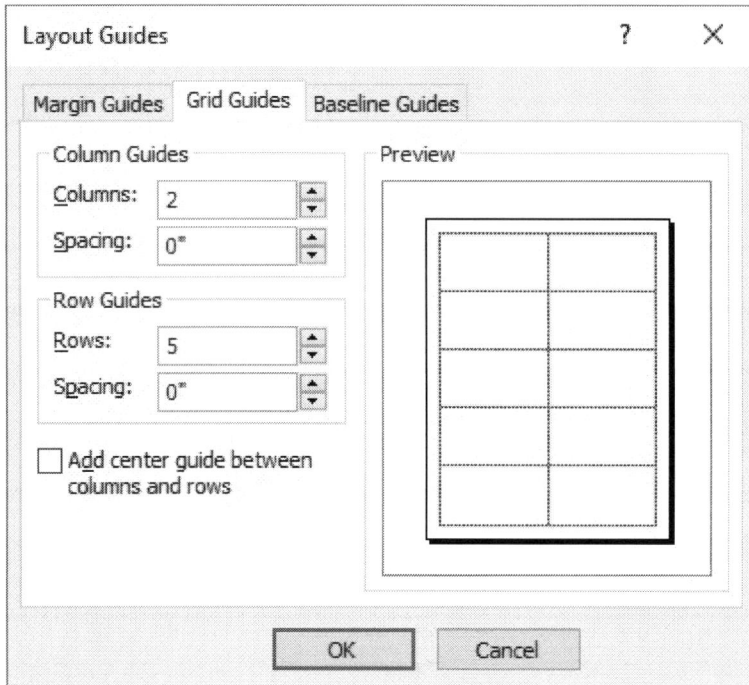

Figure 5.11

Formatting Text and Images
When you add text to your publication, Publisher will just use the default font (typestyle) and size when you create text within a text box. And when you insert a picture onto your page, it will be placed in the middle of the page and kept at its default size. In most cases, the default settings will not quite be what you are looking for so you will need to do some formatting to get things to look the way you like.

Formatting your text is a fairly easy process and most of your text editing will be done from the *Home* tab and in order to format your text, you will need to highlight it first as shown in figure 5.12.

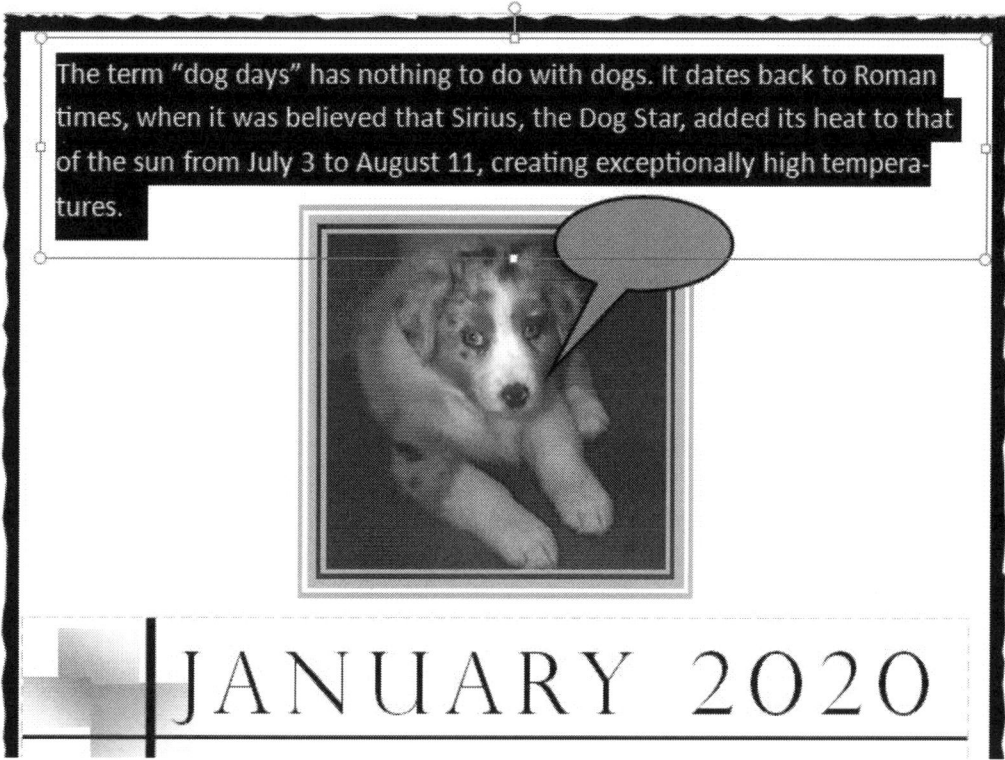

The term "dog days" has nothing to do with dogs. It dates back to Roman times, when it was believed that Sirius, the Dog Star, added its heat to that of the sun from July 3 to August 11, creating exceptionally high temperatures.

JANUARY 2020

Figure 5.12

Then you will make your formatting changes from the *Font* and *Paragraph* groups for the most part.

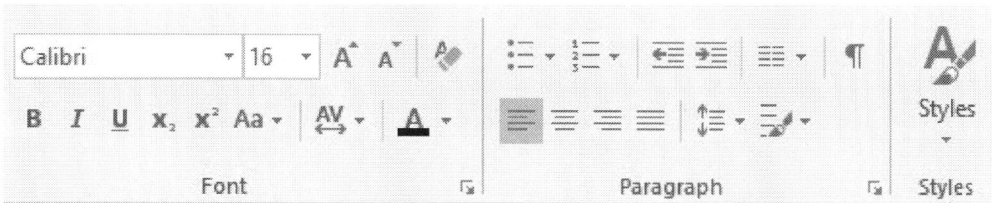

Figure 5.13

I will now change the font style and its size to something more appealing. I will also make it bold and centered. To change the font I will choose something from the dropdown box that says Calibri from figure 5.13, make it bold by clicking on the B in the Font group and then clicking on the center justification from the Paragraph group.

As you can see in figure 5.14 that the text looks more appealing and fits better within the space allocated for that text. Getting your text to look right usually takes a little trial and error until you find the look that works best for you.

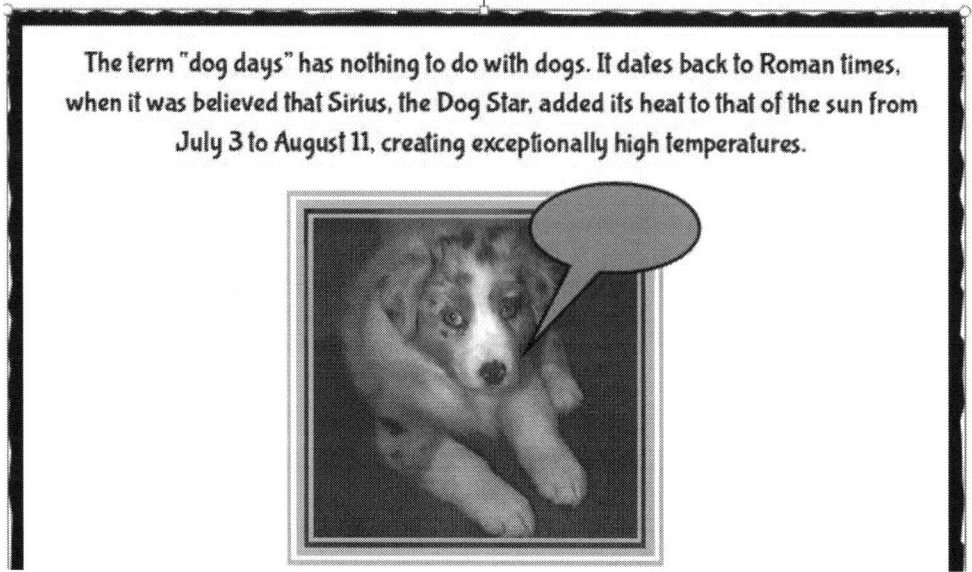

The term "dog days" has nothing to do with dogs. It dates back to Roman times, when it was believed that Sirius, the Dog Star, added its heat to that of the sun from July 3 to August 11, creating exceptionally high temperatures.

Figure 5.14

I did some image formatting in the last chapter when I added the box\frame around the dog picture that you can see in figure 5.14. There are other things you can do to your images besides add borders to them. Figure 5.15 shows my dog picture for March but I only want the dog on the left to be in the pictures so I will need to crop out the other dog.

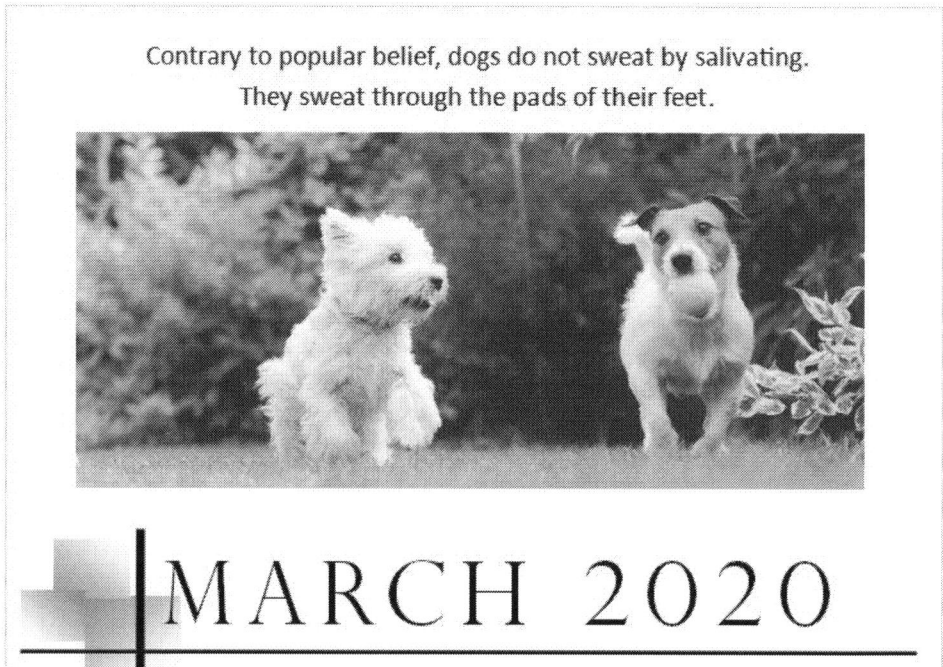

Contrary to popular belief, dogs do not sweat by salivating.
They sweat through the pads of their feet.

MARCH 2020

Figure 5.15

To do this I will double click the picture to bring up the *Format* tab and then click on the *Crop* button in the *Crop* group. This will then place black "handles" on every corner and side of the image that I can then click on and drag to crop the image.

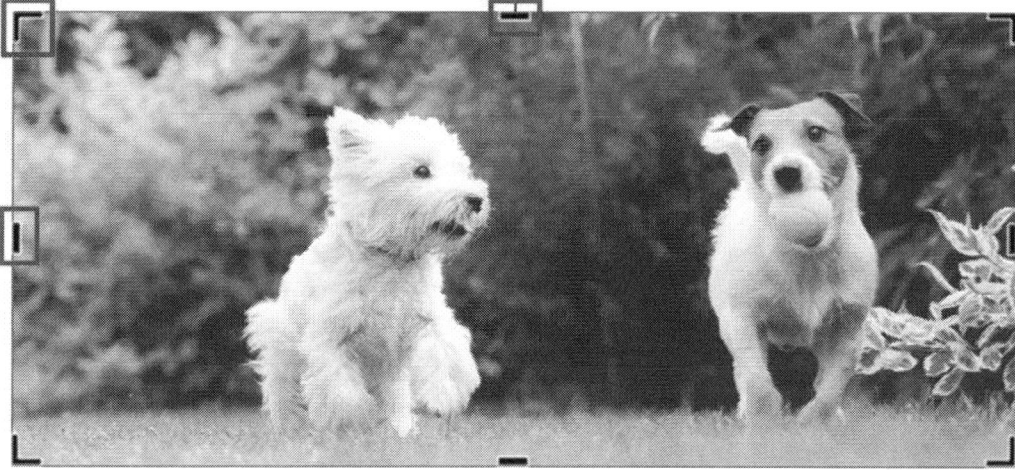

Figure 5.16

When you drag the crop handles, the part of the image that is faded out is the part that will be cropped out and the remainder of the image will be the newly cropped picture.

Figure 5.17

When you are happy with your crop, simply click anywhere off the image and you will be shown your results as shown in figure 5.18.

Contrary to popular belief, dogs do not sweat by salivating.
They sweat through the pads of their feet.

MARCH 2020

Figure 5.18

One nice feature of Publisher or any Office program is that once you crop a picture you can always go back and double click the cropped image to be able to do things like un-crop it or change the cropped area since the entire picture is stored within the publication even after you crop it.

Other ways you can format your pictures include things such as changing the brightness, contrast and colors of your images. Most of the time you would do this in a photo editing program but if you want to perform a quick change you can do this within Publisher as well.

When you right click on your picture and choose *Format Picture* you will see a tab called *Picture* and from there you can do the things I just mentioned as well as change the image's transparency levels. When you use the *Recolor* option, Publisher will simply change the picture from full color to a single tinted colored version based on the color you choose.

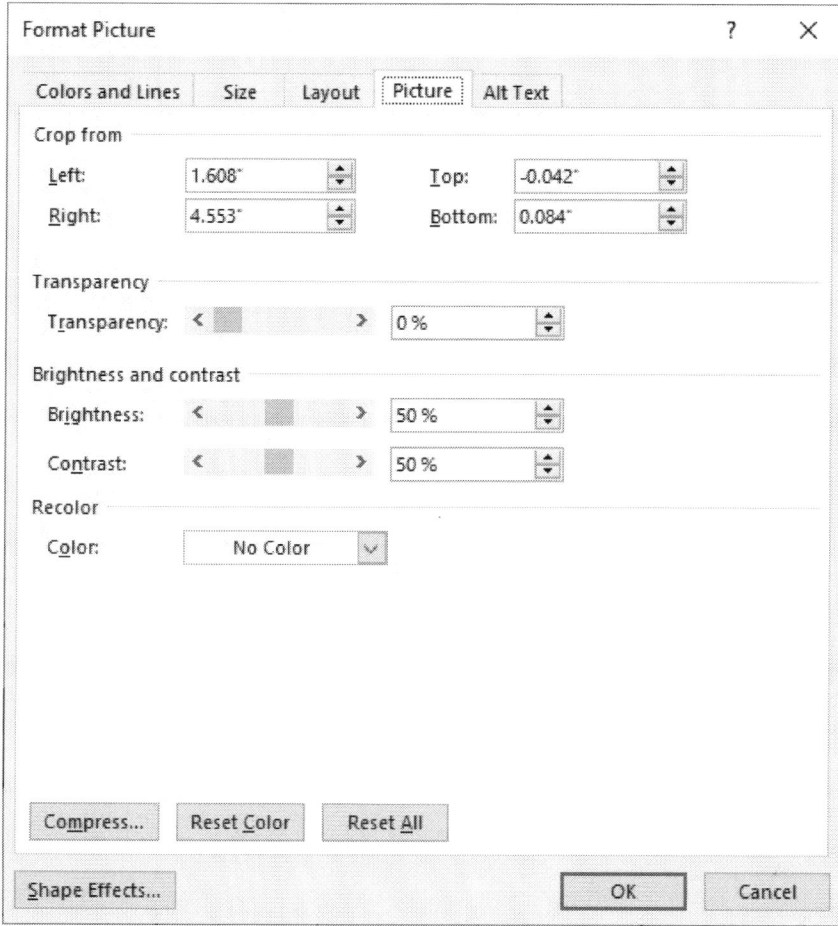

Figure 5.19

To resize a picture it's easy to simply click on it and then drag from a corner or side to change its size but you need to be careful that you don't change its aspect ratio when doing so. When you drag from a corner, the image will be kept proportional as you enlarge or reduce it but if you drag from the side or top then it will become skewed. Figure 5.20 shows the original image on the left and then how it looks when it's reduced by dragging from the left side. Notice how the image on the right looks like it's been squished?

Figure 5.20

If you want to fine tune your image size then you can go to the *Size* tab and enter in exact numbers for height and width and even rotate the image a specific amount if that is your goal.

I recommend keeping the *Lock aspect ratio* box checked so you don't end up with a skewed image when changing the numbers in the *Scale* section. If things go wrong you can always click the *Reset* button to bring the image size back to where it was before you started.

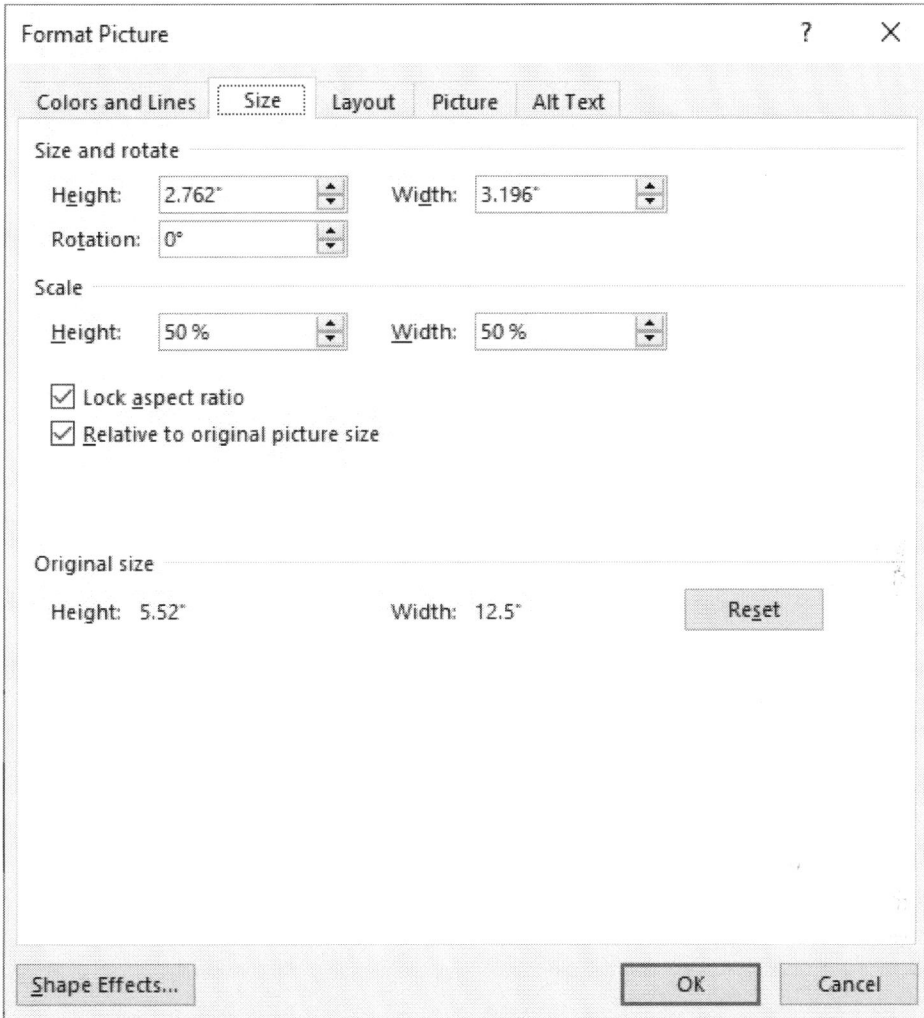

Figure 5.21

The *Shape Effects* button at the lower left of the Format Picture options has some fun ways that you can use to add some flair to your images (figure 5.22). There are many categories to choose from allowing you to add things such as shadow and glow effects to your images. Each category also has its own presets that you can choose from, so you don't need to try and figure out how all the settings work to make your own custom look...unless you want to. Figure 5.23 shows an example of the same picture with a variety of the effects applied. The applied effects are overkill for the image, but I just wanted to illustrate what you can do with them.

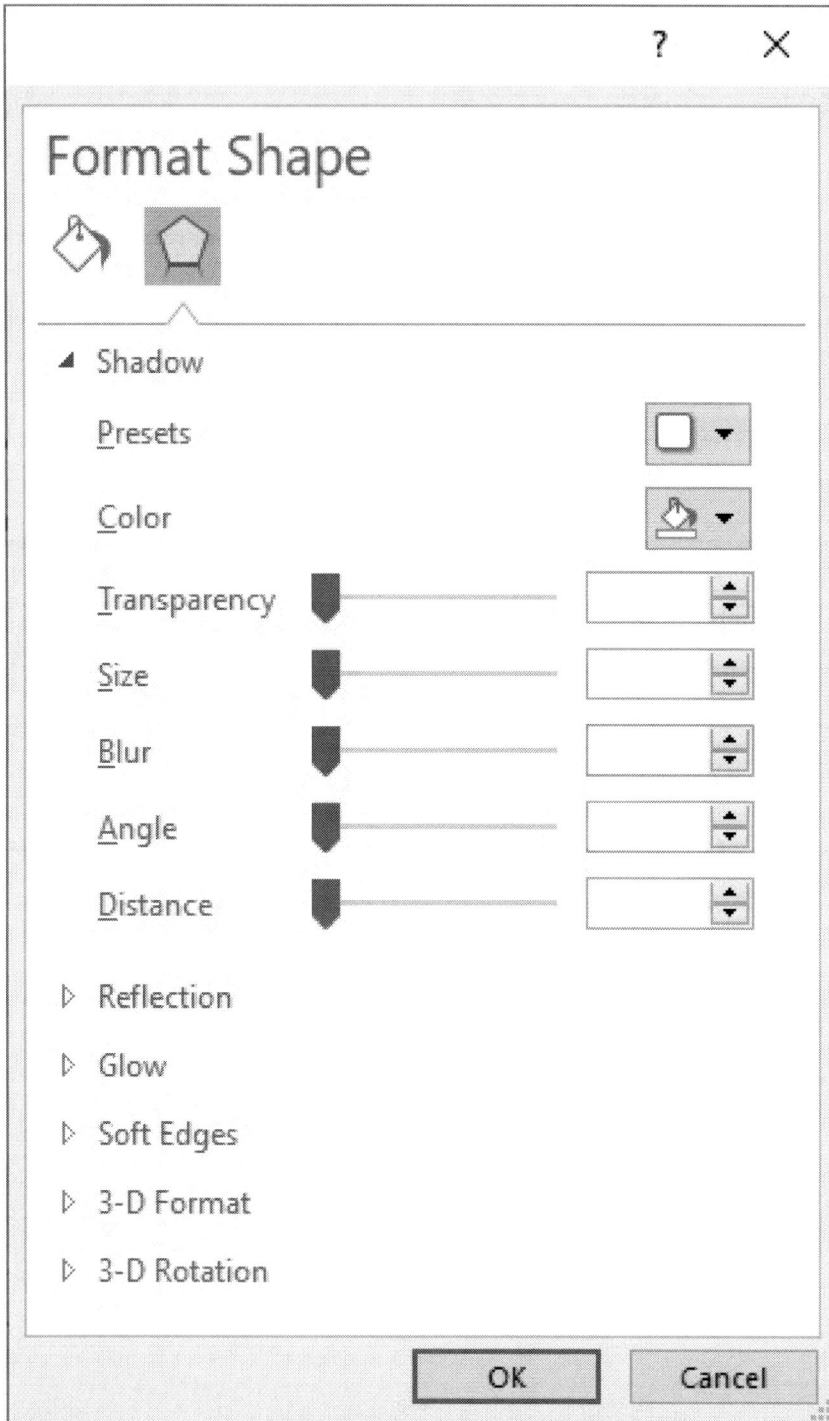

Figure 5.22

Figure 5.23

Many of these image editing tools can be found on the Format tab when you double click an image so keep that in mind if you would rather not have to right click the image and choose Format Picture each time.

Formatting Shapes

When you add custom shapes such as boxes, arrows, stars, etc. to your publication you can format these in a similar manner as you can with pictures. When you right click on a shape and choose *Format AutoShape* you will have most of the same

133

formatting options as you do when you right click a picture and choose *Format Picture*.

The main difference will be that you will have a *Text Box* tab that can be used to add text inside of your shape. Here you can set its position in the shape as well as its margins and decide how you want the text to fit within the box.

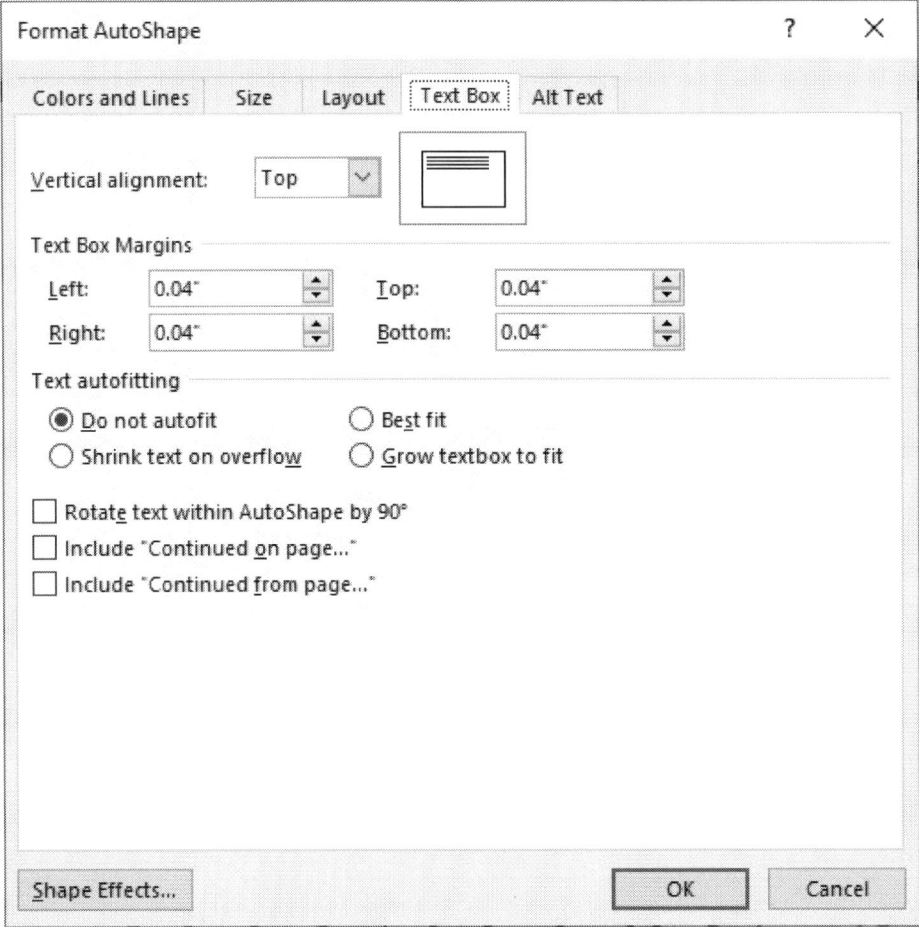

Figure 5.24

You need to pay attention to the *Text autofitting* section because that will determine how your text fits within your shape. Figure 5.25 shows what happens when I use the *Grow textbox to fit* option and add text to my speech bubble shape. When I added the text, the shape grew in size to accommodate the text which is not what I really wanted.

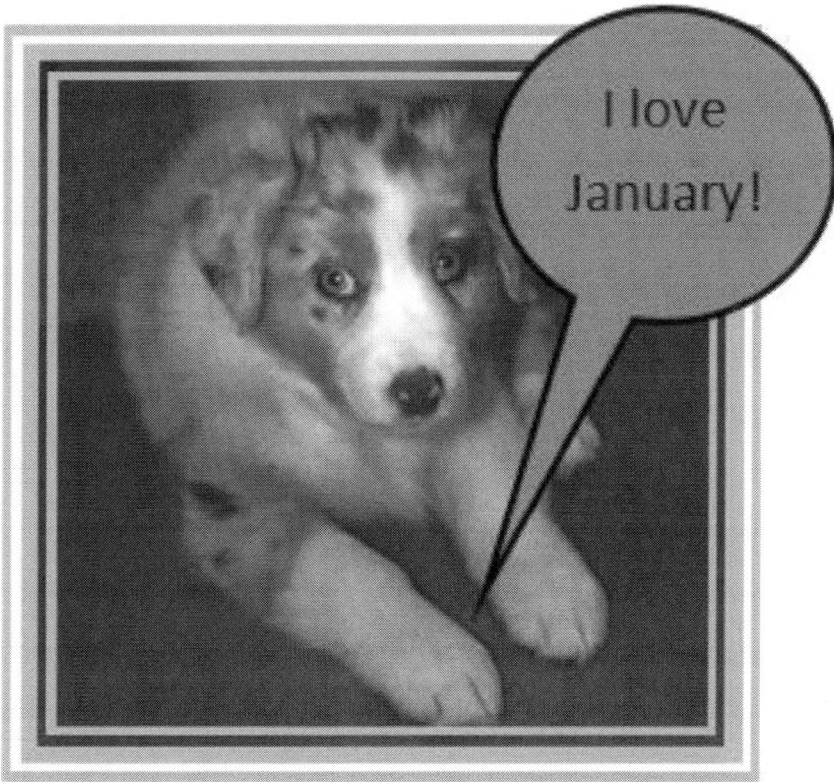

Figure 5.25

You can also add a text box from the Insert menu and place it on top of your shape if you want a little more control when it comes to making the text fit within the shape without changing the size of the shape itself. Just keep in mind that you might have to use the Bring Forward option for your text box so it's not placed behind your shape.

Changing the Background

I mentioned that it is easy to change the background for your pages but wanted to go over the topic again and get a little more in depth when it comes to your background options. When you go to the *Page Design* tab and click on *Backgrounds*, it will show you a few basic options that you can choose from and apply to your page. But if you click on *More Backgrounds*, you will have many more options to choose from.

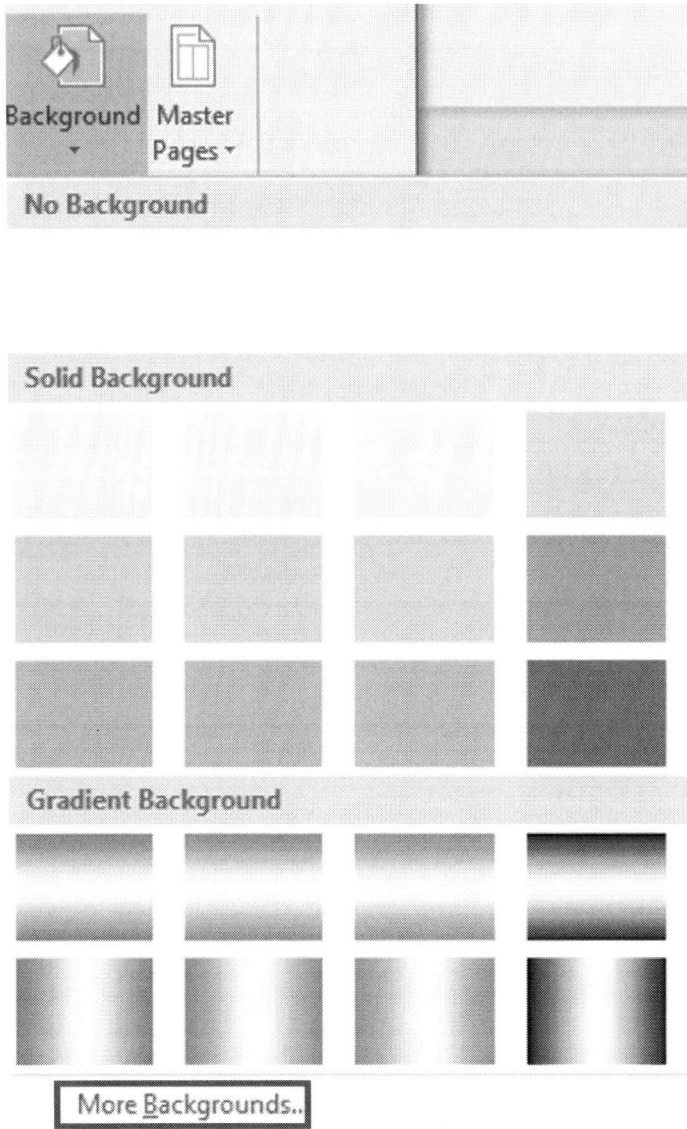

Figure 5.26

The No Fill and Solid Fill options should be pretty self-explanatory, but you can also use a gradient type fill as your background. A gradient fill is an effect that is achieved by blending one color into another using two or more colors. There are also different gradient patterns that you can apply as well as being able to create your own. And as usual, there are some preset gradients you can apply if you want to take the easy route. Figure 5.27 shows the gradient option box where you can configure your custom gradient fill. I will say that creating a custom gradient takes a little work to figure out how the color, type and direction settings work to actually look like something you would want to use for your background.

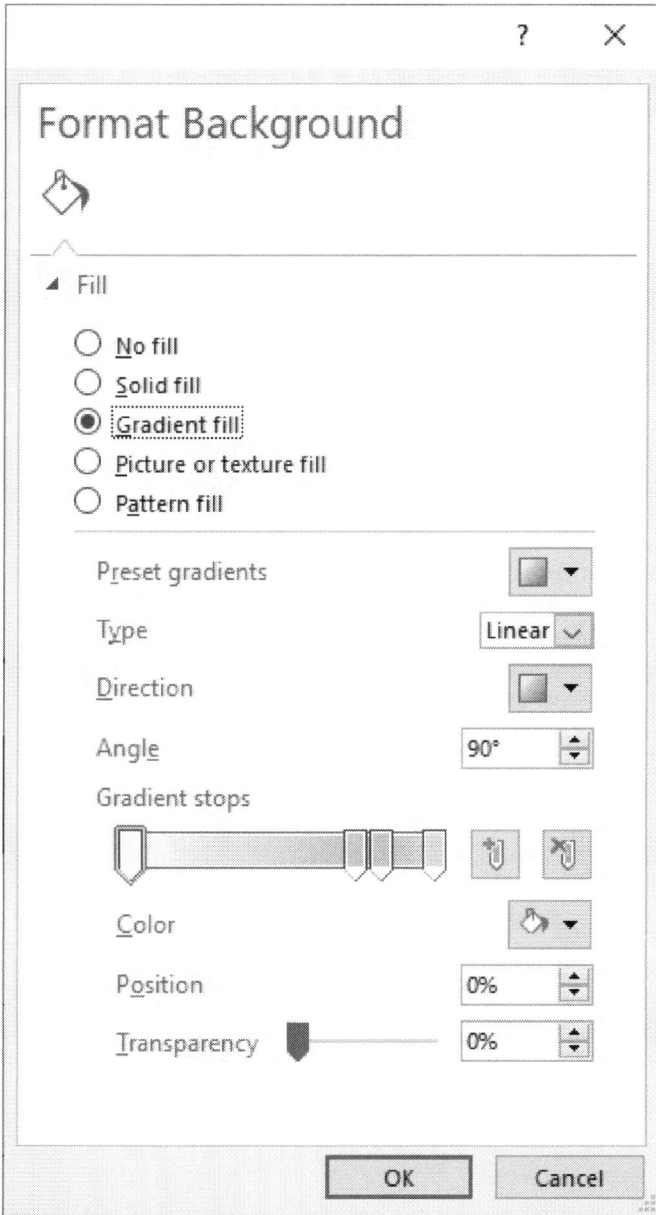

? ✕

Format Background

◢ Fill

   ○ No fill
   ○ Solid fill
   ◉ Gradient fill
   ○ Picture or texture fill
   ○ Pattern fill

   Preset gradients

   Type   Linear ⌄

   Direction

   Angle   90°

   Gradient stops

   Color

   Position   0%

   Transparency   0%

OK   Cancel

Figure 5.27

The *Picture or texture* fill option is much easier to use and all you need to do is choose a picture for your background or add one of the built in textures that come with Publisher. If you remember the cookie background that I had for my catalog in the last chapter, that was done by adding an image for my background.

If you would like to add a texture as your background you can choose one of the available textures as shown in figure 5.28.

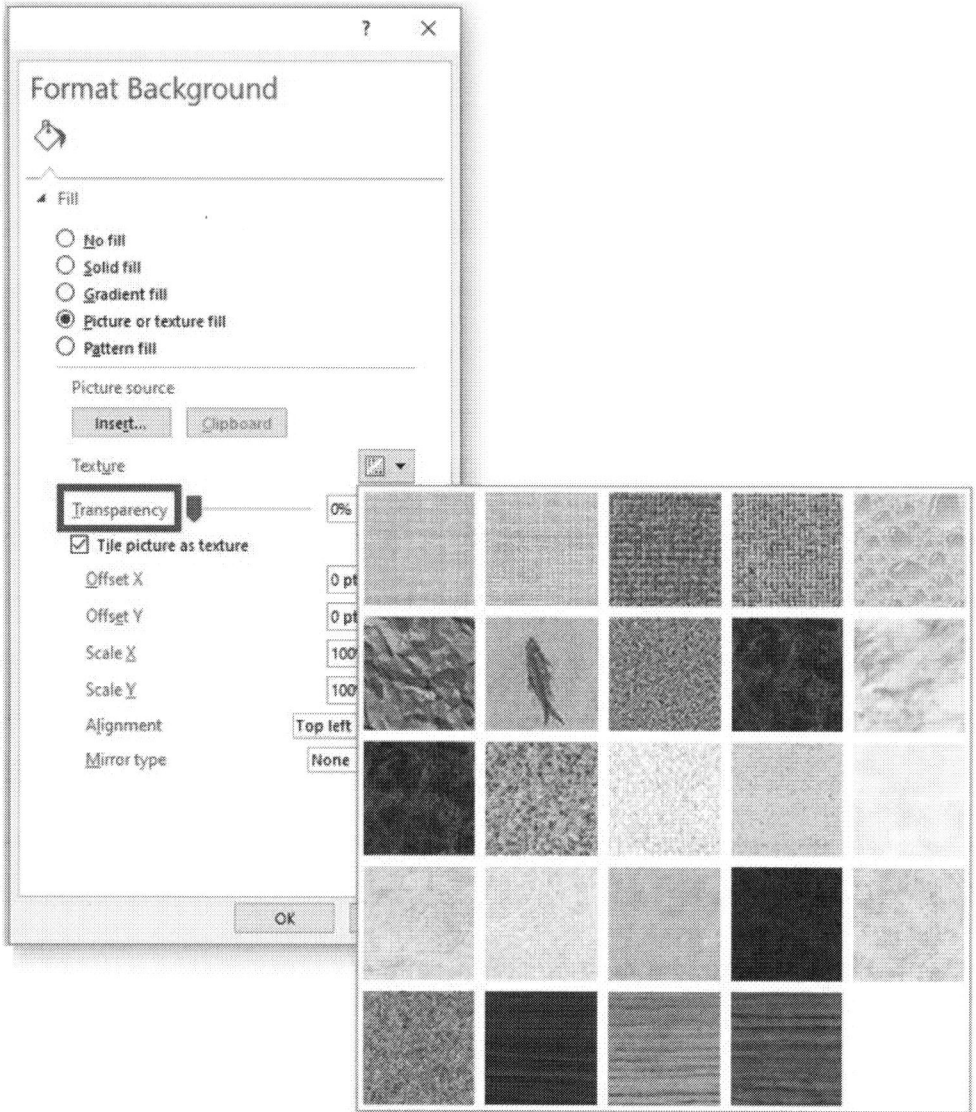

Figure 5.28

The one thing to be aware of when using one of these backgrounds is that they can be very overpowering and make the content on your page hard to read. So when using one of the darker or more complex backgrounds, I suggest using the *Transparency* slider and making the texture more transparent so it's not so bold.

Finally, you can add a pattern fill as your background but once again, these can be very overpowering as well. When choosing a pattern you can change the color and\or tint for the foreground and background which makes it possible to lighten things up so the pattern is not so strong.

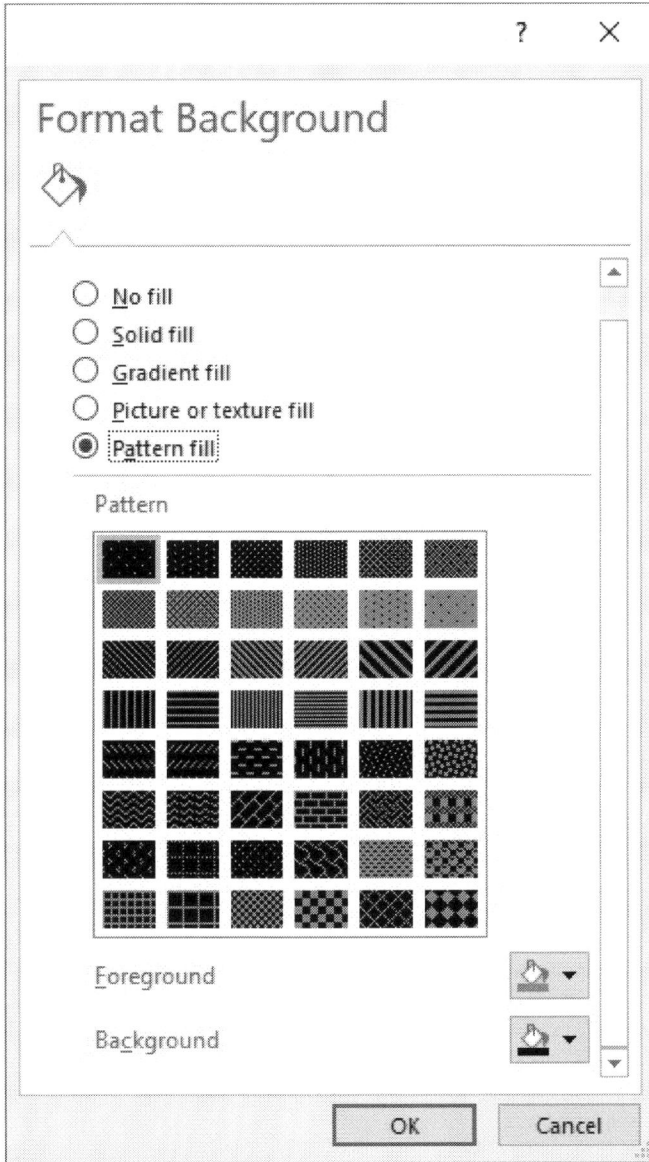

Figure 5.29

Using Mail Merge

Although Mail Merge is not really a formatting topic I thought it would fit best into this chapter since we are configuring how our publication is looking and there is some formatting involved when doing a Mail Merge.

A Mail Merge is used to take information such as names and addresses from a master list and then insert them into duplicate copies of your publication so that the only thing that is different on the page for each copy is the information you inserted from your master list.

A commonly used example of a Mail Merge is creating mailing labels where you have multiple labels on a page that are identical, but each has its own unique name and address. This allows you to take a data source like a spreadsheet that contains all of the names and addresses and import the information into your labels without having to manually type in all the names and addresses. For my example, I am going to create a book release party postcard and use an Excel spreadsheet as the source for my names and addresses. You can also manually create a list within Publisher like I did for my catalog.

To begin with, I have opened a 2 sided postcard template file that I found from the Publisher templates which I then modified to suit my needs. Next I will go to the *Mailings* tab and then click on *Mail Merge* and choose the *Step-by-Step Mail Merge Wizard*. If you have experience with Mail Merge in other programs such as Microsoft Word then you can skip the wizard and just do a manual Mail Merge.

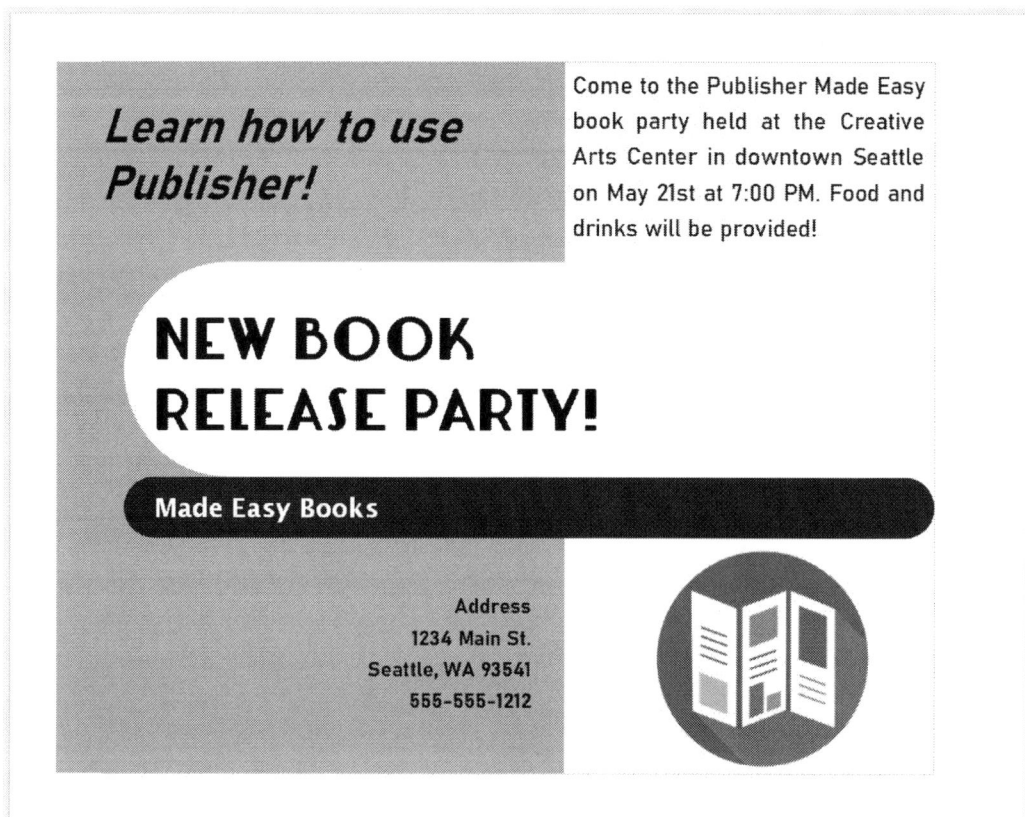

Learn how to use Publisher!

Come to the Publisher Made Easy book party held at the Creative Arts Center in downtown Seattle on May 21st at 7:00 PM. Food and drinks will be provided!

NEW BOOK RELEASE PARTY!

Made Easy Books

Address
1234 Main St.
Seattle, WA 93541
555-555-1212

Figure 5.30

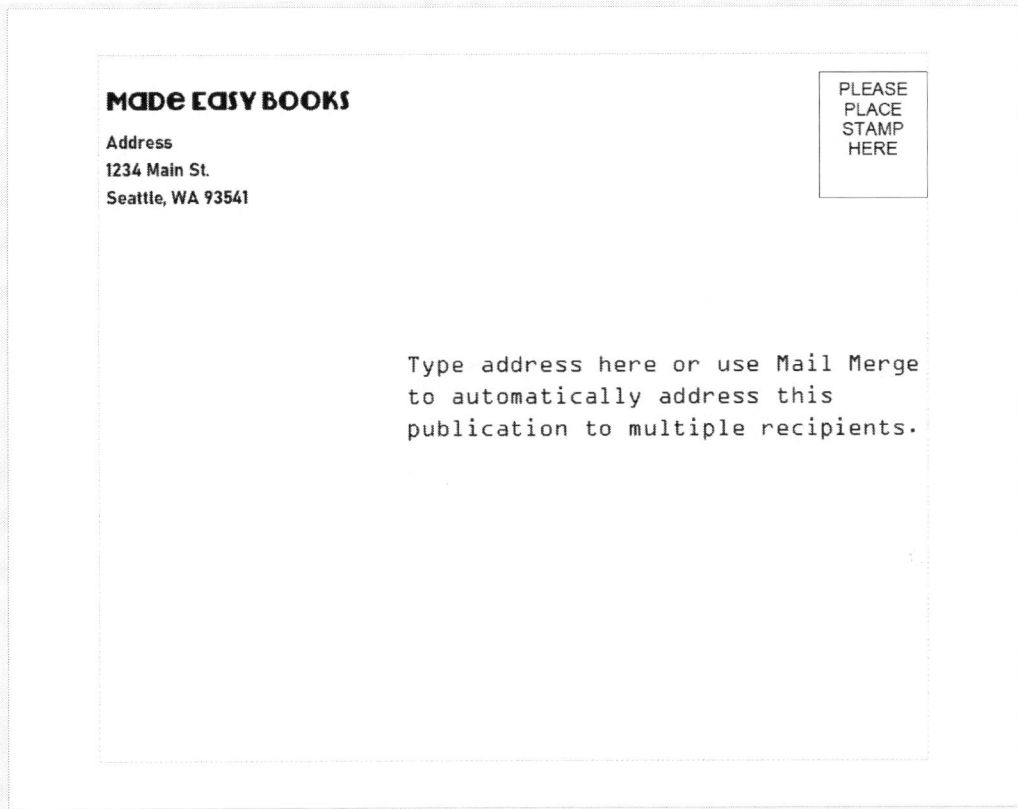

MaDe EaSY BOOKS

Address
1234 Main St.
Seattle, WA 93541

PLEASE
PLACE
STAMP
HERE

Type address here or use Mail Merge
to automatically address this
publication to multiple recipients.

Figure 5.31

When I start the wizard I get three choices for how I want to create my recipient list (figure 5.32). I can use an existing list such as a database or spreadsheet file, select the names from my Outlook contacts if I happen to use Outlook, or I can type out a new list right in Publisher. I will be using the *Use an existing list* option since I already have an Excel Spreadsheet file with my names and addresses ready to go.

Figure 5.33 shows the list of names and addresses as they appear in my Microsoft Excel spreadsheet. I will need to know the location of this Excel file when it's time to import it into my Mail Merge.

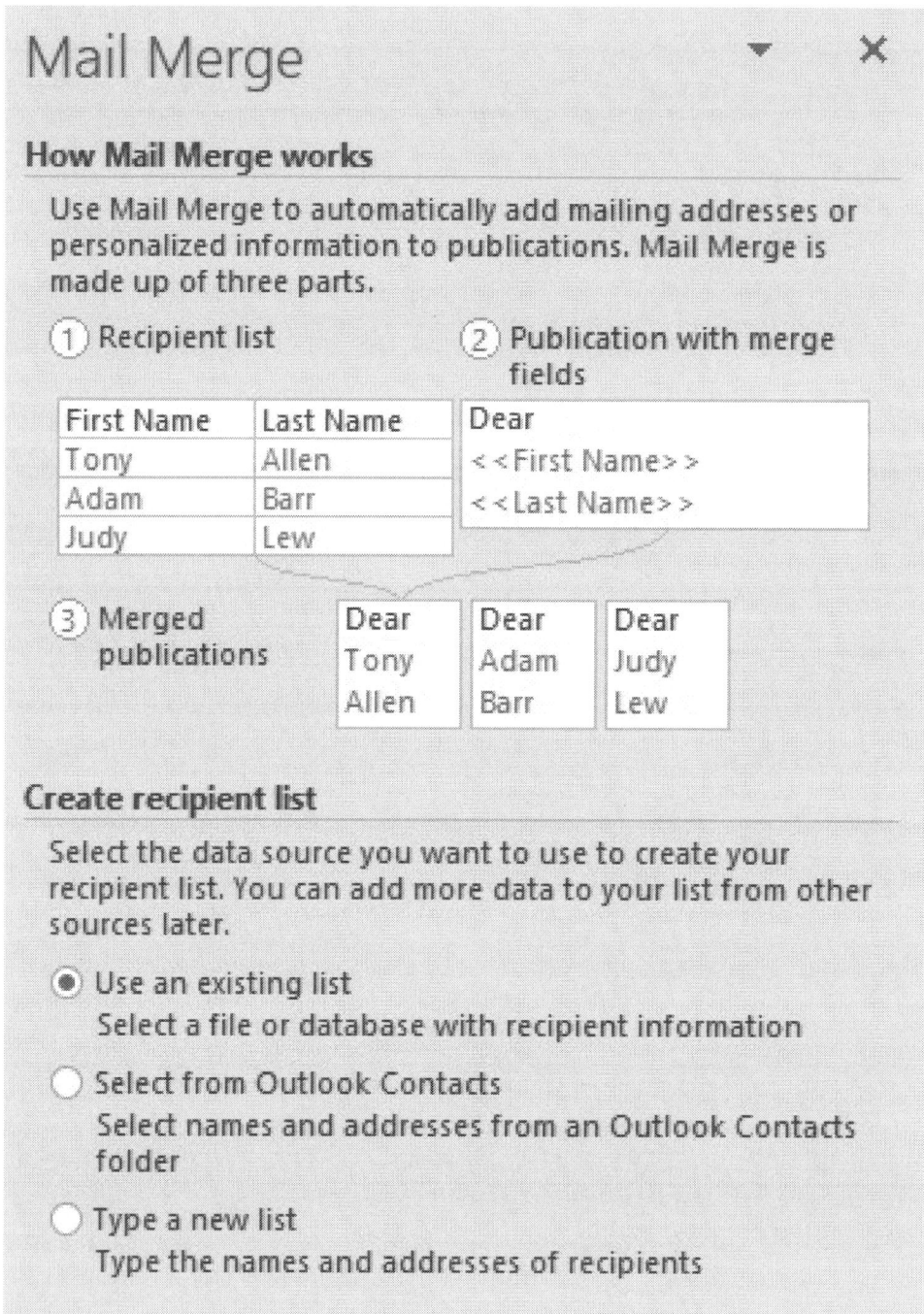

Mail Merge ▼ ✕

How Mail Merge works

Use Mail Merge to automatically add mailing addresses or personalized information to publications. Mail Merge is made up of three parts.

① Recipient list   ② Publication with merge fields

First Name	Last Name
Tony	Allen
Adam	Barr
Judy	Lew

Dear
< <First Name> >
< <Last Name> >

③ Merged publications

Dear	Dear	Dear
Tony	Adam	Judy
Allen	Barr	Lew

Create recipient list

Select the data source you want to use to create your recipient list. You can add more data to your list from other sources later.

◉ Use an existing list
  Select a file or database with recipient information

◯ Select from Outlook Contacts
  Select names and addresses from an Outlook Contacts folder

◯ Type a new list
  Type the names and addresses of recipients

Figure 5.32

	A	B	C	D	E
1	Name	Address	City	State	Zip
2	Sammy Thomas	4552 Lapine	Weschester	MN	56124
3	Rebecca Singer	493 Main St	Los Angeles	CA	85321
4	Julia Torres	9321 Birch St	Seattle	WA	75125
5	Jeff Kim	15 Maple Ave	Bend	OR	42156
6	Cynthia Jackson	453 Windsong St	Prescott	AZ	23541
7	Betty Niles	91534 S. 5th Ave	Miami	FL	99875
8	David Burns	54 Park St	Milton	AZ	33521
9	Todd Minees	876 Holley	Brenton	MN	47582
10	Sally McMann	177 Palo Verde	Alton	DE	23699
11	Jessie Garcia	756 Maple Ct	Bernville	KY	32214
12	Mandy Jones	75 Washington Dr	Venture	LA	53254
13	Bud Thompson	875 Hill Ct	Linden	MD	78963
14	Mary Wong	32 River Run Dr	Baskerville	MA	21456
15	Alice Mann	9713 Walnut St	Clinton	NM	21354
16	Debbie Simms	899 Oak Ln	Madison	OH	42357
17	Ashley McBride	9221 Union Pl	Arlington	OH	78932
18	Bill Winston	8112 San Vicente Dr	Dayton	NC	54756
19	Stephen Mills	88 Highland Ave	Burnlington	OK	43215
20	Ben Jenson	144 Lakewood Dr	Waverly	CO	45235
21	Jeff Dobson	722 Meadow Ln	Milford	GA	11224
22	Allen Knight	98877 Summit St	Riverside	VA	65211
23	Rosie Dallas	9445 Highland Dr	Ashland	WY	78544
24	Manny Smith	54 Linden St	Manchester	CA	36325
25	Marshall Adams	785 Belmont Ave	Clayton	NM	12889
26	Sam Jones	8554 Shady Ln	Marion	NV	95741
27	Vanessa Gross	482 Woodland Ave	Greenville	OK	95214
28	Holly Lamelle	8661 Fairway Dr	Franklin	MA	52143
29	Toby Wilson	733 Hickory Ln	West Abbey	DE	32514
30	Daniel Masters	621 Frontage Rd	Langston	AZ	71364
31	Jane Goodman	1554 Alpine Way	Mammoth	CA	25411

Figure 5.33

At the bottom of the wizard section, there will be a link that says *Next: Create or connect to a recipient list* and I will now click on this link and browse to where I have my spreadsheet saved. When I click on my spreadsheet file it will bring up a box asking to select a table from my spreadsheet. Since I only have the one I will click on *OK*. I will also leave the checkbox that says *First row of data contains column headers* checked since that's the case with my Excel file.

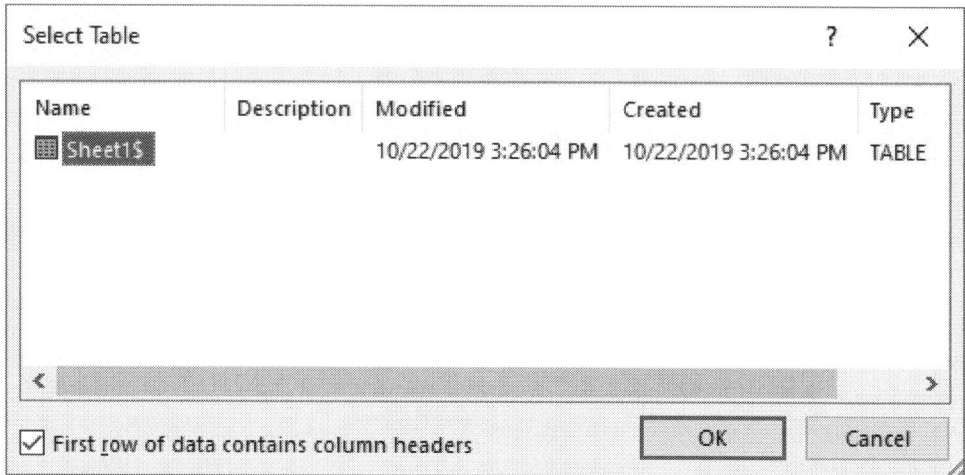

Figure 5.34

Then I will be shown my list of names and addresses and will have the option to uncheck any that I don't want to use and also do things like add to it, sort by name or other field and search for duplicate entries.

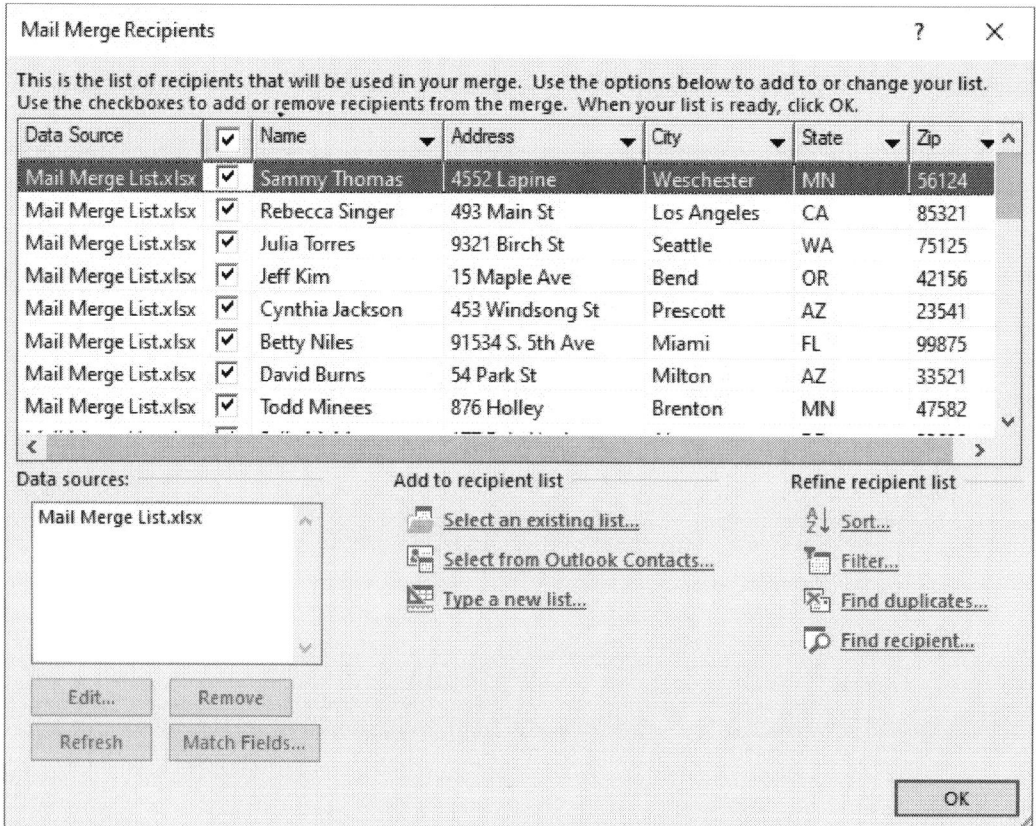

Figure 5.35

Next I can either drag and drop the recipient fields (name, address, city, etc.) to my postcard from the list that is shown in figure 5.36 or I can click the link for *Address block* under *More items* as seen in figure 5.37 and 5.38 to have Publisher add an address block with my fields automatically for me which is the choice I will go with.

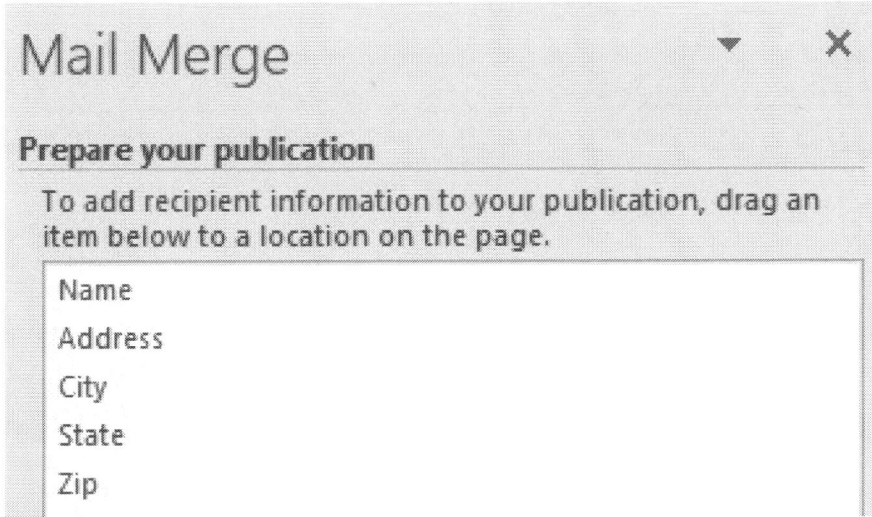

Figure 5.36

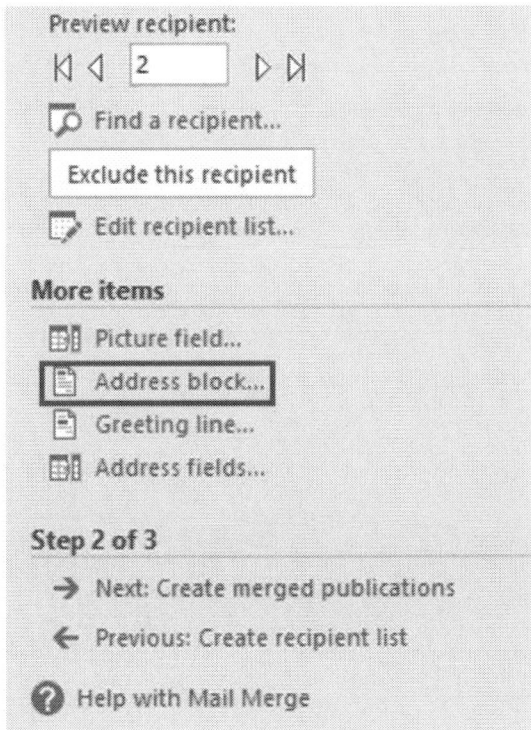

Figure 5.37

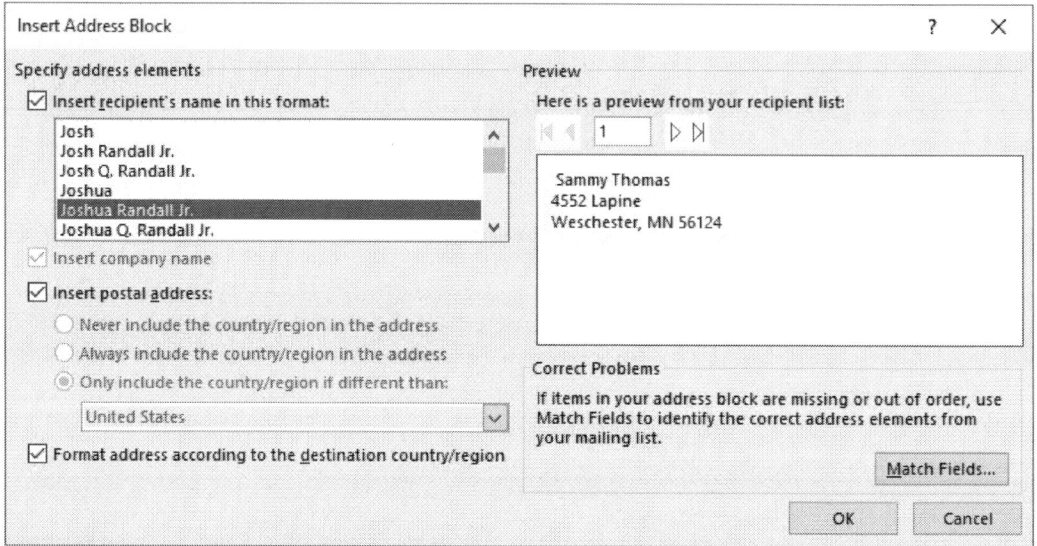

Figure 5.38

After adding the address block I will need to move it and resize it so it looks the way I want on my postcard.

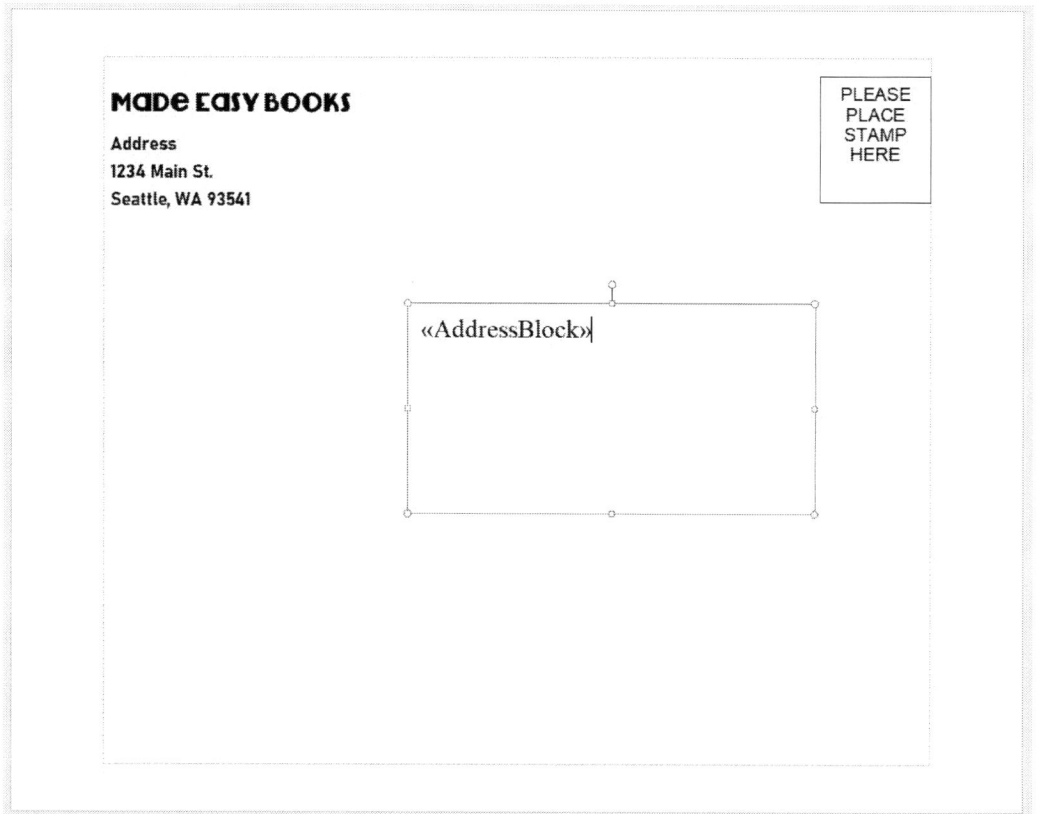

Figure 5.39

Next, I will click on the link at the bottom that says Next: *Create merged publications*. Here I will have three options to choose from. I can have my newly addressed postcards sent to my printer so I can print them out, I can have them created in a new publication or I can have them created in the publication that I am working on. I will choose the *Merge to a new publication* option so they will be kept separate from the file that I am working on to set up the Mail Merge.

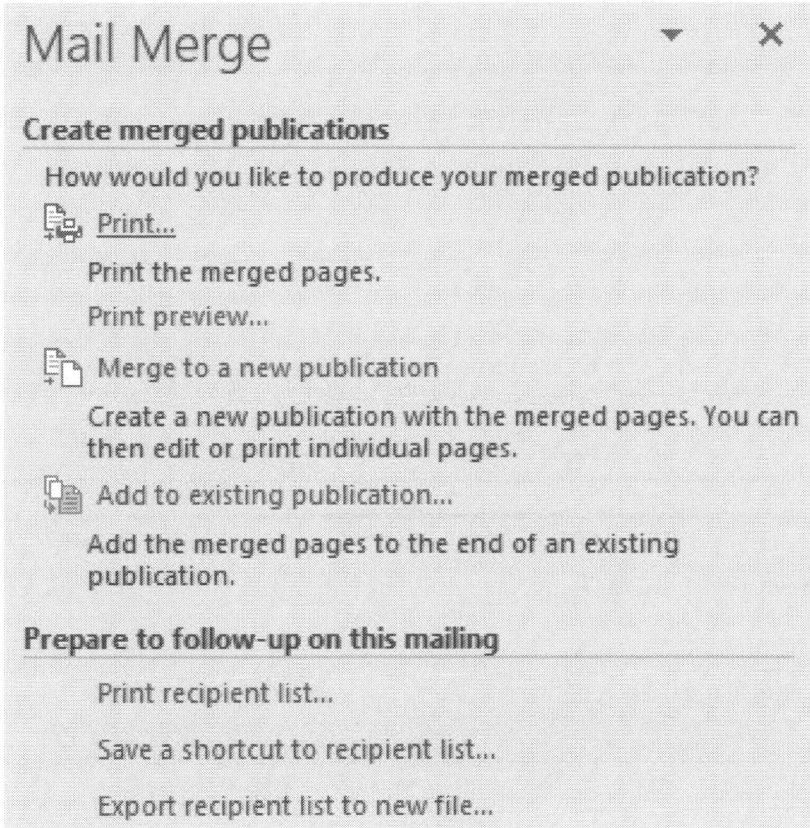

Mail Merge ▾ ✕

Create merged publications

How would you like to produce your merged publication?

Print...

Print the merged pages.

Print preview...

Merge to a new publication

Create a new publication with the merged pages. You can then edit or print individual pages.

Add to existing publication...

Add the merged pages to the end of an existing publication.

Prepare to follow-up on this mailing

Print recipient list...

Save a shortcut to recipient list...

Export recipient list to new file...

Figure 5.40

Figure 5.41 shows the results of my Mail Merge on one of the postcards. It filled in the name and address information that it took from my spreadsheet and made a separate two sided postcard for each person as shown in figure 5.42.

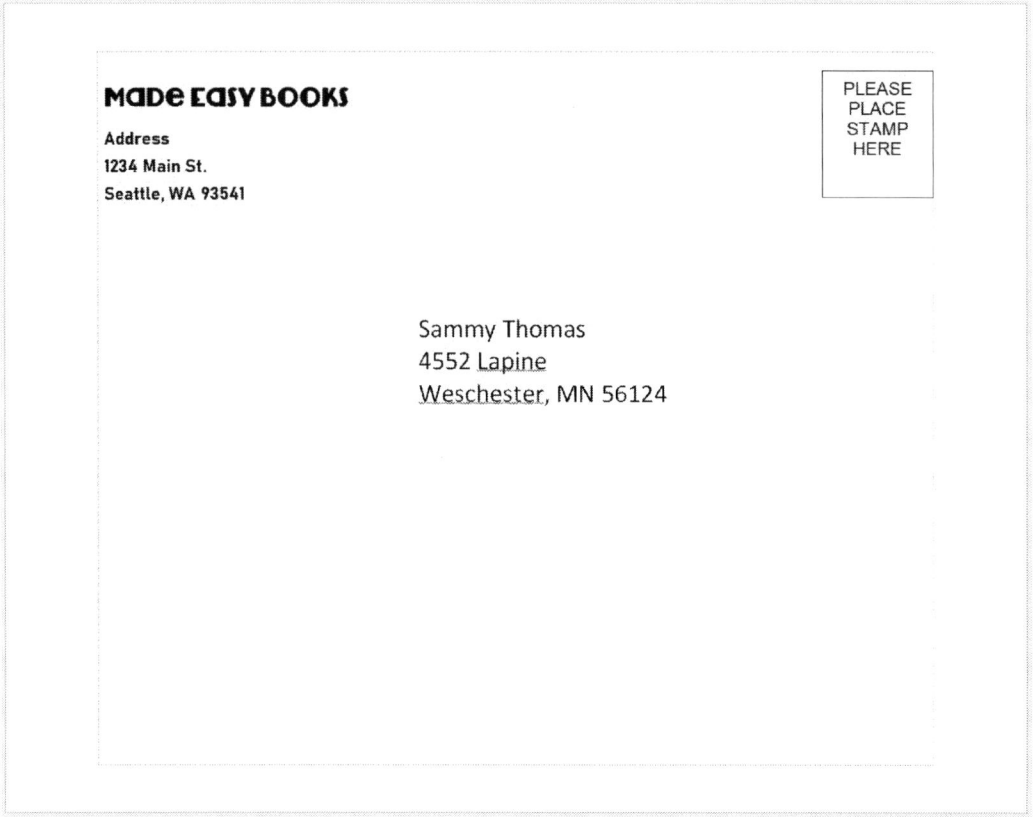

Made Easy Books

Address
1234 Main St.
Seattle, WA 93541

PLEASE
PLACE
STAMP
HERE

Sammy Thomas
4552 Lapine
Weschester, MN 56124

Figure 5.41

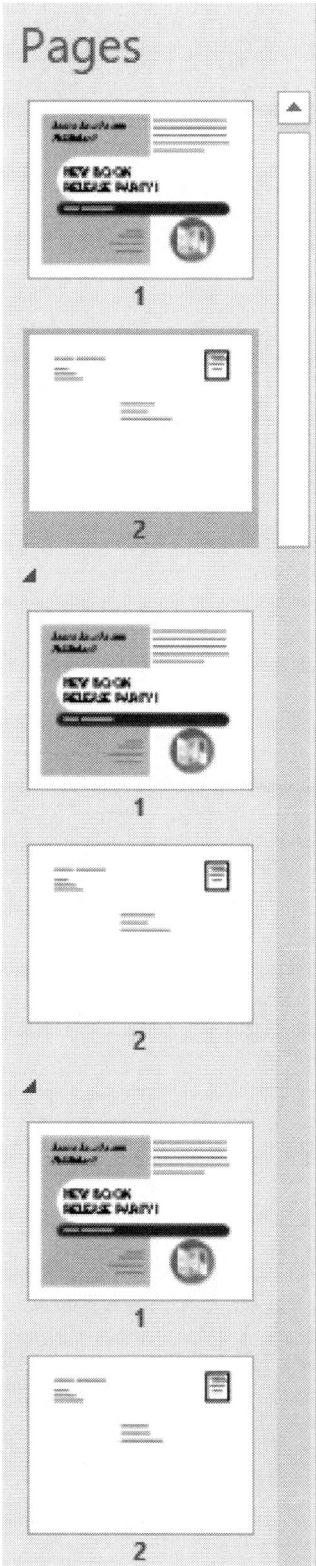

Figure 5.42

The Mail Merge process works differently depending on how you go about setting it up as well as what type of publication you are applying it to, so this was just one way of doing the process and hopefully it was enough to help get you started doing your own Mail Merge.

Chapter 6 – Saving, Sharing and Exporting Your Publication

One of the most important things you need to worry about when working on your publication is making sure that you save it on a regular basis and that you are saving it somewhere that you will have access to at any time you need. Office has a built in autosave feature where it will make periodic saves for you in case Publisher crashes so you can recover your work up until the last autosave point.

Saving Your Publication
Once you create a publication from a blank file or template you should save it with a descriptive name in a location that you will remember and maybe even create a folder for the publication and any associated files that might go with it like images that you used within it.

When you save your publication, it will be saved as a *.pub* file which is the default file type for Publisher files. File extensions are used by the operating system (Windows, Mac, etc.) to tell it what program to use to open a particular file type. So if you just save your publication as *Flyer.pub* then when you double click on that file, your computer will open it using Publisher. If you make up your own file extension or remove it then your computer won't know what to do with the file so make sure you don't change it. Sometimes your operating system will hide certain file extensions so you might not even see it even though it's really there.

Every time you click on Save from either the *Quick Access Toolbar* or from the *File* tab, the work you did from the last time you clicked on Save will be overwritten by the current state of your publication. You can also use the keyboard shortcut Ctrl-S to save your work (Command-S for Mac). If you want to keep your current changes separated from your previous changes then this is where the *Save As* feature comes into play.

When you use the Save As option, you will need to save your file with a different name since you can't have two files with the same name in the same folder. If you want to keep the same name then you will need to save your file in a different folder. Having different files with the same name can get confusing so be careful when doing this.

Publisher publications can be saved as other types of files as well and there are cases when you might need to save your publication as a different kind of file. If you go to the *File* tab and then click on *Save as,* and then click on the drop down arrow next to the Save button you will see that there are many different types of files that you can save your publication as (figure 6.1). You will see that *Publisher Files (*.pub)* is the default file type. Even though are many other types of files that you can save your publication as, you will most likely not use many of the other choices.

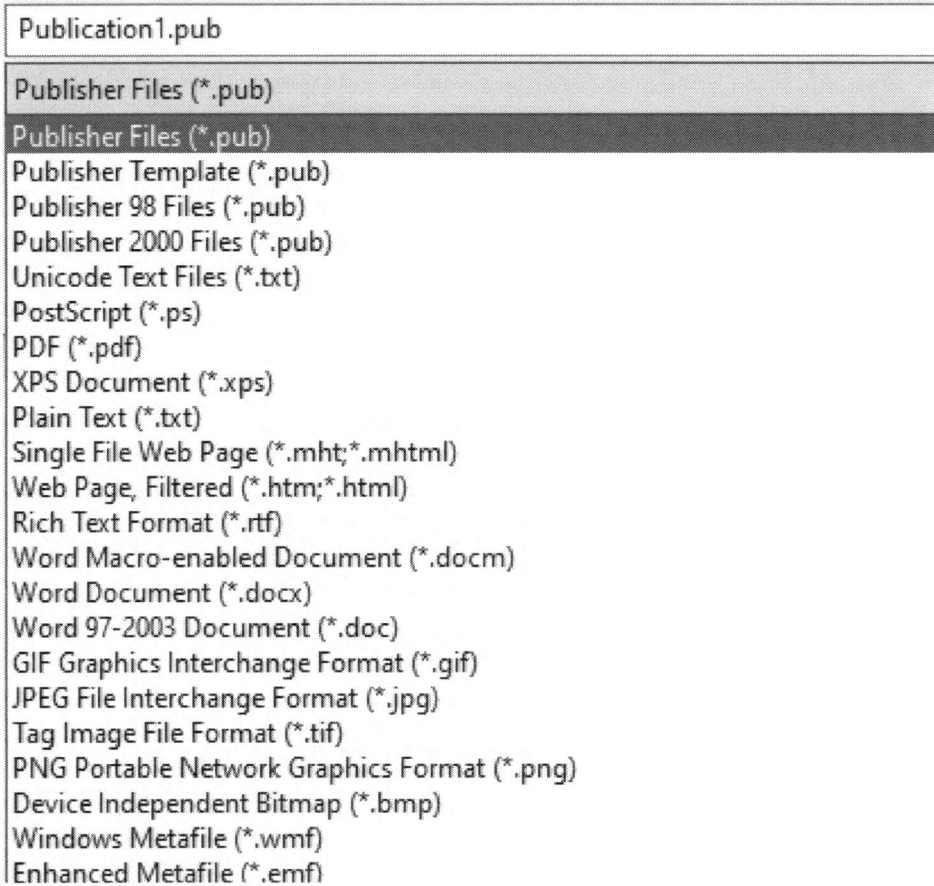

Publication1.pub
Publisher Files (*.pub)
Publisher Files (*.pub)
Publisher Template (*.pub)
Publisher 98 Files (*.pub)
Publisher 2000 Files (*.pub)
Unicode Text Files (*.txt)
PostScript (*.ps)
PDF (*.pdf)
XPS Document (*.xps)
Plain Text (*.txt)
Single File Web Page (*.mht;*.mhtml)
Web Page, Filtered (*.htm;*.html)
Rich Text Format (*.rtf)
Word Macro-enabled Document (*.docm)
Word Document (*.docx)
Word 97-2003 Document (*.doc)
GIF Graphics Interchange Format (*.gif)
JPEG File Interchange Format (*.jpg)
Tag Image File Format (*.tif)
PNG Portable Network Graphics Format (*.png)
Device Independent Bitmap (*.bmp)
Windows Metafile (*.wmf)
Enhanced Metafile (*.emf)

Figure 6.1

Now I would like to take a moment to go over some of the other file types that you might use just so you have an idea of what types of files you can save your publication as.

- **Publisher Template** – If you have a publication that you have formatted a specific way and would like to use this as a template file for future publications then you can save it as a Publisher template file.

- **Publisher 98 or 2000 Files** – If for some strange reason you know someone who has a very old version of Publisher and needs to open your file then you can save it as one of these older versions.

- **PDF** – Portable Document Format files are very common and are a great way to send your publication in a smaller sized file while making where the person on the other end is not able to edit your publication. They will not be able to open the file with Publisher ether.

- **GIF, JPEG, PNG, BMP or TIFF** – Saving your publication as an image file allows you to have one or all of your pages converted to that image type making it easy to send someone just one slide or let someone see your publication without needing to open it in Publisher. You can also use this for other things such as posting one of your pages on your website or even making it the background image on your computer.

Sharing Your Publication with Others

Collaboration is a big thing when it comes to how businesses operate these days and there is an increasing need to be able to quickly and easily share information in order to increase productivity and keep things running smoothly.

Other Office programs such as Word and PowerPoint have some more advanced sharing options such as uploading your file to your OneDrive online cloud storage and then letting others access it from there but for some reason, Publisher only gives you Email options from the *Share* section under the *File* tab. Figure 6.2 shows the choices you have for emailing your publication which I will now go over.

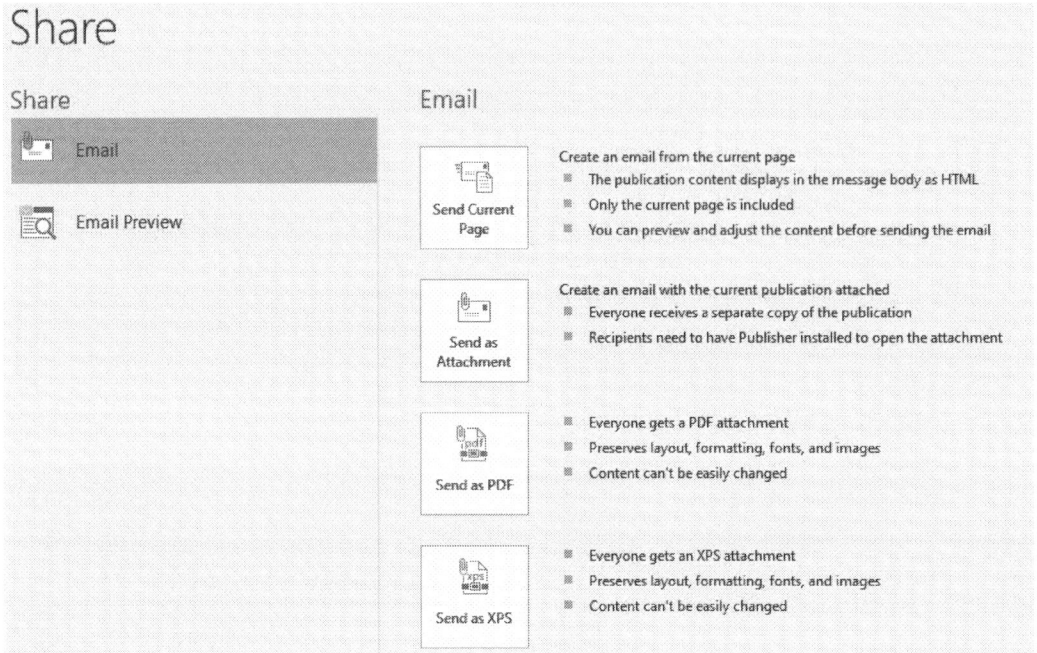

Share

Share

- Email
- Email Preview

Email

Create an email from the current page
- The publication content displays in the message body as HTML
- Only the current page is included
- You can preview and adjust the content before sending the email

Send Current Page

Create an email with the current publication attached
- Everyone receives a separate copy of the publication
- Recipients need to have Publisher installed to open the attachment

Send as Attachment

- Everyone gets a PDF attachment
- Preserves layout, formatting, fonts, and images
- Content can't be easily changed

Send as PDF

- Everyone gets an XPS attachment
- Preserves layout, formatting, fonts, and images
- Content can't be easily changed

Send as XPS

Figure 6.2

Send Current Page

If you have an email client such as Microsoft Outlook configured on your computer then you can send one of your pages as an email for the person on the other end to then be able to look over. They will not be able to edit the page or open it in Publisher though. All you need to do is enter in their email address and the subject (figure 6.3) and Publisher will send the current page that you are on as an email. Figure 6.4 shows how it looks at the recipient's end within a standard email client.

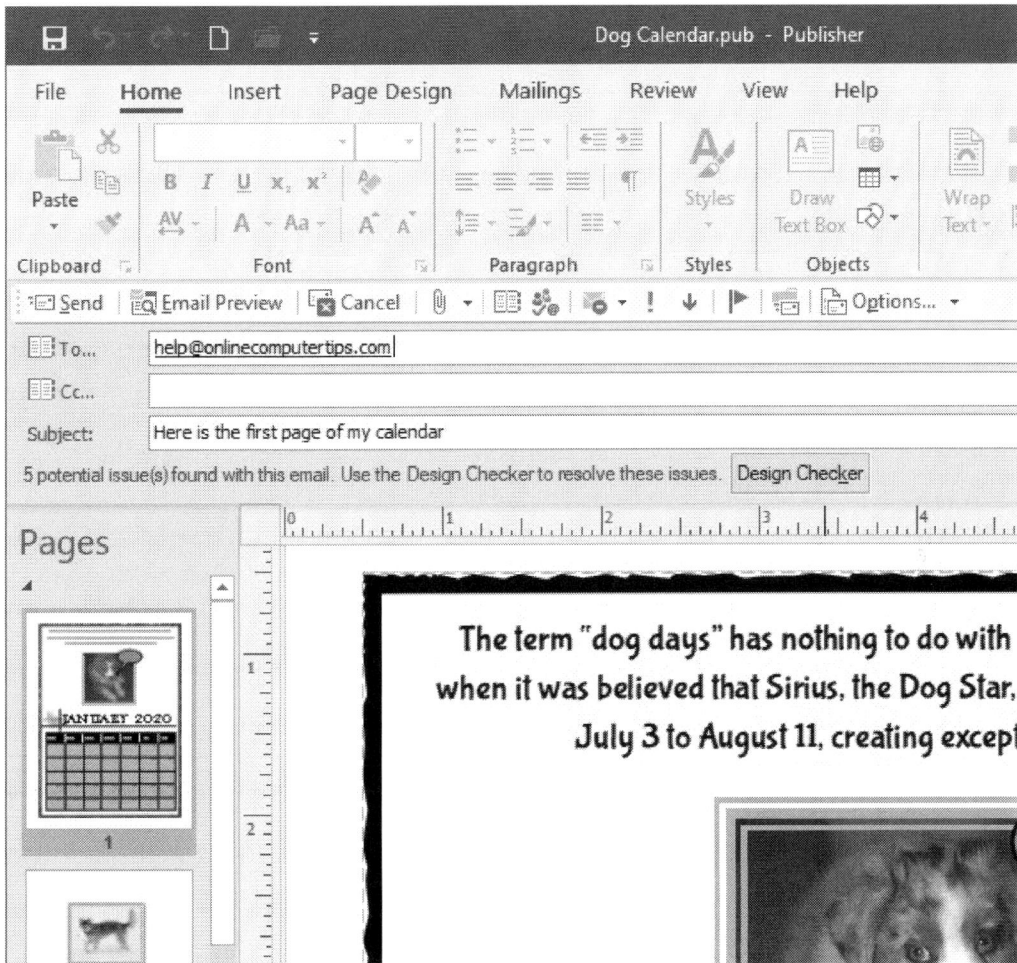

Figure 6.3

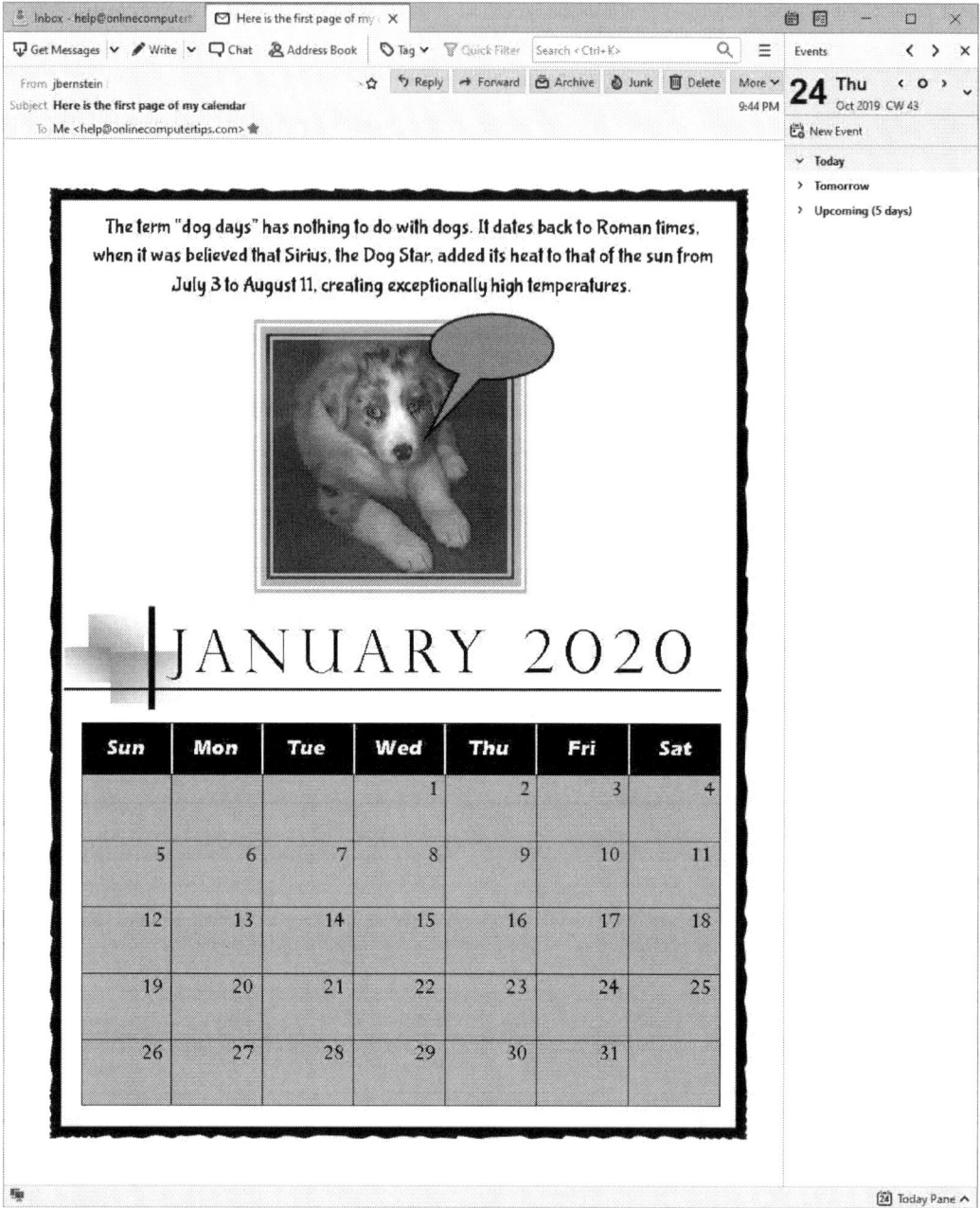

Figure 6.4

Send as Attachment

This option simply takes your Publisher file and adds it as an attachment to a new email (figure 6.5) assuming you have an email client installed on your computer.

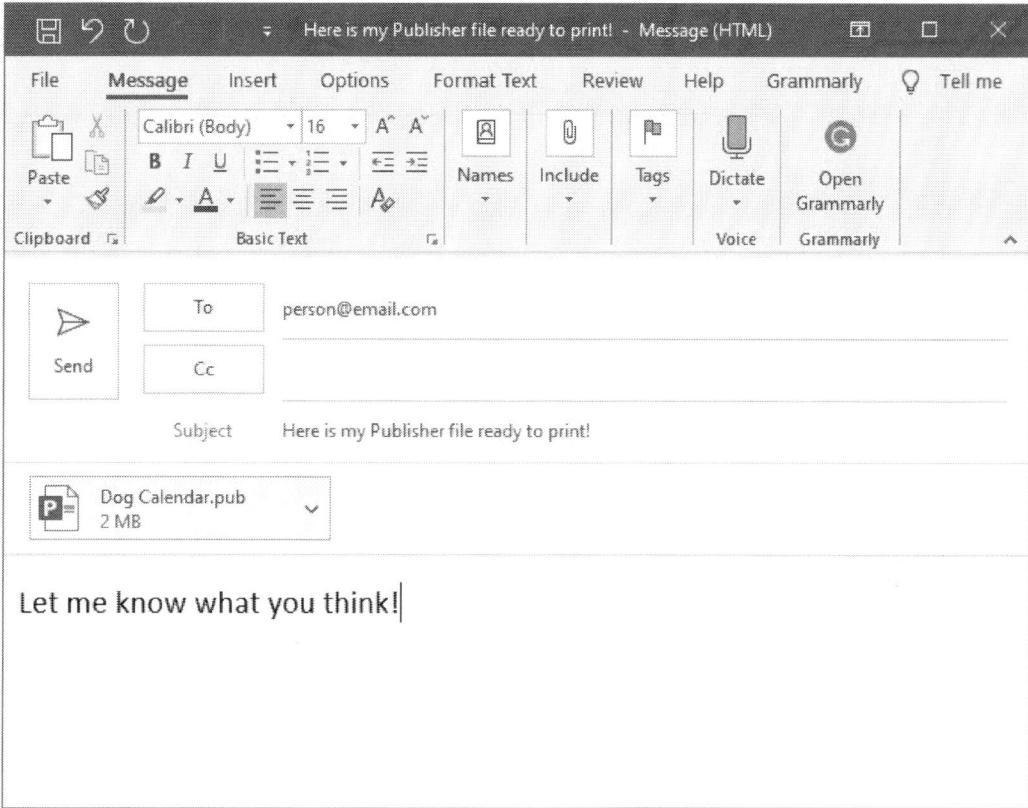

Figure 6.5

Send as PDF
This will do the exact same thing as the Send as Attachment option but will first convert your publication to a PDF file before attaching it.

Send as XPS
This is similar to the Send as PDF option but will convert your publication to an XPS file which is sort of like Microsoft's version of a PDF file and not used nearly as often as a PDF file.

Finally, the *Email Preview* button will open an HTML version of the current page in your web browser to show what it will look like as an HTML email message.

Exporting Your Publication
Publisher comes with several ways to export your publication as different file types or for printing purposes and these Export options can be found under the File tab as seen in figure 6.6. I will now go over what each one of these options will do.

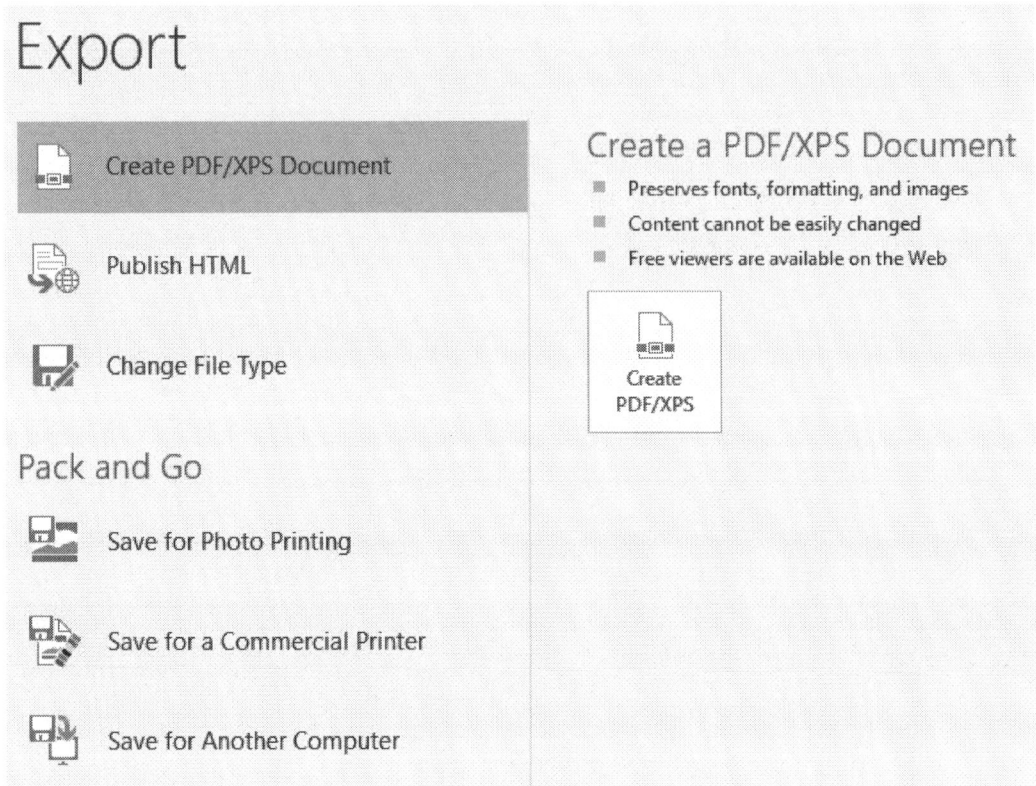

Export

Create PDF/XPS Document

Publish HTML

Change File Type

Pack and Go

Save for Photo Printing

Save for a Commercial Printer

Save for Another Computer

Create a PDF/XPS Document

- Preserves fonts, formatting, and images
- Content cannot be easily changed
- Free viewers are available on the Web

Create
PDF/XPS

Figure 6.6

Create PDF/XPS Document
I discussed sending your publication as a PDF and XPS in the previous section and here you can do the same thing, but this time save it to places such as your local computer, network drive, flash drive and so on.

Publish HTML
If you are thinking of adding one of your pages to your website then you can export it to either a web page (HTML) file with its associated images in a separate folder or single web page file MHTML that keeps everything within one file. These types of files can also be opened with a web browser.

Change File Type
The *Change File Type* option is very similar to the Save As option that I previously discussed. In fact, there is even a Save As button at the bottom of the Change File Type interface making it easy to choose additional file types to save your publication as. Figure 6.7 shows you all of the file types you can change your file to.

Save Publication

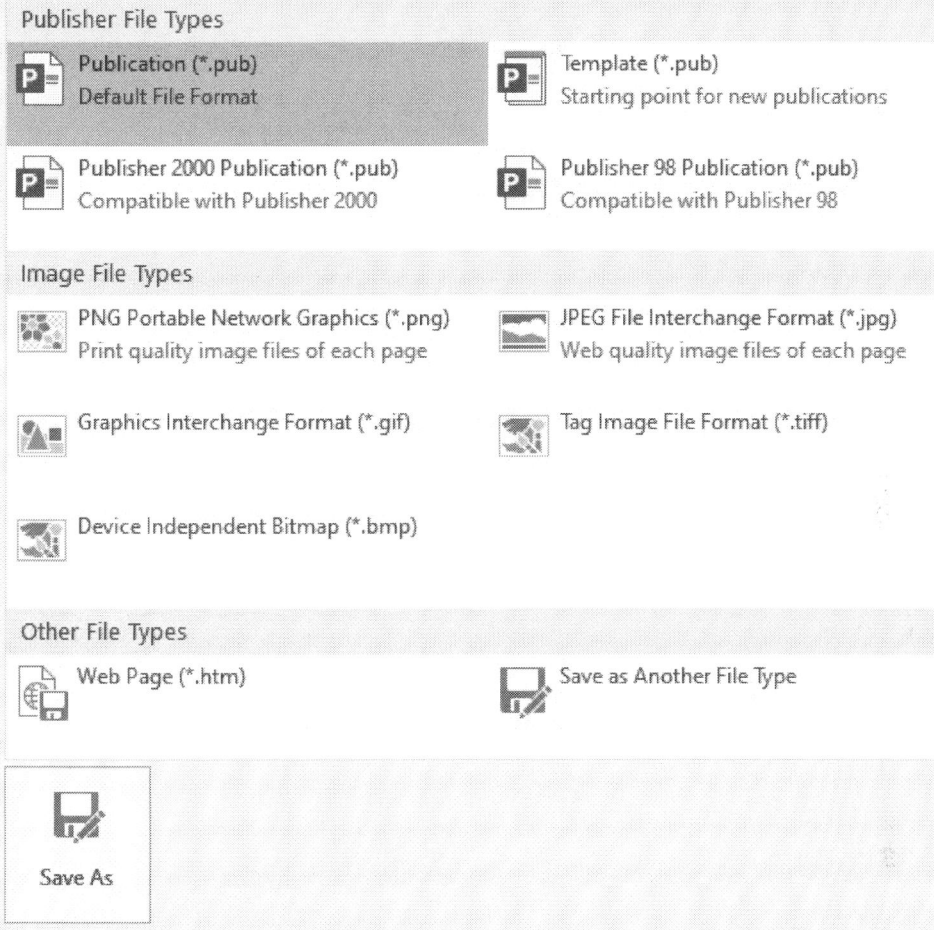

Publisher File Types

Publication (*.pub)
Default File Format

Template (*.pub)
Starting point for new publications

Publisher 2000 Publication (*.pub)
Compatible with Publisher 2000

Publisher 98 Publication (*.pub)
Compatible with Publisher 98

Image File Types

PNG Portable Network Graphics (*.png)
Print quality image files of each page

JPEG File Interchange Format (*.jpg)
Web quality image files of each page

Graphics Interchange Format (*.gif)

Tag Image File Format (*.tiff)

Device Independent Bitmap (*.bmp)

Other File Types

Web Page (*.htm)

Save as Another File Type

Save As

Figure 6.7

Save for Photo Printing

If your pages contain photos that you want to have printed on a high resolution printer then you can use this option to have each page of your publication saved as a high quality image file. Each page will be either a separate JPEG or TIFF image file depending on what type you specify during the save process. Then you will just need to tell Publisher where to save this image set so you can then find a way to get the image files to your printer.

page01.jpg

page02.jpg

page03.jpg

page04.jpg

Figure 6.8

Save for a Commercial Printer

If you plan on having your publication professionally printed then you might want to use this option to have your files packaged together into a printer package that you can then give to the print shop so they will have the best quality files to work with. There are several choices when creating this type of package.

- **Minimum size** – Creates a small file suitable for on-screen display and not recommended for high quality print jobs.

- **Standard** – Creates a moderately compressed file suitable for online distribution since the file sizes will be smaller.

- **High quality printing** – Creates a large file optimized for at home or copy shop printing.

- **Commercial Press** – Creates the largest size file for the highest quality suited for commercial printers.

- **Custom** – here you can select the exact options for your package based on your needs.

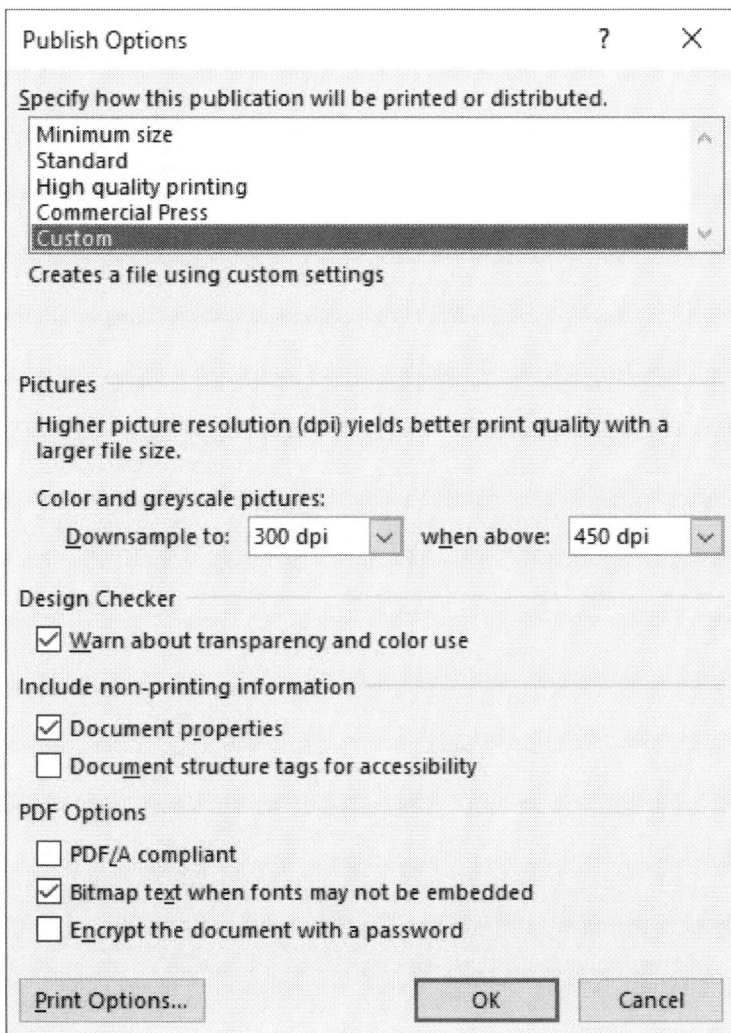

Publish Options

Specify how this publication will be printed or distributed.

Minimum size
Standard
High quality printing
Commercial Press
Custom

Creates a file using custom settings

Pictures

Higher picture resolution (dpi) yields better print quality with a larger file size.

Color and greyscale pictures:

Downsample to: 300 dpi   when above: 450 dpi

Design Checker
☑ Warn about transparency and color use

Include non-printing information
☑ Document properties
☐ Document structure tags for accessibility

PDF Options
☐ PDF/A compliant
☑ Bitmap text when fonts may not be embedded
☐ Encrypt the document with a password

Print Options...   OK   Cancel

Figure 6.9

After you choose your options you can click on the *Pack and Go Wizard* button to go through the process of creating the printing package. Before doing so you should decide if you want a Publisher file and PDF file or just one or the other. Many printers prefer high quality PDF files to print from.

You will then be prompted as to where you want to create the files. You can do things like burn them to a CD\DVD, copy them to a flash drive or copy them to your local hard drive.

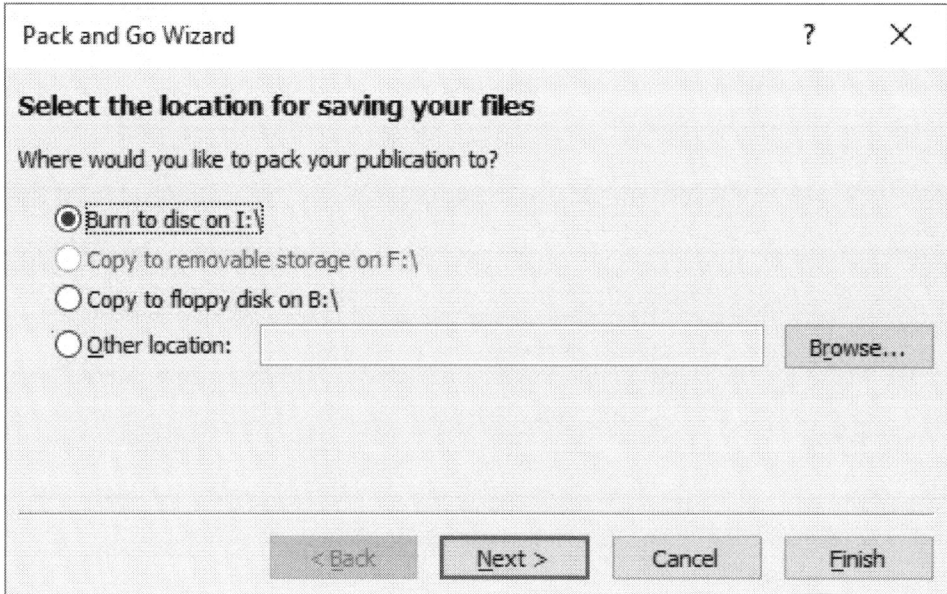

Figure 6.10

Save for Another Computer
If you want to transfer your publication to a different computer and make sure that everything you need will be there when you open the file on that computer then you can use the Save for Another Computer option. Normally you can just copy your Publisher file over and be ok but if the computer you are copying it to doesn't have the same fonts or access to your images then it might not look the same when you go to open it on the other computer.

The wizard for the Save for Another Computer option looks similar to the one for the Save for a Commercial Printer procedure but you will have the choice of whether or not you want to embed your fonts into your file as well as include linked graphics (figure 6.11). If you are going to use this option you might as well check all the boxes to make sure everything you need gets included even though it will increase your exported file size.

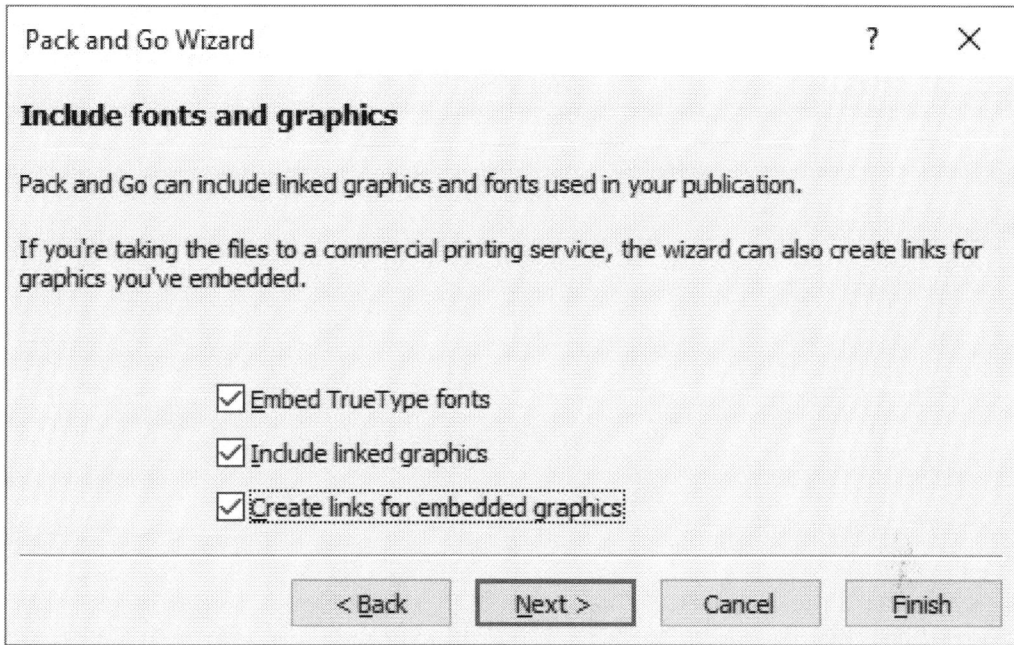

Pack and Go Wizard   ?   X

Include fonts and graphics

Pack and Go can include linked graphics and fonts used in your publication.

If you're taking the files to a commercial printing service, the wizard can also create links for graphics you've embedded.

☑ Embed TrueType fonts
☑ Include linked graphics
☑ Create links for embedded graphics

< Back   Next >   Cancel   Finish

Figure 6.11

Chapter 7 - Printing Your Publication

Now that you have your publication looking the way you like, its time to put it on paper so you can share it with those who want to see it. But before printing out your work, you should make sure its really ready to go so you don't waste time and money printing out a bunch of copies you can't use, especially if you are paying to have it printed.

I always like to double check my formatting before printing to make sure things are aligned the way I want them to be and there are no objects covering up other objects when they shouldn't be. It's easy to miss something like part of the text in a text box being cut off or not being formatted to match the rest of the text in your publication.

For example, figure 7.1 shows some text with a dog picture and there are two problems here. Can you see what both of them are?

Dogs are capable of
locating the source
of a sound in
6/100ths of a sec-

Figure 7.1

The first problem should be fairly obvious and its that the picture is covering up the rest of the text box so you can't see the rest of the dog fact. The other issue is that the last word that you can see is hyphenated and that may, or man not be ok with you depending on how picky you are. If I send the picture backward and stretch out my text box so the word second is not hyphenated I get the results shown in figure 7.2.

Dogs are capable of
locating the source of
a sound in 6/100ths
of a second by using

Figure 7.2

I also like to zoom in on my images and graphics to make sure they are really aligned properly since its harder to tell when you are looking at the entire page on your screen. If you are using guide lines then it's easier to make sure that everything is in the right spot but zooming in will still help even if you are using the guides.

Other things you might want to check are your page margins and make sure you have the paper size correct as well. Running a spell check from the Review tab is always a good idea as well.

Choosing a Printer and Changing Printer Options

Just like with anything you print, you will need to make sure you are printing it to the correct printer if you have more than one and then you should check the printer settings to make sure it's set to print the way you want it to print.

When you go to the *File* tab and then click on *Print* you will see a print settings page similar to figure 7.3. There are two main sections in this area, and they are *Printer* and *Settings*. Publisher will print to your computer's default printer if you don't change it to a different printer from the dropdown printer selection, assuming you have another printer installed to choose from.

If you have a Print icon on your Quick Access Toolbar it will print to your computer's default printer when you click on it. If you change to a different printer and then print something, the next time you click on the Print icon it will use the last printer you printed with so if you need to change printers, use the File tab.

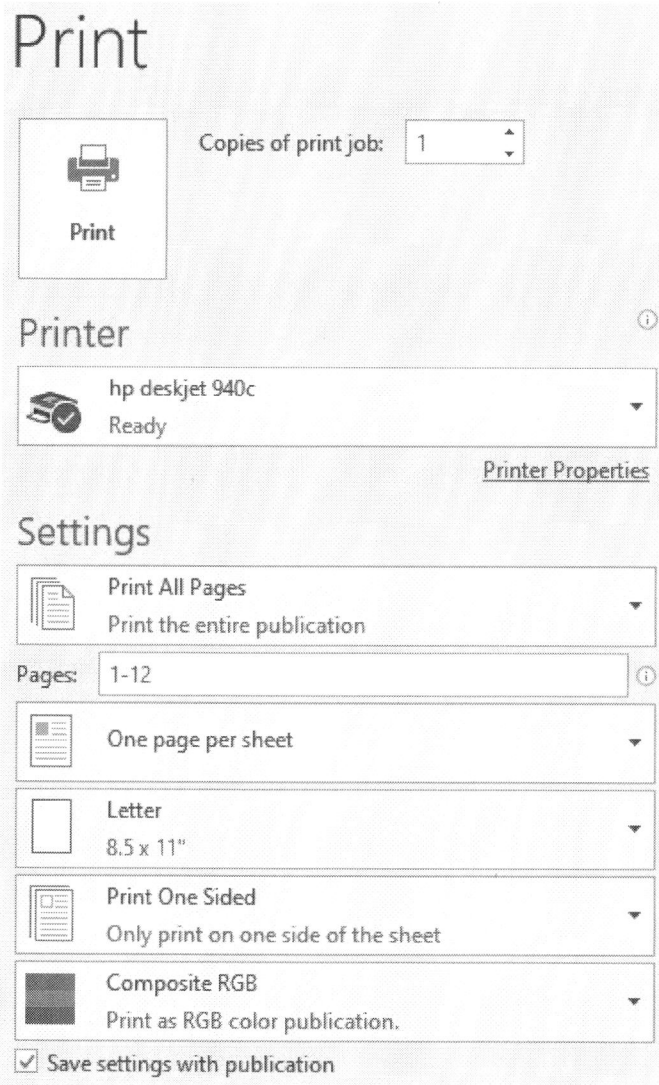

Print

Copies of print job: 1

Print

Printer

ⓘ

hp deskjet 940c
Ready

Printer Properties

Settings

Print All Pages
Print the entire publication

Pages: 1-12 ⓘ

One page per sheet

Letter
8.5 x 11"

Print One Sided
Only print on one side of the sheet

Composite RGB
Print as RGB color publication.

☑ Save settings with publication

Figure 7.3

If you take a look back at figure 7.3 you will see that there is a link named *Printer Properties* underneath the printer choice and that is where you can go to change printer specific settings. You might want to do this before printing to save yourself from having to print your file again in case something is not configured correctly.

Figures 7.4 and 7.5 show some common printer settings such as layout configuration (portrait and landscape) and page printing order. You can also do things such as tell Publisher what printer tray to use and what quality to use for printing. The settings here will vary depending on what printer you are using.

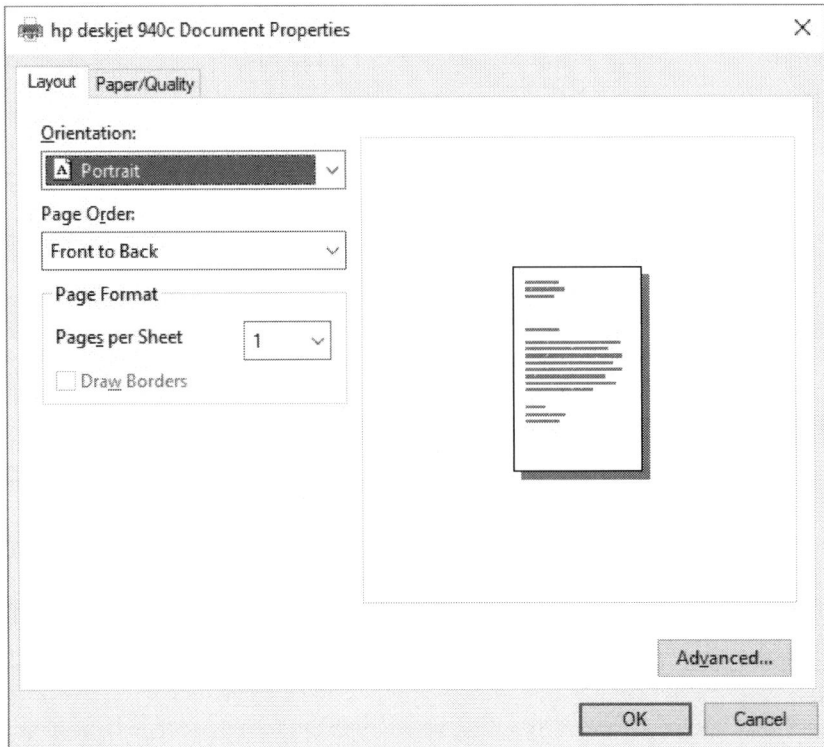

Figure 7.4

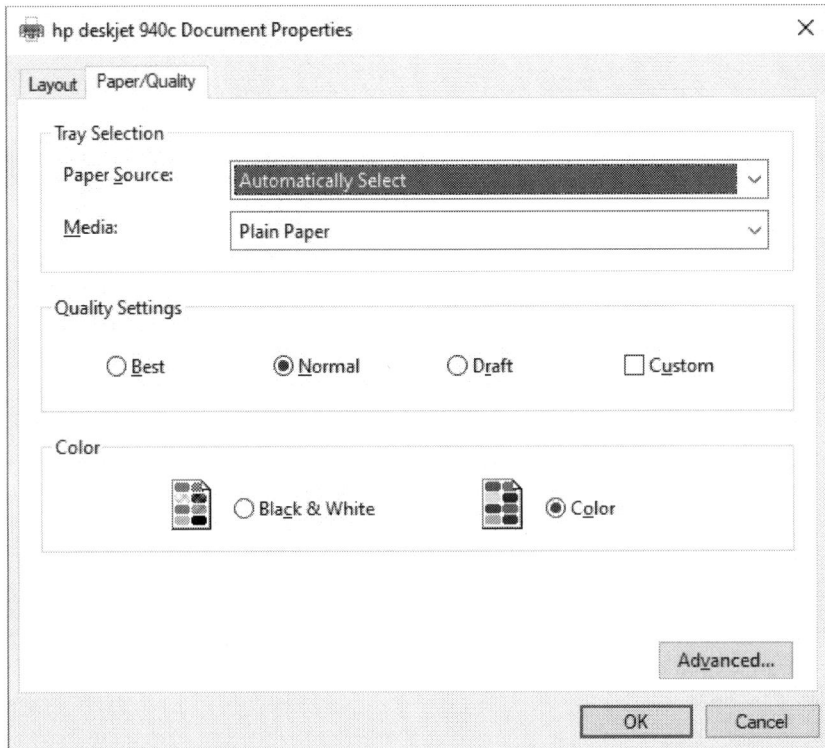

Figure 7.5

Changing Publication Printing Options

There are multiple ways to print out your publication in Publisher and the way you choose will most likely depend on how your publication is formatted and how you want it to come out on paper. When you go to the print options area right under Settings you will see that you have several ways to print your slide.

- **Print All Pages** – This will obviously print out all the pages within your publication.

- **Print Selection** – With this choice, you can highlight specific pages in the Pages Pane and then go to Print Selection and it will only print out the pages that you have selected.

- **Print Current Page** – This will print out the page that you are currently on. So if you are looking at page 3 and choose this option, then only page 3 will be printed out.

- **Print Custom Range** – Here you can type in specific page numbers that you want to print such as **2-5** or **1-3, 5, 8** which will print out pages 1 through 3 and also pages 5 and 8.

Under the page range section you have the choice to either print one page per sheet of paper or to have each page be tiled in order to have it stretch across a multiple sheets so you can tie them together to make a banner for example.

The final sections should be pretty obvious as to what they do. You can change the paper size from here before printing, enable double sided printing if your printer supports that feature and also choose to have your publication printed in color or greyscale (black and white with some greys basically).

At the bottom of the printer options, there is a checkbox that says *Save settings with publication* and if this is checked, Publisher will save the print settings that you made within your file so they will be set the same way when you open the file the next time.

When printing always be sure to look at all your pages in the *Print Preview* and scroll down using the scroll bar or the number selection box at the bottom of the screen before risking wasting time (and ink) on a print job that might not come out the way you want it to.

What's Next?

Now that you have read through this book and taken your Publisher skills to the next level, you might be wondering what you should do next. Well, that depends on where you want to go. Are you happy with what you have learned, or do you want to further your knowledge of Publisher and become a Publisher expert?

If you do want to expand your knowledge, then you can look for some more advanced books on Publisher, if that's the path you choose to follow. Focus on mastering the basics, and then apply what you have learned when going to more advanced material.

There are many great video resources as well, such as Pluralsight or CBT Nuggets, which offer online subscriptions to training videos of every type imaginable. YouTube is also a great source for instructional videos if you know what to search for.

If you are content in being a proficient Publisher user that knows more than your friends and coworkers, then just keep on practicing what you have learned. Don't be afraid to poke around with some of the settings and tools that you normally don't use and see if you can figure out what they do without having to research it since learning by doing is the most effective method to gain new skills.

Thanks for reading Publisher Made Easy. If you liked this title, please leave a review. Reviews help authors build exposure. Plus, I love hearing from my readers! You can also check out the other books in the Made Easy series for additional, computer-related information and training.

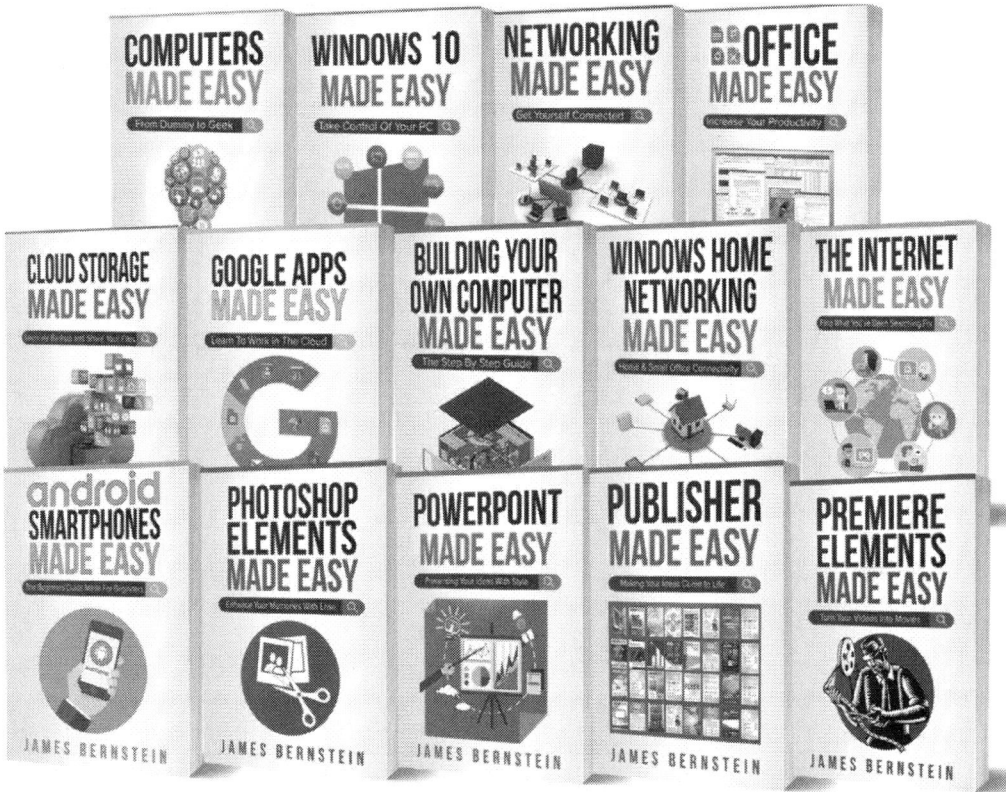

You should also check out my website at www.onlinecomputertips.com, as well as follow it on Facebook at https://www.facebook.com/OnlineComputerTips/ to find more information on all kinds of computer topics.

About the Author

James Bernstein has been working with various companies in the IT field since 2000, managing technologies such as SAN and NAS storage, VMware, backups, Windows Servers, Active Directory, DNS, DHCP, Networking, Microsoft Office, Photoshop, Premiere, Exchange, and more.

He has obtained certifications from Microsoft, VMware, CompTIA, ShoreTel, and SNIA, and continues to strive to learn new technologies to further his knowledge on a variety of subjects.

He is also the founder of the website onlinecomputertips.com, which offers its readers valuable information on topics such as Windows, networking, hardware, software, and troubleshooting. James writes much of the content himself and adds new content on a regular basis. The site was started in 2005 and is still going strong today.

Printed in Great Britain
by Amazon

35604911R00099